Judgment at Tokyo

Judgment
at Tokyo
THE JAPANESE WAR CRIMES TRIALS

TIM MAGA

THE UNIVERSITY PRESS OF KENTUCKY

Scholarly publisher for the Commonwealth,
serving Bellarmine College, Berea College, Centre
College of Kentucky, Eastern Kentucky University,
The Filson Club Historical Society, Georgetown College,
Kentucky Historical Society, Kentucky State University,
Morehead State University, Murray State University,
Northern Kentucky University, Transylvania University,
University of Kentucky, University of Louisville,
and Western Kentucky University.
All rights reserved.

Editorial and Sales Offices: The University Press of Kentucky
663 South Limestone Street, Lexington, Kentucky 40508–4008

05 04 03 02 01   5 4 3 2 1

Library of Congress Cataloging-in-Publication Data

Maga, Timothy P., 1952-
    Judgment at Tokyo : the Japanese war crimes trials / Tim Maga.
        p. cm.
    Includes bibliographical references and index.
    ISBN 0-8131-2177-0 (cloth : acid-free paper)
    1. Tokyo Trial, Tokyo, Japan, 1946-1948. I. Title.

KZ1181 .M34 2000
341.6'9'026852135—dc21   00-028670

This book is printed on acid-free recycled paper meeting
the requirements of the American National Standard
for Permanence of Paper for Printed Library Materials.

Manufactured in the United States of America

To Kenneth Maga, USMC-Guam and Chichi Jima.
And to those who remember.

Contents

Preface

They're "plain, ordinary murderers," cried Chief Prosecutor Joseph Keenan. Known for his courtroom theatrics and his out-of-court booze parties and womanizing, Keenan was a 1940s preview of 1990s "political incorrectness." He was also a central figure in a two-and-one-half-year-long trial drama that was barely noticed in its day and has received little attention since. But those "plain, ordinary murderers" included four prime ministers, three foreign ministers, three economic and financial leaders, two ambassadors, four war ministers, two navy ministers, and numerous senior military officers. They were the former leaders of World War II–era Japan, and their fate played a significant role in the shaping of their country's postwar future, in modern U.S.-Japan relations, and in the debate over what constitutes a war crime. Although far from the final word on the subject, *Judgment at Tokyo* tells the tale of this amazing endeavor to punish "evil" and to do "the right thing."

Doing "the right thing" has rarely been associated with the Tokyo War Crimes Trials of 1946–1948. The few analysts who have written books on the subject have been quick to denounce the "victor's justice" there, Allied racist agendas, Keenan crucifixions, and slipshod lawyering. In reality, the trials were more complex than these sound bite–style labels suggest. The commitment to justice was firm, although the trial effort itself was beset with problems and controversies.

The very suggestion that there might have been good intentions behind the Tokyo trials and that they might even have done good work is not a popular one to many in academe, certain political circles, and the press. Yet that is the general thesis of *Judgment at Tokyo*. As the research and writing of this book progressed, I discussed my findings with colleagues both inside and outside of the university setting. Nearly all of them yelled, "Stop now!" The topic is a "political mine field," I was warned. It was best to "let it go." Certain descriptive adjectives and nouns, I learned, had crept into educational lesson plans to help define the postwar war crimes trials at both Tokyo and Nuremberg. By the 1990s those descriptions had become something of a mantra in classrooms and newspaper background accounts of the trials. Nuremberg, it was said, had been a "noble" exercise and the product of "good" lawyering. Tokyo was a "racist" exercise, the product of "vengeance." One well-intentioned American friend and academic suggested that a book on the Tokyo trials could only be accomplished, and accepted as worthy by academics and many interested journalists, if those trials were compared and contrasted to the ones in Nuremberg. The Tokyo topic could never stand on its own, she said, unless the comparison-contrast model was built. Without a doubt or a question raised, she also assumed the Nuremberg-Tokyo tale was more of a study in ugly contrast than it was decent comparison.

I informed my professional colleagues in Japan (where I taught and wrote for several years) what my old friend had said. To a man, they were shocked by her advice, but not surprised. It suggested to them that a matter most important to their modern history was irrelevant to Americans unless a European foil was present. It suggested that Japanese history still required "acceptance" by American academe. It suggested that Americans pull the "race" card too quickly and that perhaps the primary issue at hand was an obvious ignorance over what took place in Tokyo. The alternative to these cerebral conclusions, of course, was yet another racial slur. Hence, I was told that the "real" reason behind the American reluctance to examine the Tokyo trials as a singular topic was that many American academics might be as "racist" as the Tokyo War Crimes Trials judges that they are so quick to condemn. Given this assessment, it was ironic that my American friend thought a Nuremberg-Tokyo contrast would better expose Allied "racist" policies in the Pacific. In any case, this is a book about the Tokyo trials. Nuremberg is noted when it makes sense to do so.

There are many in academe and elsewhere who do not see the Tokyo trials as an ugly tale of Western racism, hatred, and conspiracy. History is never that simple, and it should never be left to the "politically correct." Unfortunately, the level-headed, analytical majority has not been making itself heard on this subject. For the moment, the noise is being made by Western writers largely concerned about the influence of race in World War II policymaking and by Japanese writers defending a strong nationalist point of view. Most of the time liberal humanitarians and right-wing nationalists make strange bedfellows. But not here. Indeed, the debate over what did or did not take place at the postwar trials has become an important part of the current debate in Japan over Japan's precise role and responsibilities in World War II. Stimulated by the fiftieth anniversary of the war's end, that debate rages on in Japan. The past and the present come together in discussing the Tokyo trials, and the controversy may never end.

Charges and countercharges of "racism" are not unusual when the topic of the Tokyo War Crimes trials is brought up. Sadly, few of the debaters know the facts, and the history of the trials becomes a tool for a present-tense political agenda far removed from the late 1940s. No one wins this debate. In short, the topic of the Tokyo War Crimes Trials remains an emotional one, even after the fiftieth anniversary of the event. It should be. The crimes were horrible, and the general indictment mentioned some of them, including "plundering public and private property, wantonly destroying cities, towns and villages beyond any justification of military necessity; [perpetrating] mass murder, rape, pillage, brigandage, torture and other barbaric cruelties upon the helpless civilian population of the over-run countries."[1] Yet, in the face of popular movies like *Judgment at Nuremberg* in the 1960s and *Schindler's List* in the 1990s, public knowledge of Japanese war crimes and war crimes trials, as opposed to Nazi crimes and trials, is limited. If one leaves the "race" card in the deck, it could be concluded that this limited public interest and knowledge has also led numerous analysts to shy away from the topic. This book does not shy away from the facts and controversies.

In the usually staid and gentlemanly halls of academe, the issue of Japanese war crimes trials can create a shouting match that few other topics in modern history can equal. The denunciation of the Japanese "Rape of Nanking" is quickly met by a denunciation of the "American-led nuclear holocaust" at Hiroshima and Nagasaki. The Japanese murder of Allied POWs on Truk in the Caroline Islands is countered by the American killing of Japanese nurses on Okinawa. And on it goes. Announcing that "war is hell" is the usual way one bows out of this type of sparring match. It is an unsatisfying conclusion, for issues of moral, ethical, and legal significance are often lost in what becomes, essentially, a bizarre tit-for-tat debate.

Technically, the term Tokyo War Crimes Trials refers to the work of the International Military Tribunal for the Far East (IMTFE) in Tokyo between May 3, 1946, and November 12, 1948. Generically, it refers to a wider, more ambitious effort. Trials were held across the entire Asian/Pacific region, or wherever Japan's "Co-Prosperity Sphere" had been established. The U.S. military even began a series of trials in Tokyo months before the IMTFE was organized. There were other military tribunals in the Pacific islands, and trials took place in ten different locations within China alone. Some of these trials continued into the 1950s, but the most spectacular ones were always associated with the IMTFE prosecution of Japan's senior wartime leadership. It is not my purpose to survey each trial in every far-flung location of this mammoth endeavor. *Judgment at Tokyo* is not an encyclopedic account, throwing in a paragraph or two about every trial held. Although I do encourage, for the record, a large, multivolume work to match the scope of this Asian/Pacific mission, I stress here the efforts of the IMTFE and the most significant military tribunals and their trials. The goal is to acquaint the reader with the general facts and results of the trials, resurrect the life-and-death drama of the period, and examine the controversies and legacies that live on today. Hence, this story does not end when the trials end. Another goal is to acquaint those already in the know with some interesting revelations, precedents, and previously unknown issues. The latter is particularly important in the face of new war crimes trials efforts that are going on at the time of this writing.

There are literally miles and miles of bureaucratic records and trial transcripts in the underused Tokyo trials archives. Already sensitive to the charge of "victor's justice," the Asian/Pacific trials justices insisted on keeping a detailed account. The result was a mountain of paperwork; the original trial transcripts can be found at the National Archives. Even more important for the serious researcher are the archives of the Douglas MacArthur Memorial in Norfolk, Virginia. The complete trial transcript copy is located there, along with the private papers and oral histories of dozens of lawyers, defendants, politicians, and others associated with the trials. Other vital sources, particularly in reference to senior policymaking decisions relevant to the trials, can be found at two U.S. National Archives–administered presidential libraries: the Franklin D. Roosevelt Library in Hyde Park, New York, and the Harry S. Truman Library in Independence, Missouri. Additional important primary documentation is available at the Herbert Hoover Institution of War, Revolution, and Peace at Stanford University and at the Micronesian Area Research Center (MARC) at the University of Guam. Sifting through these complete records, including the private papers of participants as well as oral history transcripts, requires a grand commitment even on the part of a veteran researcher and writer. It can be frustrating, time-intensive work. But the story merits that effort.

One of the great dangers in the endeavor to examine and describe the Japanese war crimes trials is to become as cold and detached as some of the bureaucrats who were involved in the matter at the time. The "rooms" full of reports and memos at the MacArthur Archive tempt the researcher, in a sense, to summarize quickly or to tell a bland and basic tale. The Tokyo trials were never bland, and the story is complex. Throughout the trials, emotion tended to rule the day, influencing prosecution arguments, defense arguments, and even sentencing decisions. With that fact in mind, certain spectacular cases are offered in detail in this book. A spectacular case did not have to involve a well-known figure from Japan's militarist government. Often, Allied foot soldiers and Japanese citizenry alike were more spellbound by the trials of Japanese Imperial Army privates and junior officers than by the fate of former prime ministers and foreign ministers. World War II was called "the common man's war," and the "common man" faced his fair share of war crimes trials. These so-called less important trials were soon forgotten, but they constituted the bulk of the entire war crimes effort.

In the many trials outside of the Tokyo area, one endeavor particularly stood out. John Murphy, a civil libertarian turned chief prosecutor, made it a point to transform his mission, war crimes prosecution on the Western Pacific island of Guam, into a showpiece of democratic justice. He hoped to create the fairest and most ethical war crimes court of all time, leaving a positive legacy that would be difficult for the legal profession to ignore. Although he came close to achieving that goal, his mission, like so much associated with the Tokyo trials era, has been long forgotten. It is remembered with a whole chapter here.

To many it appeared that Japan could not move forward into its democratic postwar future until its militarist past was tried and punished. Both the Japanese government and the American Occupation authorities agreed with this thesis. Although glossed over or simply not considered at all in diplomatic history, the trials period had a profound impact on the postwar relationship between Japan and the United States. A chapter is dedicated to that influence; I suggest that the immediate impact and significance of the trials was sometimes too easily overlooked both by contemporary observers and by postwar historians.

Sadly, there is not much of a legacy remaining from the Tokyo trials period. The justices of the IMTFE, for instance, had planned to leave an important, working, and "Proper Legacy" behind: the International Permanent Court. That court, they hoped, would always be at the ready to prosecute war crimes and would stand as a discouragement to those who even contemplated war crimes. It took fifty years for this 1948 suggestion to see the light of day. Then, the only member nation of the United Nations that could assure and defend the ambitious new court's international jurisdiction, the United States, voted against its creation. Yesterday's war crimes prosecutor had changed its view on war crimes prosecution. The fact that nothing had been done to investigate yet another, more recent war crime in the Asian/Pacific region (the Cambodia holocaust of the 1970s) made this change of heart even more dramatic. The death of the IMTFE's dream of a "Proper Legacy" is the topic of the epilogue of this book.

This has been an immense project. For Bradley and Stanford University librarians, FDR and Truman Library archivists, and others, I am hoping a general thanks will be acceptable. A special thanks is reserved for James W. Zobel, an archivist at the MacArthur Memorial and perhaps the world's greatest expert on the mechanics of the Tokyo War Crimes Trials. His assistance was invaluable. Another grand debt of thanks is owed to former Japanese Foreign Minister, Finance Minister, and Prime Minister Kiichi Miyazawa for his fine insights on the Japanese view of the trials. The advice, support, and selfless assistance of the following individuals was most welcome: Dr. Dirk Ballendorf, Professor of Micronesian Studies and founding director of the Micronesian Area Research Center (MARC) at the University of Guam in Mangilao, U.S. Territory of Guam; Dr. James Weland, Professor of Japanese History at Bentley College in Waltham, Massachusetts; Dr. Joseph Arden, Director, University of Maryland–Asian Division at Yokota Air Base–Japan; Dr. Walt W. Rostow, former National Security Council Advisor for Presidents John Kennedy and Lyndon Johnson and Distinguished Professor of Economics at the University of Texas at Austin; Dith Pran, focus of the 1980s film "The Killing Fields" and director of the Dith Pran Holocaust Awareness Project, Inc., in Woodbridge, New Jersey; and Mark McGuire, formerly of Emory University, for his wicked good humor and amazing knack for putting things in "perspective." But my warmest thanks, as always, go to the center of my universe, Patsy Maga, for enduring yet another book project.

"Evil" must never go unpunished. But that is easier said than done. The Tokyo trials were controversial as they made history. Today, that very history is the controversy. I explain here why that happened.

Chapter 1

The Stage Is Set

From "Little Glass Eye" to "Joe the Key"

War and treaty-breakers should be stripped of the glamour of national heroes and exposed as what they really are—plain, ordinary murderers.

Joseph Baker Keenan

His victims nicknamed him "Little Glass Eye." Quite thin, less than five feet tall, and wearing his trademark coke-bottle-thick glasses, Tatsuo Tsuchiya looked more like a librarian than a sadistic killer. Indeed, he had once worked in a bookstore during his prewar life, and none of his friends from those peaceful days described him as a violent man, a militarist, or even a staunch supporter of the government. Tsuchiya had not been a member of Japan's World War II regime. He was not a famous general, an admiral, or a policymaker of any kind. Stationed at Mitsushima Prison Camp throughout much of the war, Tsuchiya had been one of many young troopers assigned to guard American prisoners of war. Yet his trial was the first war crimes case held in postwar Japan, eventually becoming part of the general trial record associated with the International Military Tribunal for the Far East (IMTFE). The IMTFE would come to symbolize the Allied effort in the Pacific to punish the evils of Japanese militarism, although there were many war crimes trials held from Tokyo to Guam and often administered by U.S. military tribunals alone.

Although this first trial, in grand contrast to the trials of prime ministers, foreign ministers, and other senior policymakers soon to occur, might not have been regarded as a significant, precedent-setting event by the *New York Times* and later historians, it was extremely important to the lawyers involved, American veterans, and Japanese everywhere. To them the drama of the case involving this "simple soldier" symbolized the entire trials effort to come. They were right.

The Tsuchiya case was prepared in the late fall of 1945 during the very opening weeks of the U.S. military occupation of Japan. At that time the IMTFE, which was also expected to serve as a postwar example of continuing Allied harmony, was still in its organizational phase. This did not stop the work of individual U.S. military–run trials, and "Little Glass Eye" would be the defendant in one of those trials.[1] Allied participation or not, the Tsuchiya case would set a number of precedents and procedural examples important to the IMTFE's own ambitious endeavor in the years to come.

Although one could argue that the Tsuchiya case was irrelevant in the face of larger matters at hand, this was not the view of the tribunal involved and especially not the view of those Allied soldiers who were or might have been Tsuchiya's victims. Tsuchiya was tried not only in the name of justice but also in the name of good politics within the Allied relationship. Thousands of veterans of the Allied campaigns in the Pacific were watching this trial closely, and it offered them an obvious preview of the upcoming IMTFE commitment. Nevertheless, to much of the 1945 press corps, the Tsuchiya case was not a major matter of concern. The man had been a "cog in the wheel," a young soldier caught in troubled times. It was his policymaking superiors who deserved judgment, attention, and to be made examples.[2]

This opinion reflected a general misunderstanding of the war crimes trials in Japan. To the prosecution in this case, Tsuchiya represented a regime that encouraged brutality and aggression throughout all of its ranks. Given this reality, which the IMTFE later attempted to demonstrate in its general indictment of the entire Japanese wartime leadership, there could be no "cog in the wheel." Sanctioned by an evil government, Tsuchiya, the prosecution argued, was responsible for his actions, rewarded by his superiors, and as guilty as the brutal policymaking defendants who occupied the headlines associated with the trials.[3] The Tsuchiya trial was not a forgettable legal footnote to the Tokyo trials. It was the foundation for the trials, whether the IMTFE itself and later analysts wished to admit it or not. The problem, of course, was the defendant and his crime. In a world gone mad, he was, as his defense counsel sometimes argued, only a product of the madness.

The larger concern of the Tokyo trials involved the fate of eighty indicted men who represented the power and madness behind Tsuchiya. Classified as Class A war criminal suspects, the eighty were tried between May 3, 1946, and November 12, 1948, in Yokohama, near Tokyo. The Tsuchiya trial took place in December 1945. These eighty suspects included

Class A war crimes defendants enjoy hamburger steak at Sugamo Prison, Tokyo. (Courtesy of Douglas MacArthur Memorial)

four former premiers (Tojo, Hiranuma, Hirota, and Koiso), three foreign ministers (Matsuoka, Shigemitsu, and Togo), four war ministers (Araki, Hata, Itagaki, and Minami), two navy ministers (Nagano and Shimada), six former generals (Koihara, Kimura, Matsui, Muto, Sato, and Umezu), two ambassadors (Oshima and Shiratori), three economic and financial leaders (Hoshino, Kaya, and Suzuki), one imperial advisor (Kido), one radical theorist (Okawa), one admiral (Oka), and one colonel (Hashimoto). They were accused of plotting and carrying out a war of conquest; murdering, maiming, and ill-treating civilians and prisoners of war; plunder; rape; and "other barbaric cruelties." But were these trials truly necessary, and were they conducted in the name of justice and fair play? I suggest that they were required and that they were as just as they could be, given time, place, and circumstances. Yet there are many who support a different view.

Considering the nature of the charges, there was little Allied questioning of the necessity for trials in 1945. In contrast, Allied motives and objectives were especially questioned in the years after the trials.[4] Today many of these questions come from the Japanese themselves, and few of the works asking the questions have appeared in English. Particularly for the Japanese, the Tokyo trials are not a long-ago affair or a footnote in history. Tatsuo Tsuchiya could be a neighbor. Given Japan's growing foreign population, some of his former victims could also live next door. The legacy of World War II and the postwar trials is a part of everyday life, especially in an era of great reflection over the meaning and significance of the Japanese role in the war. Moreover, the controversies associated with the Tokyo trials live on in the present debate over whether Japan was, indeed, a villain in World War II, whether it needs to apologize for that villainy, and whether it can move forward through the twenty-first century while ignoring or denying its recent past. Hence, the record of war crimes trials in the 1940s connects to a turn-of-the-century debate. For instance, historian and Japanese legal expert Hiro Nishikawa makes this connection loud and clear. He suggests that the trials did not involve the punishment of individual violators of the social order. The Allied effort, he insists, put Japanese life and culture on trial, finding it evil and sickening to Western palates. Describing his politics as "mainline LDP" (Liberal Democratic Party, postwar Japan's most popular and dominant political party), Nishikawa notes that his views do not result from some nostalgic admiration for Japanese militarism. He even says that, like many of his countrymen, he is "apolitical" and just a "concerned citizen." In any event, his point of view is not unusual in Japan.

Nishikawa believes that the primary mission of the trials was part of a racist agenda, whereby the victors punished an "enemy race" once again. The Allies in the Pacific were not seeking justice for the perpetrators of genocide, as they had been in the war crimes effort in Nuremberg. They were, he explains, seeking revenge for early wartime defeats, for the embarrassment of Japanese success over western European and American colonial power in the Pacific, and for raw emotional reasons totally divorced from the pursuit of justice.

Guiding this racist agenda, Nishikawa concludes, were years of Western misunderstanding of Japanese culture. One of the charges against Tsuchiya in the "Little Glass Eye" case involved the defendant's slapping of American POWs; but Nishikawa points out that Japanese Imperial Army superiors always slapped subordinates. Several senior Japanese officers faced charges of "forced marching POWs"; but Nishikawa reminds his audiences that Japanese troopers from New Guinea to China underwent forced marches ordered by their own commanders. And finally, few Japanese soldiers welcomed a world of dishonor and disservice to the emperor via surrender and imprisonment; but those same soldiers, according to Western-designed rules, were expected to treat captured Allied troops with respect and consideration. This might have been too much to ask, Nishikawa insists, of a culture that viewed military service in a different light than did the Americans and the Europeans. The westerners never gave an inch, Nishikawa complains, to understand and accept cultural differences. Instead, the Japanese were labeled "evil," he says, and many guilty verdicts in the war crimes trials were predetermined because of it.

Nishikawa concedes that the Americans offered much to the successful reconstruction of postwar Japan. America's generosity to a defeated enemy was kindly welcomed, he admits, although that generosity was more connected to Washington's Cold War objectives at the time than a "sudden love of Japanese culture." And meanwhile, America attempted to punish Japan for its past, its own history, and wartime heroism. The war crimes trials symbolized the effort, he said, and it was unfortunate that a "guest culture" (the American Occupation Government of 1945–1952) had dedicated itself to this task. All of these sad goals and ambitions were fully exhibited in the "Little Glass Eye" case alone, Nishikawa notes. The hundreds more cases to follow were "just more of the same," although few Americans at the time or later American analysts of the trials paid much attention to the fate of Tatsuo Tsuchiya. Tsuchiya, Nishikawa remembered, was a poor, young foot soldier who represented "the soul of a nation captured by war and militarism." His predicament was Japan's predicament, and his trial by foreigners made the tragedy of Japan's defeat even more tragic.[5]

A similar view was echoed by historian Yuki Tanaka in his 1996 book *Hidden Horrors: Japanese War Crimes in World War II*. Particularly concerned with reports of cannibalism and biological warfare experiments, Tanaka explained that Japan's wartime behavior was a temporary state of mind influenced by "Emperor ideology" politics. He attacked the Allies for committing plenty of atrocities of their own. He noted further that the victors set too many murderers free after the war, both Japanese and Allies. Tanaka's work suggested to some that Japan was beginning to deal with its past, even though his "temporary madness" and "everybody did it" thesis was strangely reminiscent of 1950s German wrangling over the crimes of the Third Reich.[6] Tanaka's investigations revealed shocking details of specific atrocities. His account was also incomplete, presenting a bizarre portrait of a nation that flirted with madness for a few years but then returned to peaceful "normalcy" and in which all is well today.

To Saburo Ienaga, nothing was well with Japan, and history should not be left to Tanaka, and certainly not to the Japanese government. Ienaga was a historian, but his name was not known outside Japan until he was nearly ninety years old. He claimed that many of his fellow historians had missed the point. Japan committed war crimes throughout the Pacific region, he said, and even pacifist postwar Japanese governments could not admit it, much less examine the facts. As early as 1965, Professor Ienaga challenged the constitutionality and legality of the Japanese government's long-standing legal right to screen history textbooks before they were published. Any mention of Japanese wartime atrocities in those books (including one of Ienaga's) was eliminated or reduced to vague, overly general terms. In 1970 the Tokyo district court agreed with Ienaga's challenge, declaring the Ministry of Education's screening system "censorship." The Japanese Supreme Court overturned that decision in 1982, and for the next fifteen years Ienega fought to have another day in court. Carrying petitions that eventually included the names of more than twenty thousand history teachers and other instructors in Japan, Ienaga demanded that history be recorded accurately. The governments of South Korea and Taiwan, former Japanese colonies, echoed Ienaga's demand, making it an international cause and an issue in Pacific region relations. The aging Ienaga won his case to change specific war crimes–related references in new history books; however, the court did not assault the constitutionality of general government involvement in textbook screening. Ienaga's long argument filled fourteen huge volumes of legal discussion, and his victory constituted a first step in the creation of a truly meaningful Japanese national dialogue on war crimes issues. Yet, to some, Ienaga was a tired old man, obsessed with the details of specific atrocity tales, who did not appreciate the larger issues of Western-imposed justice, racism, imperialism, and cultural conflict. According to this anti-Ienaga view, the Ministry of Education had been wisely protecting the nation's youth from Western interpretations of alleged Japanese crimes during World War II. Consequently, the screening system was a cultural protection device deserving respect rather than derision.[7]

Few Western analysts of Japanese war crimes could disagree with Ienaga's victory. Most felt uncomfortable with the very existence of screening systems. Yet some of them, at least, could agree that Ienaga did indeed ignore so-called larger issues throughout his long complaint. Professor John Dower, for example, a well-respected U.S.-based historian with strong interests in the problem of Japanese-American cultural misunderstanding, has critically examined America's postwar imperial mission in Japan, the oftentimes personal agenda of Gen. Douglas MacArthur, who led the Occupation Government, and the difficult relations and unfortunate, long-lasting impressions that resulted from the occupation period. To Dower, American racism and elitism help explain the thrust and direction of the occupation period itself and the war crimes trials that took place during those years. Nevertheless, the war crimes trials have not been a focus of his work. They remain a small piece of his big-picture story of cross-cultural misunderstanding, struggle, and misery.[8]

In author Richard Minear's view, the trials are not part of a larger story at all. They are the story! Written in the early 1970s, Minear's *Victors' Justice* accused the American government of "sham trials" based on pure vengeance, power, and privilege. Influenced by the then ongoing Vietnam War and the American antiwar movement, Minear saw great relevance in the "fact" (often repeated by him) that the U.S. government seemed as anxious to crush the North Vietnamese as it had been to hang the Japanese at the war crimes trials. The wartime leadership of Japan fell victim to America's imperial agenda in the Pacific, and the North Vietnamese, he claimed, were next.[9]

Near the fiftieth anniversary of the beginning of the trials, Harvard University sponsored a special seminar on the war crimes topic, supported by Harvard's famous Reischauer Institute for Japanese Studies. The audience included a former prime minister, Yasuhiro Nakasone, then a visiting fellow at the institute; aides to Massachusetts senators Edward Kennedy and John Kerry; Kimberly Dubois, of Massachusetts governor William Weld's protocol office; noted academics from across New England; and a good number of graduate and undergraduate students from the Boston area. The issues of Allied-led "racial conspiracy," American-championed "cultural hegemony," "allied crucifixion" of Japanese wartime leaders, and "sham trials" were well voiced by both American and Japanese speakers. Those issues represented the dominant view of the seminar participants. Little was said about the actual work of the war crimes trials, the atrocities they examined, the precise crimes involved, the many victims of those crimes, and the militarist Japanese regime, which ruled its wartime occupied territories with a ruthlessness rivaled only by its ally Nazi Germany. The consequences of Japanese wartime aggression were strangely absent from the discussion.[10]

Without question, academic concern over the issue of race in big-power politics merits further expression. Cultural misunderstanding has polluted a truly happy and healthy U.S.-Japan relationship for years.[11] American interests in postwar Japan were indeed often dominated by self-interest, and the war crimes trials were conducted under the watchful eye of the "American Caesar," Douglas MacArthur. But the war crimes trials themselves also deserve further consideration before they are lost within these intellectual considerations of race, culture, and détente. There were good reasons for the trials. Horrible atrocities had been committed. Both prosecution and defense teams often did excellent work. And evil should never go unpunished.

In the effort to prosecute evil, the Tsuchiya or "Little Glass Eye" trial did certainly set the stage. Much of today's politically correct argument does in fact echo the arguments of Tsuchiya's defense team of over a half-century ago. Those arguments have been lost and forgotten within the comprehensive history of the trials, but they are worth resurrecting in order to understand the thrust and direction of the trial debates and procedures.

Whether an anxious public opinion in 1945 thought the "Little Glass Eye" case wasted time vis-à-vis the larger trial matters at hand was irrelevant to Louis Geffen, an American army major and the chief prosecutor in that case. To Geffen, Tsuchiya represented the execution of the "cruelties" soon to be highlighted in the general indictment of the wartime regime. Tsuchiya's fate, Geffen noted over and over again, was important to soldiers in the Allied armies throughout the Far East. The POW has rights, he reminded everyone, and brutality to POWs was "unacceptable behavior." Tsuchiya's trial suggested to combat veterans that the Allied leadership cared about the concerns of the common soldier in addition to the sweeping questions of ethics in war and the administration of prisoner-of-war camps. Particularly to the "dogface" or common foot soldier of the American military in the Pacific, the "Little Glass Eye" case was as important as the upcoming trials of Japanese generals and political leaders. The U.S. military–administered *Pacific Stars and Stripes* daily newspaper accorded Tsuchiya (whose name sometimes appears mistakenly as "Tsuchiyo" there and in the English-language *Nippon Times*) headline coverage for days. The courtroom was filled with off-duty U.S. military personnel, competing for spectator seats with Japanese civilians, who also packed the courtroom throughout the trial. Indeed, with the exception of only a few of the senior wartime leaders' trials, no other trial stimulated this much excitement in the American Occupation community and among the Japanese populace. That surprised Geffen. Some, he believed, thought the trials would be overly

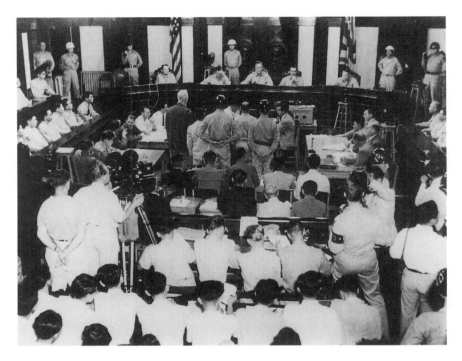

A packed courtroom was typical of the early U.S. military tribunal–administered trials before the 1946 arrival of the IMTFE. (Courtesy of Douglas MacArthur Memorial)

fast-moving affairs, whereby the defendants were quickly sent to the gallows in a demonstration of the victor's peace and justice. Pretrial pronouncements by Geffen himself attempted to dispel such concerns, but the he still worried about the "appearance" of shoddy courtroom procedure, to say nothing of bad law. Hence, during the trial itself, he even abstained from several opportunities to object to defense counsel tactics and arguments. Those objections, he later argued convincingly, would have succeeded. But the defense "needed visibility and credibility" more than his own endeavor did. Meanwhile, Geffen trusted the mountain of evidence behind his prosecution effort, and a longer trial would be better than a short one, he once suggested, if the "kangaroo court" issue was still a matter of concern.[12]

Also setting a precedent for defense tactics in the trials to come, John Dickinson, a U.S. Army lieutenant colonel and the chief defense counsel, led a vigorous defense on behalf of his client's plea of innocence. Tsuchiya faced charges involving "cruel, inhuman and brutal atrocities which re-sulted in death for one American prisoner and torture for many others." Before entering the not guilty plea, Dickinson successfully demanded the removal of Col. John H. Ball from his role as trial judge on the grounds that he had been a prisoner of the Japanese for more than three years and had suffered through the "Death March" at Bataan during the successful Japa-nese invasion of the Philippines. Maj. Harold H. Emmons, a member of Dickinson's defense team, even tried to eliminate most of the charges brought against Tsuchiya on the grounds that the case had been formulated against him by vengeance-minded American ex-POWs masquerading as objective representatives of the law. Eight specific charges of torture and cruelty to American prisoners of war had been leveled against Tsuchiya, and the court partially agreed with Emmons by eliminating two of the most damning ones. Both matters involved unsubstantiated charges of Tsuchiya's "gleeful torturing" of American prisoners; dropping them temporarily hurt the prosecution's contention that Tsuchiya "enjoyed his work." Tsuchiya's personal lawyer, Jiko Watanabe, especially welcomed the downplaying of Tsuchiya's alleged "sadistic side." Instead of suggesting that his client had "just followed orders," Watanabe condemned the prowar hysteria that had "infected Japanese life and culture during World War II." Tsuchiya was a youthful product of that hysteria, he said, not its architect. Watanabe urged the court to consider the pressures on common soldiers trapped within an evil dictatorship and to save its wrath for those evil policymakers them-selves. Geffen countered that he had little interest in a psychological inves-tigation about the state of mind of Japanese foot soldiers. The task at hand, he argued, was the brutality of Tatsuo Tsuchiya. Tsuchiya, Geffen con-tended, also encouraged seven other guards at Mitsushima Prison to beat American prisoners regularly, with clubs, knotted ropes, boards, and even shoes. These were the issues at hand, he insisted, rejecting the attempt to transform the trial into a review of recent Japanese history. Tsuchiya had not been a policymaker. The defense counsel's depiction of him as "everyman," trapped in the horror of war and dictatorship, was a broad, overly general theme that, according to the prosecution, had little relevance in the case. Instead, Geffen focused on one of the remaining six charges against Tsuchiya, the torture and death of nineteen-year-old Pfc. Robert Gorden Teas of Streator, Illinois.

Geffen produced nine sworn affidavits bearing the detailed testimony of American witnesses to the Teas torture. The gruesome account shocked the court, offering a preview of prosecution efforts to shock and dismay for the remainder of the war crimes trials. According to witness Gordon Gavard, under the instigation of Tsuchiya, Mitsushima Prison's Red Cross parcels, destined for the American prisoners, had been stolen by the prison guards for their own use as well as for black market sales. By accident, Teas found the hidden parcels and was discovered by Tsuchiya. What followed in the harsh winter of 1943 were five continuous days of torture for Teas. Stripped and left to freeze in the snow-covered courtyard of the prison, Teas was beaten with clubs on one day, with boards the next, and with wet knotted ropes the following day. If rendered unconscious, he would be revived, stood up, and beaten again. Gavard was amazed that the gaunt, young Teas survived as long as he did. Although Tsuchiya was assisted in the torture by his colleagues, Tsuchiya did most of the beating himself.

Gavard's testimony became critical to Geffen's case. Given the location of Gavard's cell, other ex-POWs admitted that Gavard was in an excellent position to witness the beatings. As the "Little Glass Eye" trial continued into late December 1945, Tsuchiya's predicament made some Japanese observers wax poetic on the trial's significance to Japan. The foremost among them was Dr. Toyohiko Kagawa. Known even on the lecture circuit in the United States as a prewar champion of Christian values, pacifism, and social reform, Kagawa favored a postwar Japan that embraced humane government, rejected war, and granted the downtrodden, especially women, a better, happier place in society. Much of what he favored would indeed soon typify postwar Japanese government, but his December 1945 reflections stressed the issue of brutality in war by the common man and what that should mean for Japan. Kagawa said that Tsuchiya was no different from the American Marines on Guam who shipped home the skulls of dead Japanese soldiers as "souvenirs." He was no different from the American army personnel on Okinawa who used the flamethrower to root out, if not incinerate, Japanese defenders. Foot soldiers on both sides of the war, he insisted, had a little of Tatsuo Tsuchiya in them all.

Kagawa made these remarks at one of the opening postwar sessions of the Social Democratic Party of Japan. They were not well received. The party published an official press release noting that Kagawa needed to study the facts of the Tsuchiya case, accept the reality of Japanese brutality in much of the Asian/Pacific region throughout World War II, and return to his causes of pacifism and moral values. Kagawa rejected the criticism. Explaining that the Tsuchiya case was the beginning of Japan on trial, Kagawa predicted that the result of the many trials would be the end of the emperor system and, possibly, a way of life. Indicating that he would love to return to the championing of the causes that had made him famous, Kagawa said that he had his doubts that Japan would ever be the same again after America's trials were over. He ended these public remarks with shouts of "banzai" and praises for Emperor Hirohito (whom he incorrectly predicted would be tried and convicted as a war criminal).

To this day, it remains unclear how many Japanese shared Kagawa's view and reaction to the Tsuchiya trial. Kagawa's position was well reported in most Japanese newspapers and in radio broadcasts. In any event the biggest problem with Kagawa's message was the messenger himself. Kagawa's visibility and criticisms raised the question, especially among the Allies, of what he had done for a living during World War II. The answer was a surprising one, especially to those Japanese who were curious about his Christian-influenced beliefs or were admirers of his bold opposition to the prewar government. Early in the war, Kagawa embraced the militarism he once questioned. Some of his wartime remarks would be quoted by Japanese government propagandists. Coming to the conclusion that World War II was a racist war prompted by the colonial policies of the Europeans and the Americans, Kagawa said he could not tolerate the hypocrisy of the Allies' allegedly noble objectives in World War II. "Forged in a spirit of racial superiority," he said in 1943, "while they speak of liberty and freedom, America and her allies wage an unjust war on the Oriental race. Ah, woe to America for so degrading the name of Christ by this butchery!"[13]

By the end of the war, Kagawa was living in Japanese-occupied China, where he made a fortune looting and confiscating Chinese property and commodities. He then sold his holdings at fantastic prices to the Japanese Imperial Navy, hid his fortune in Japan, and masqueraded there in late 1945 as a pauper and an intellectual who only wanted to help create a peaceful, reformed postwar Japan. In reality, Kagawa intended to use his money to create a new nationalist party someday, as well as to maintain a fund to assist the emperor should he fall victim to Allied persecution. Given these facts, Kagawa was arrested by both the American military and the Tokyo police shortly before Christmas 1945 and charged as a war criminal.[14] If anything, the arrest put into question the credibility of Tsuchiya's out-of-court defenders. Tsuchiya's lawyers proved to be more talented in that defense.

On December 22, 1945, Tsuchiya's defense team asked for the dismissal of the entire case. Producing a respected medical doctor, who once volunteered his services to the Mitsushima Prison clinic in the winter of

1943, the defense provided new compelling testimony. Teas's official cause of death was "natural causes," and the doctor remembered examining the body and writing the official death report himself. The doctor also believed that prisoners had been moved from an especially frigid corner of the prison to a different location, thereby making it impossible for Gordon Gavard to have witnessed any beatings. Since Chief Prosecutor Geffen had rested his case on the Teas torture matter, the defense argued that there was no case at all.

In addition to a Japanese witness, the defense produced several American POWs from Mitsushima. In a move that was critical to this phase of the defense strategy, Chief Defense Counsel Dickinson attempted to prove that the former POWs were motivated by wartime-stirred hatred of the Japanese and not by the facts. For instance, Pvt. Vincent P. Vigil stated that Tsuchiya was known as "Little Glass Eye" because of his glass right eye. He swore under oath several times that the man who "often" beat him was the diminutive guard who wore a right glass eye beneath thick glasses. Vigil stated that as long as he lived, he would never forget the gleam in that right glass eye. Pfc. Fred Kolilus offered a similar account. Both men were introduced to the defendant upon their testimony, and both men learned at that moment that Tsuchiya wore his glass eye on the left side.

Cpl. Peter George added a twist to the tale by noting that the Mitsushima guards sometimes ordered American prisoners, under threat of death, to beat each other while these same guards supervised the event. George suggested that some of his colleagues might have been so outraged, so ashamed, and so determined to get back at their former tormentors for this type of treatment that they would do anything to see any one of them suffer and die. Hence, the "story" of Tsuchiya-inflicted beatings. It was a conspiracy, George concluded, "just like Roosevelt conspired to get us in World War II." The court was instructed to ignore George's final opinion.

To Dickinson, the twin issues of revenge and contradictory testimony seemed fine reasons for dismissal. Furthermore, most of the written eyewitness accounts presented at the trial were written two to two and a half years after the fact; they contributed, Dickinson charged, to a "hearsay argument which has no place in a court of law." Major Geffen insisted that Tsuchiya's victims would remember their torture in detail for the rest of their lives. Dozens of survivors had come forward, and their accounts were identical. Dickinson's effort to raise "reasonable doubt" and even imply "conspiracy" on the part of Mitsushima survivors was "understandable," said Geffen, in the face of "overwhelming evidence" against Tsuchiya.

Although Geffen exaggerated his claim of "overwhelming evidence," the defense motion for dismissal was denied. The trial continued.

There is also no solid evidence to suggest it, but the court's quick dismissal of Dickinson's argument about a postwar conspiracy of Mitsushima survivors against Tsuchiya might have been, at the least, influenced by coinciding events and a disgust for American conspiracy arguments. At the time of Dickinson's call for dismissal, the U.S. Congress had begun its investigation into the reasons behind America's lack of preparedness for World War II. These hearings were well covered by the press in Japan. During late December 1945, the Congress focused its attentions on a possible "conspiracy" of senior American military officers in the Pacific to "permit" the Japanese attack on Pearl Harbor. Sen. Scott D. Lucas of Illinois charged that one of the witnesses in this open hearing, Adm. Richmond Kelly Turner, knew that Japan was on war footing in late November and early December 1941 but that he had done nothing to put U.S. Navy forces on alert in the Pacific. He also did nothing to coordinate navy and army intelligence operations at a critical time. Gen. Sherman Miles, former chief of U.S. Army Intelligence, had told the Congress that as U.S.-Japan relations collapsed, the army and the navy needed to pool their intelligence resources. He had asked Turner to cooperate in the endeavor, but Turner had quashed the operation in the hours just before Pearl Harbor. Senator Lucas hoped in his tough questioning of Turner that the besieged admiral might also implicate his former commander in chief, Franklin Roosevelt, in the "conspiracy"; but Turner spent his days on Capitol Hill vehemently rejecting and denying the accusations. Roosevelt and the navy would have stopped at nothing to get America into the war, Lucas and a bipartisan coalition of congressmen charged.

Years later, Geffen remembered how much the U.S. military in Japan resented the conspiracy talk, the soiling of a recently deceased president's good name, and the implication that American military men would have encouraged the deaths of so many and for unexplained political benefits. Likewise, it seemed "fantastic" that a group of American POWs would concoct a conspiracy against a former guard. Whether it concerned POW survivors from Mitsushima or senior officers at the Pentagon, there was little interest in or evidence of "conspiracy" throughout the ranks. Geffen's connections between the Tsuchiya trial and the congressional hearings were artificial ones; however, the military's disgust for this turn in the congressional investigation was more profound than he suggested. Urging all those serving with the occupation in Japan to contain their anger against the

Congress's "attack on the military," the *Pacific Stars and Stripes* even asked its military readers to "go easy" on American civilians working with them "who might have connections with Congress." "Conspiracy" issues were indeed on the minds of those involved in the Tsuchiya trial, and most resented the very implication of their existence.[15]

The ending days of the Tsuchiya trial were dramatic ones, and both the Americans and the Japanese focused their attention accordingly. Huge crowds of Japanese civilians and U.S. military personnel now competed daily for the few spectator seats available. Some stayed outside the courtroom, under the close watch of police, even though they could hear or see nothing of the proceedings. Max Pestalozzi, a Red Cross representative in Japan during the last half of the war, testified about the sadistic behavior of the guards and the horrific living conditions of the prisoners at Mitsushima (although he never personally witnessed the beatings). A large man with a booming voice, Pestalozzi was also present every day of the trial in a spectator seat. Not opposed to outbursts, gesticulating, and other emotional reactions to trial testimony (especially defense efforts), he became a spectator for the spectators (and the press) to watch. One of the more dramatic moments (especially for the prosecution) involved the testimony of Capt. Nobaru Nakajima, the former commandant of Mitsushima. Considered a "soldier's soldier" who found the brutal behavior of the Japanese military beneath the pride and dignity of Japan itself, Nakajima apologized to the court for the "evil" of Tatsuo Tsuchiya. Blaming himself and his entire generation, Nakajima urged the court "to find justice in the matter." Nakajima surprised some observers. Geffen, for instance, expected a vigorous defense of everything that took place at Mitsushima. This did not happen; however, Dickinson and the defense wondered if the official translation of Nakajima's interesting testimony was truly correct. Dickinson now even questioned whether any Japanese-in-translation testimony was done properly and accurately. If not, the trial, he said, was over.

Dickinson's questioning of translation work, like many other defense tactics first trail-blazed here, would become part of common defense procedure in the many trials to come. Sho Onodera, a Japanese American and a U.S. Army second lieutenant, was the chief translator at the Tsuchiya trial. He admitted that his task was a difficult one, for much of the "pedestrian Japanese and English" used at the trial was "virtually impossible" to translate directly. Some mistakes in verbal translation often drew outbursts of laughter from the Japanese or American spectators, leading one group to question the other's humor as well as to official threats to "clear the court" if the disturbance did not cease. "Little Glass Eye," for instance, some-times became "Big Glass Eye" in translation and even "Big Glass Tooth" in one verbal exchange. During another cross-examination, Geffen attempted to make clear the distinction between a beating with a "stick" and a beating with a "club." The latter he considered especially brutal; however, there is no adequate distinction in the Japanese language between a "stick" and a "club." A larger problem arose after a full day of testimony about Tsuchiya and several "soldiers" beating Private Teas. The official translation simply read "soldier," implying singular blame for Tsuchiya alone.

Dickinson raised all of these points at the trial, calling it a "travesty of justice" in reference to his client's basic right to be heard and judged accu-rately. Yet the court examined the translation record, finding Dickinson's complaint more a semantic argument than a legal one. The court, Dickinson was told, "anticipated" problems with translation, and instead of the objection's leading to the dismissal of the case, as Dickinson once again hoped, the defense was praised by the court for its identification of difficult translation issues.[16]

After a brief recess for the 1945 Christmas holidays, the Tsuchiya case resumed with its final drama. Tsuchiya himself was called to the wit-ness stand. At first Geffen had opposed this "theater," but given the defendant's cold, unemotional reaction to the testimony against him, the prosecution team thought whatever words he had to offer could be easily turned against him. They would not be disappointed.

Tsuchiya admitted on the witness stand that he had struck prisoners eight or nine times with open palms. He denied the prosecution's allega-tions that he had used his fists and various instruments against helpless POWs. Tsuchiya also claimed that he did not recall a Private Teas, much less days of torture. Answering Geffen's questions for nearly three hours straight, Tsuchiya remained a portrait of composure. He also denied all the allegations, noting that a war wound received in China during August 1941 rendered his right arm rather useless. Consequently, it would have been impossible, he said, to beat anyone with force. Nevertheless, both Ameri-can and Japanese witnesses had remembered seeing Tsuchiya carrying heavy food parcels throughout his years at Mitsushima. He carried these items with both arms. At the least, the prosecution pointed out, those parcels weighed eighteen pounds apiece. Given the strength required for that task, the beatings were more than possible for Tsuchiya. In response, Tsuchiya continued to insist that all he had done was to slap POWs now and then, especially during the ending days of the war when food was scarce and discipline was poor. It was customary, added Tsuchiya's lawyer, Jiko Watanabe, for Japanese soldiers to slap other Japanese soldiers. Thus, a cultural infraction had been committed by his client, Watanabe pointed out, and little else. "I feel I treated the prisoners fairly," Tsuchiya concluded, "and under orders from my superior. I always looked after their protection and their interest. I don't think the prisoners had any grievances against me."[17]

On December 28, 1945, Tokyo's first war crimes trial ended. Without a trace of emotion, Tsuchiya stood at ramrod stiff attention as the eight-man U.S. military tribunal who oversaw his case read the verdict. He was found guilty and sentenced to "life imprisonment at hard labor." Tsuchiya had beaten Pfc. Robert Gordon Teas to death, they said, and also had ordered a total of one hundred prisoners to beat each other during his days as a Mitsushima guard. Tsuchiya's final words to the court simply reiterated his previous testimony, claiming that he was innocent of all cruelties and that he had tried to make prisoners "more comfortable" at Mitsushima. In a rare and emotional moment, a tearful Watanabe asked to address the court and was given permission to do so. Not only Tsuchiya's lawyer, Watanabe was the recently elected president of the Yokohama Lawyers Association. In that capacity and in the name of all of Japan, Watanabe said his tears were not for his client but in response to the "fairness of the proceedings." Dickinson's vigorous defense efforts and the general commitment of the court to seek the truth had been unexpected, Watanabe noted. He had joined the defense team in an effort to prevent the "easy lynching" of his client by an "occupying army." That effort was never made, and justice prevailed. He thanked the court for setting a "noble precedent."[18]

There had been reason for Watanabe's original concerns and fears. The U.S. military tribunal that heard the Tsuchiya case was not bound by the procedural rules, guidelines, and protections that are part of both the court-martial and civil court systems. Guilt could have been quickly determined and without apology. The IMTFE, given its Allied makeup and the diplomacy that had created it, was expected to be the best example of the victor's justice. It was with that in mind that Watanabe's tears of surprise and thankfulness were best understood. At the time of the Tsuchiya trial, the IMTFE was not expected to begin its work until spring 1946.

In the meantime, there were more military tribunals and trials. Tsuchiya's case was quickly followed by that of Lt. Kei Yuri, commandant of Prison Camp 17–B, who had allegedly ordered his subordinates to bayonet an American soldier to death in front of his fellow prisoners. Another commandant, Lt. Chotora Furushima, was accused of denying adequate food and clothing to American POWs in both Camps 1D and 3B, where he had been in charge. Both commandants were tried at the same time and both found guilty. There were many to try. Col. Robert V. Laughlin, the Eighth Army judge advocate in Japan, established five new military tribunals in early 1946. The caseload numbered 250 and would grow to over 300 in just a few months.[19]

Yet, to many observers of the Japanese war crimes matter, the first case of "significance" was not "Little Glass Eye's" but that of Gen. Tomoyuki Yamashita and the involvement of the U.S. Supreme Court in his fate. Given the press attention to and the general public knowledge of Yamashita's successful military campaigns, his late-1945 trial by military tribunal in the Philippines, which soon coincided with the Tsuchiya case, offered a further interesting preview of the many trials to come. Whereas the Tsuchiya case had had relatively little publicity outside of Japan, the Yamashita case had world press attention, leading contemporary and later critics to complain of a Hollywood-like atmosphere. That fact, combined with Gen. Douglas MacArthur's well-known attraction to showmanship, made the Yamashita trial quite the spectacle. MacArthur might have been Japan's future, but he also represented the passing of the American era in the Philippines. He had loved the place, and to a large degree he held Yamashita responsible for the misery it now faced. Thanks to the brutality of the Japanese occupation there, few Filipinos disagreed with the importance MacArthur accorded to the case. Nevertheless, like Tsuchiya's, the Yamashita case was a forerunner to the IMTFE's work and therefore officially labeled a "lesser" trial at the time. Since the case was destined for Supreme Court review, the "lesser" label merited some second thought. Nevertheless, both the prosecution and the defense in the Yamashita trial believed that the real precedents in war crimes–related law would be made in Tokyo by the IMTFE. Contemporary news reporters and latter-day analysts, fascinated by the symbolism of the Philippines' great liberator, MacArthur, punishing Yamashita, a legendary hero of Japan's Co-Prosperity Sphere over the Philippines, would embrace the type of showmanship in their depiction of the trial that MacArthur welcomed. And few of them liked that side of MacArthur. Today, a Japan war crimes specialist often finds that historians and others have heard more about the Yamashita trial than about the entire trials effort in Tokyo. At the time, the legal profession, whether Yamashita received a Supreme Court review or not, still awaited the larger "show" of the IMTFE in Tokyo.

Whereas Tsuchiya's defense team raised the issue of the evil of war as a means to shield their client from accusations of representing evil itself, the prosecution in the Yamashita case made the connection between institutionalized and personal evil. Yamashita would be hanged in late February 1946 not because he ordered his men to commit evil acts or because he made evil decisions, but because he was the officer in command of men who committed atrocities. Yamashita's predicament did indeed make headlines, and his hanging raised a number of legal, moral, and political questions that have since become the focus of both interested writers and documentary filmmakers.

More than sixty thousand Filipinos died at the hands of Japanese troops during Yamashita's one year of generalship in the Philippines. Without full military honors or respect for his rank, Yamashita was executed near Los Banos, where American POWs had been tortured. Many Japanese were shocked by the means of his execution even more than by the guilty verdict. The situation was not lost on Yamashita himself, who, in his final statement from the gallows, said he had done his best as a military commander and that was all. Poorly translated or not, his statement served, in a sense, as a warning to all those who thought they might be exempt from the unspeakable actions of their subordinates. That translation also symbolized Yamashita's inability to communicate with his troops, for he had truly failed to prevent their many atrocities. "As I said in Manila Supreme Court that I have done with all my capacity, so I don't ashame in front of God for what I have done when I have died. But if you say to me, 'you do not have any ability to command Japanese Army,' I should say nothing for it, because it is my nature. Now, our war criminal trial going on in Manila Supreme Court, so I wish be justify under your kindness and right. I don't blame my executioners. I will pray God bless them."[20]

Standing at six feet and weighing more than two hundred pounds, Yamashita was an imposing figure. His wartime victories in Southeast Asia had created something of a heroic reputation in Japan, and there were some Japanese who found it difficult to believe that the Americans would consider a great soldier a war criminal. One popular Japanese rumor following Yamashita's execution was that the whole trial and hanging had been a ruse. Given the Cold War tension between Washington and Moscow at the time, the rumor suggested that the Americans had brought Yamashita back to Japan through a top secret arrangement. Yamashita, according to the tale, was secretly training Japanese troops at home to fight alongside the Americans in the "inevitable" war between the United States and the Soviet Union. To some, this anticommunist resurrection of Yamashita made better sense than the trial and execution reports coming out of Manila.[21] Meanwhile, there were plenty of Americans who were shocked by the Yamashita hanging for other reasons. Hanson Baldwin of the *New York Times* wrote that the American people were seeing justice done in Europe with the Nazi trials at Nuremberg. In the Pacific, he said, too much time had been wasted in the name of fair play for "killers." He insisted that most of his newspaper's readers shared this sentiment, although he had no evidence of it.[22] One of those readers might have been Ellis Fuqua, one of New York's top attorneys. In the first extensive legal analysis of the Yamashita trial, Fuqua wrote, as early as spring 1946, that Yamashita had been a victim of the American need for scapegoats and that no one man could legally represent the actions of thousands of men in war.[23]

In the end, Yamashita believed he had received a more than adequate defense. He thanked each defense counsel personally moments before his hanging (although none of them were present). The U.S. Supreme Court agreed with his praiseworthy assessment of the defense team. Nevertheless, a minority of the Supreme Court justices also worried that an unfortunate precedent had been set in the case. On the same day as the opening arguments in the Tsuchiya trial in Tokyo, the Supreme Court granted a stay of execution in the Manila-based Yamashita case. Yamashita's American defense lawyers especially wanted the case transferred to a U.S. civil court. The stay was written as part of an effort to provide clear legal precedent for the upcoming trials. Yamashita had faced 123 atrocity counts during his trial by a U.S. Army commission. Arguing that Yamashita did not condone, approve, or encourage the men under his command to commit atrocities, his lawyers appealed the guilty verdict. At the same time, the Supreme Court saw an opportunity to break new legal ground in war crimes matters. More than seven hundred pending cases involving Japanese war crimes depended on the Supreme Court's action. One of the more headline-making ones involved Lt. Gen. Masaharu Homma, who was charged with the Bataan Death March and the demise of sixty-seven thousand American and Filipino troops.[24] As in the Yamashita case, critics of this non-IMTFE trial would complain of the introduction of "hearsay" evidence and that the defendant, Homma, was convicted because of this alleged mockery of justice. A more accurate and focused criticism might have been against the rules of evidence within the Yamashita or Homma tribunal. The U.S. military tribunal procedure differed from the typical Stateside court, and therefore it would always be easier to dismiss or reject something as "hearsay" in the latter than in the former. Joseph Keenan would later complain that the "lesser" trials outside of Tokyo were too quick to introduce "hearsay" evidence, but the proud, flamboyant chief prosecutor was always quick to praise whatever happened in Tokyo over trials on Guam, the Philippines, or elsewhere.

Landmark case or not, it was late December 1945 when the Supreme Court accepted the Yamashita case and then adjourned for the Christmas–New Years holidays. The delay created a considerable amount of tension; even Homma's lawyers said the Court's decision to "take a vacation at a critical time in world history" was difficult to understand.[25] Homma faced forty-three specific charges of crimes against humanity, and the witnesses against him included an impressive list of American war heros, foremost among them Gen. Jonathan Wainwright. Left in command of the Philippines defense following Gen. Douglas MacArthur's exit (under presidential order) to Australia, Wainwright's gallant defense of Corregidor and the resulting surrender had made his name a household word in America. Wainwright became America's most senior POW in Japanese captivity, and he was proud of the fact that he never bowed to his Japanese captors during the surrender ceremony and during his difficult postsurrender imprisonment. Wainwright testified that Homma's brutality extended beyond the maltreatment of combatants, including noncombatant Filipinos and U.S. civilian internees. Lt. Col Frank Meek, the chief prosecutor in the Homma case, especially emphasized Homma's responsibility for the infamous Bataan Death March. But it would be all for naught, he worried, if the Supreme Court ruled in favor of Yamashita's appeal.[26]

While everyone waited for the Court to return from its holiday break, a pro-Yamashita campaign was hastily organized in Japan. Led by Toichiro Araki, a Tokyo consulting engineer, the campaign put together a petition, bearing the names of eighty-six thousand Tokyo residents alone, to be presented to General MacArthur personally at his Tokyo residence. Mail-in forms were provided by a number of Japanese newspapers, and Araki turned a rubble-strewn vacant lot on the Ginza (downtown Tokyo) into his Yamashita campaign headquarters. Araki's petition did not ask for clemency. Instead, it asked for one of two sentences for Yamashita. Hanging, the petition suggested, was an insult to Yamashita's family, his gallant service to the nation, and Japan's regard for his heroism. A lighter sentence of life imprisonment was requested, and if that was not possible, then the "soldier's right to harakiri" should be honored by MacArthur's command. The sister of Yamashita's wife headed the list of names on the petition; it was she, more than Araki, who insisted that the list be given to MacArthur personally. No other American would do. Araki's petition concluded that "General Yamashita has been a man of good reputation among our people and has done his duty to his mother country just as all your men have done bravely to your country."[27]

Col. Herbert B. Wheeler, MacArthur's military secretary, accepted the petition on behalf of General MacArthur. The latter concluded that the petition effort was part of the politicking and lobbying associated with the early-January 1946 elections. He was right. This was the first Diet (parliamentary) election under American-supervised democratic rules. Without question, many of Araki's petitioners were associated with the campaigns of old-line nationalist politicians running for Diet seats, and that fact annoyed General MacArthur no end.[28] He postponed the elections, noting that the friends of war criminals in elective office might be bad for the new Japan. The elections would be rescheduled, he promised, once his office amassed a petition or list of its own. This list included "ineligible politicians" (i.e., former activists and supporters of the wartime regime) for Diet service. MacArthur's election postponement was a short one: the new elections were held after Yamashita was hanged.[29]

MacArthur's role in the Yamashita trial has always been a matter of fascination for the few analysts of the Pacific region war crimes trials. To the first scholars to investigate the matter, such as John Alan Appleman in his 1950s writings on military tribunals, Richard Rovere and Arthur Schlesinger Jr. in their general work on Douglas MacArthur, and Charles Fairman in his analyses of Supreme Court early postwar decisions, the Yamashita case appeared to involve General MacArthur's arrogance, interference, and personal view of war crimes trials, as well as the trials' significance to postwar Japan. According to these writers, MacArthur had too much power and influence in the Pacific, and Washington, they complained, was negligent in even permitting this situation during a critical time in postwar policymaking.[30]

Few analysts would disagree today with the general conclusions, or at the least with the tenor and tone of these early accounts. In any event, as the Tokyo trials began, America's number one hero of the Pacific War was indeed Gen. Douglas MacArthur. In charge of the postwar Japanese Occupation Government, MacArthur often defined Japanese political change in his own terms. Although his orders to rebuild a peaceful and progressive Japan enjoyed certain "liberties of interpretation" granted by President Harry Truman, MacArthur's power did have limits.[31] Did he cross the line in the Yamashita matter?

MacArthur's position in the Yamashita case was influenced by a variety of sometimes contradictory motives and objectives. They included a soldier's vengeance and a military governor's expressions of power. They concerned his insistence on justice for the Philippines (soon to become the Republic of the Philippine Islands), the host of his military career for years. And they involved the political need for the closure of an ugly past before moving on to a new era of Japanese progress, prosperity, and peace. Because of the unusual charge of command responsibility violations in specific reference to Yamashita, MacArthur could even agree with Supreme Court Justices Frank Murphy and Wiley Rutledge when they complained that the Japanese general had been convicted of "an unrecognizable crime." Nevertheless, MacArthur argued that Yamashita had broken the recognized "codes" of the "social order." That was the point behind the war crimes charges, he said. Furthermore, thanks to Yamashita's tolerance, if not sponsorship, of evil in his own ranks, the Japanese general was also declared unfit to wear a soldier's uniform during his own trial.

In its majority opinion, the Supreme Court, represented by Chief Justice Harlan Fiske Stone, concluded that the primary charge against Yamashita (failing to control the actions of his own troops) constituted a violation of the laws of war and military conduct. But did Yamashita receive "due process" during his own trial? Even a fallen enemy, Yamashita's lawyers had argued, enjoys basic civil rights, and they had a long list of prosecutorial "maltreatment and insults" to their client. Mindful of this accusation, Justice Rutledge worried that the defendant had not received a fair hearing at all. Official documents, translations of documents, diaries, affidavits, photographs, and even hearsay testimony were virtually nonexistent in the case. The lack of evidence was disturbing to Rutledge, even though his argument seemed concerned more with the quantity of paperwork than with any other factor. Consequently, Rutledge argued, Yamashita had been convicted on "ex parte evidence," or raw opinion as opposed to the facts. Such a procedure, he concluded, would never be permitted in a Stateside court of law.

According to MacArthur, the Yamashita trial had been conducted "to ascertain the full truth unshackled by any artificialities of narrow method or technical arbitrariness."[32] He claimed that the latter was a serious problem inherent in the American court of law. Although this comment might have solicited a firm response from the Supreme Court, Chief Justice Stone ignored the issue. The Supreme Court had no further comment on the matter of MacArthur-influenced military tribunals. More to the point, it had no jurisdiction to comment on it. It would be MacArthur who reviewed the findings and sentences of the U.S. Army military tribunals in the Pacific. It would be MacArthur, and not the Supreme Court justices, who made the final judgment in the Yamashita case and succeeding cases. One post–Yamashita trial analyst, A. Frank Reel, in a strong attack on "MacArthur's execution of Yamashita" and the Supreme Court's "ineptness" in the face of the MacArthur wartime "legend," even claimed that the general deliberately arranged the ending trial date (December 7) to serve as fitting revenge for the Japanese attack on Pearl Harbor, which had taken place exactly four years earlier.[33] Reel began to write his critique just hours after the end of the trial, finally finding a publisher (Octagon Books) three years later. His book constituted the first analysis of the Yamashita trial written for a general audience, and it would serve somewhat as the definitive work for years to come. Yet there was no evidence to support the December 7 account, and his charges concerning MacArthur's "executioner" objectives and the Supreme Court's "ineptness" were never substantiated. Reel's work did remind its many readers, however, that the decisions of both MacArthur and the Supreme Court in the Yamashita matter would always be controversial ones.

Given the Supreme Court's Yamashita decision, numerous Japanese officers could now be tried before military commissions for crimes they might have had little knowledge of at the time when they were committed. Ignorance of the crimes of one's subordinates was not a defense. Especially in reference to the maltreatment of prisoners of war, nearly all command officers standing trial could now be easily found guilty. If one of those officers had failed to institute an orderly system of care for POWs, guilt was also certain, or if he had failed to take action against those in his command who beat prisoners. The Supreme Court's decision essentially echoed the opening statements of Robert M. Kerr, the chief prosecutor in the Yamashita case. Kerr had claimed that the defendant "must have known" of the atrocities in the Philippines, "and if he did not know of them, he nonetheless had a responsibility to learn of them."[34]

In addition to being pleased that the war crimes trials could now proceed with "vigor," MacArthur in his official response to the Yamashita ruling took some Washington officials by surprise. In a low-key and little-known lobbying effort, MacArthur insisted that the Truman administration make the "command responsibility" decision part of U.S. military law as well. These were not just rules for the "enemies of the past war," he noted.[35] In any event, the new postwar nation of the Philippines would apply the "command responsibility" law to its armed forces within a matter of months.

Referencing "America's Yamashita case," the Philippine law stated precisely that "a commander alone is responsible for all that his unit does or fails to do."

That responsibility, the law concluded, could not be "shifted to another person," and it called for a commander's "strict discipline among those under his immediate command."[36]

Following the lead of the Philippines would take time for the United States. President Truman said he favored this "military reform in principle" but that the Pentagon needed to study "its implications." At first it appeared that Truman, as commander in chief, hoped to avoid the impact of the Yamashita case in his military, but this was far from the case. Truman wanted "command responsibility" spelled out in even more precise terms than it was in the Philippines statutes. America's "law of land warfare" would be written without much room for interpretation. "A commander is responsible if he has actual knowledge, or should have knowledge, that troops or other persons subject to his control are about to commit or have committed a war crime and he fails to take the necessary and reasonable steps to ensure compliance with the law of war or to punish violators thereof."[37]

Although the "law of land warfare" became a little-recognized U.S. benefit of the Yamashita case, there were those who saw the case as a precedent for a more gruesome agenda. Sen. Theodore Bilbo of Mississippi, for example, told MacArthur that the Yamashita case paved the way to "punish Japan." He asked him to look into the possibility of "mass sterilization," thereby sparing future generations of Americans from "another war with the Japs."[38] The exiting high commissioner of the Philippines, Paul McNutt, even advocated the "Bilbo solution" in a series of public speeches, adding that "sterilization might be too good for Japan."[39] Justice Murphy of the Supreme Court, who had dissented in the majority Yamashita decision, said he had worried that the case might unleash "the vengeance seekers." It might even be expected, he said. But it was his colleagues on the Court that troubled him. He feared they might have given way to the emotions of the moment rather than representing "judicial statesmanship of the highest order."[40]

Although it has been often forgotten in the rush to examine the "command responsibility" aspects of the Yamashita trial, there was more to the case than "command responsibility" arguments. In fact, much of the trial addressed issues divorced from what Yamashita's subordinates did or did not do. The prosecution in the Yamashita case spent much time describing the Japanese general's personal supervision of the destruction of Manila and the killing of many of its residents. Hence, even Chief Prosecutor Kerr wondered if the case had become more about Yamashita's own violation of the laws of war than about the "command responsibility" charge. It had been a fast-moving case, and that in itself always remained an issue of concern with regard to adequate resources, evidence-gathering, and testimony. The military commission hearing the case also had trouble balancing the arguments and the evidence, concluding that Yamashita "might have" ordered the destruction of the people of the Philippines during his military campaign there. Kerr produced plenty of witness testimony that explained that dozens of Yamashita's subordinates believed they were acting on his personal orders of destruction. But Kerr never saw this phase of the trial as particularly convincing or compelling. He would feel the same way decades later.[41]

The reason for Kerr's doubt involved the history of the Japanese campaign in the Philippines. As early as December 1944, Yamashita had been trying to evacuate his troops from impending doom. Following his capture, he even told American interrogators that he had hoped Manila might be spared from the battle, implying an interest in saving the lives of innocent civilians. MacArthur also regarded his Japanese opposition in the battle for Manila as poor troops, renegades, not representative of Yamashita's best and brightest. Manila was sacked by the Japanese, but was it under Yamashita's order? The order for destruction was more a generally accepted rumor than fact, and MacArthur was more satisfied with the rumor than with the further investigations of the facts.[42] Some have taken this satisfaction another step, arguing that MacArthur conspired to depict Yamashita as an obvious "villain" and himself as a "hero liberator" in the eyes of the Filipinos. According to this account, MacArthur planned to form a glorious new government, personally designed by him, after exposing the corruption of the previous regime.[43] Such accounts accord with the many tales of MacArthur's arrogance and showmanship. But it could also be said that MacArthur simply wanted Yamashita held responsible for war crimes in the Philippines. Furthermore, MacArthur was already a "hero liberator," and the political fate of the Philippines had not been his decision.

Commenting on the decision to execute Yamashita, the *Nippon Times* quoted an old Japanese proverb: "By killing one bird, many others will be saved." This respected Japanese newspaper suggested that Yamashita symbolized the punishment of an entire army, which, by the time of the battle for Manila, behaved like a demoralized, angry mob. With that in mind, the *Nippon Times* challenged the generally held belief in Japan, and even in MacArthur's headquarters, that Yamashita had been a great general. A true leader, the paper implied, would not have permitted his army to sack neighborhoods, murder civilians, plunder for plunder's sake. This position was not a popular one, and the paper raised a point that was often overlooked by those who debated the outcome of the Yamashita verdict. Too many Japanese war criminals might now escape justice, the paper's editors complained, for Yamashita was expected to die for all of their sins.[44]

"Hundreds of killers are now absolved," added Tokutaro Kimura, a Japanese judge, soon to be the justice minister in the cabinet of Prime Minister Shigeru Yoshida, a strong advocate for war crimes trials and a lively speaker on behalf of new Japanese commitments to democratic justice. "The allies might take solace in personifying the evil of wartime Japan through the career of Gen. Yamashita," Kimura observed, "but too many precise war crimes may go unpunished."[45] Why must there be "one representative of guilt," he asked, when there was so much more to be investigated and tried? He even worried that the Allies would, despite public comments to the contrary, put little effort into the coming trials. A few "symbols of evil" would be found, a "spectacular but brief" trial held, denunciations of the "old Japan" made, and "the process would end before it started" (Kimura, 32-33). This would be a "mockery of the justice so needed in the New Japan." To Kimura, the Tsuchiya trial had been more valuable to the cause of justice than Yamashita's. An individual had been punished for individual war crimes in that case. Given the role of famous Japanese lawyers such as Jiko Watanabe in the "Little Glass Eye" trial, a "proper statement" had been made on behalf of Japan's new commitment to justice and fair play. Kimura had his doubts that the Yamashita trial would be remembered in such a light, but at least, he noted in an effort to find some sarcastic humor in the matter, the "Yamashita case was a Philippines case. Such things can never happen in Occupied Japan" (Kimura, 34).

Kimura would never be satisfied with the allegedly weak Allied caseload, but he was mistaken about the Allied commitment to proceed with the trials. Most American observers saw the Yamashita verdict as a precedent that would facilitate the conviction of many senior wartime policymakers and military leaders. Indeed, the machinery to proceed with this commitment had been long in place. Only days after the Japanese attack on Pearl Harbor, President Franklin Roosevelt had cabled the Tokyo government, asking that they comply with the rules of war and all international agreements that addressed the treatment of prisoners of war. In August 1942, as the reports of Japanese atrocities and maltreatment of American prisoners flooded his office, Roosevelt warned Japan that "barbaric crimes" would be punished after the war.[46] Victory in the Pacific was far from assured at the time of Roosevelt's warnings. It was not until early 1944, during the successful U.S. assault on Japan's forward (once considered unassailable) navy base in the Truk group of the Caroline Islands that American diplomats began to work with the Allies on the mechanics of postwar trials.

In the latter months of the war, the State Department's Herbert Pell served as the president's representative on the United Nations Commission for the Investigation of War Crimes. Although preoccupied with the imminent collapse of Hitler's Germany and the need to try the architects and enforcers of his "Final Solution" for European Jewry, the commission entertained a variety of Asian/Pacific-based proposals concerning Japan. It was a difficult process. Pell was especially pressured by the Chinese government, which in 1944 declared Japan "an evil race." The Chinese ambassador, Wellington Koo, even asked for several international military tribunals. Much of their work, of course, would be centered in China. Each would have sweeping powers to detain thousands of suspects and conduct investigations whereby few Japanese civilians and soldiers would be exempt from scrutiny. Pell understood the reasons behind the Chinese hatred of Japan, but the Chinese position only delayed the creation of the type of legal apparatus, divorced from motivations of hatred and revenge, that the American government could support.[47]

Whereas the Chinese desired a huge and expensive operation, the chairman of this UN commission, England's Sir Cecil Hurst, worried about jurisdiction, balancing budgets, and the worthiness of the many rumored Japanese atrocity reports versus the known reality of Hitler's genocide. Pell found Hurst to be Eurocentric, overly conservative in his assessment of atrocities in the Far East, and too generous in his depiction of Japan as "just a distant ally to Nazi Germany." The Free French, Belgian, and Dutch delegations had views similar to Hurst's, explaining that the Japanese situation had low priority in contrast to the Nazi terror in their own German-occupied homelands. When the atrocity reports emerge from Allied-liberated Far East French or Dutch empires, said the French and Dutch delegations, "that will be the time for review and consideration." Hence, Pell was caught between the Chinese and the western European view of the war crimes scene, but he noted that "in the long run it was a decent place to be."[48] Although not fond of the Chinese view, he helped champion a Chinese request to create a specific Far East panel to investigate Japanese war crimes. Especially because of Australian support and lobbying, Pell's special investigation panel became reality.

The Australian government had already laid a foundation for Pacific-region war crimes trials. The chief justice of Queensland, Sir William Webb, had led an investigation into Japanese atrocities in the southwest Pacific. Webb was a friend of both Pell and Douglas MacArthur, and, more to the point, he insisted that the Allies must not ignore Japanese crimes against humanity. Even in Australia itself, Webb told Pell in late 1944, the Australians were simply grateful for the fact that Japanese invaders had never touched their shores. Japanese shootings and beatings paled in comparison to the reports of death camps in Europe. Perhaps to some Australians, Webb observed, the Japanese war crimes trials would be more trouble than they were worth. This type of sentiment worried Webb as much as the Chinese desire for revenge worried Pell. "People here, as you yourself have seen on more than one occasion," Webb wrote Pell from Australia, "are rather apt to forget the Japanese side of this global conflict." The war criminals "must not go free," the chief justice told his friend. He volunteered himself to stand as "Chief Booster" and supporter of Pell's call for "fair and just trials in the Orient."[49]

In the latter weeks of his life, President Roosevelt aligned himself strongly with what some French and Dutch delegates called "Pell's cause."[50] Roosevelt took a strong moral tone in that support, explaining that the postwar world must be a united and humane one divorced from the type of madness championed by fascists and militarists.[51] At the time of Roosevelt's April 1945 death, the battle for Okinawa had just begun. The outcome of the war in the Pacific had yet to be determined, and the war crimes issue had been largely an ideological matter for the four-term president. In comments obviously connected to the type of idealistic goals expressed earlier in the war through his Atlantic Charter, Roosevelt described the upcoming trials as "democracy's case against fascism." It was his successor, Harry Truman, who would concentrate on the practical aspects of the trials.

A living symbol of that practicality was Joseph B. Keenan, a former assistant to the U.S. attorney general and director of the Criminal Division of the Justice Department. In late November 1945, Truman appointed him chief prosecutor for the IMTFE effort in Tokyo. Nicknamed "Joe the Key," Keenan had been one of the early New Dealers. He had personally prosecuted famous, headline-making gangsters of the era, such as "Machine Gun Kelly." Also a tireless lobbyist for White House–sponsored legal initiatives in Congress, he persuaded a majority of congressmen to pass tough new antiracketeering laws. His successful wheeling and dealing on Capitol Hill won him the "Joe the Key" nickname. He liked it.[52]

A rare photograph of Chief Prosecutor Joseph Keenan without his trademark bow tie. Here (*third from left*), Keenan prepares to leave Washington National Airport for Tokyo with his new IMTFE staff. *Left to right,* Col. Thomas Morrow, John Darsey, Keenan, Henry Hauxhurst, Carlisle Higgins, John W. Finelly, and Otto Lowe. (Courtesy of Douglas MacArthur Memorial)

Usually wearing his trademark extra-large bow tie, Keenan was known for his courtroom theatrics and unique facial expressions. One aide remembered that Keenan "was quite a character," who could be more persuasive with a jury by "strategically raising a bushy eyebrow" than by offering grand analytical summations. Accused by critics of "having an ego as tall as the Empire State Building," Joseph B. Keenan found it especially annoying when he was confused in the late-1940s press with the Truman administration's labor policy advisor, Joseph P. Keenan. The war crimes trials would make him more recognizable than the latter; on occasion, though, he would introduce himself to reporters covering the trials as "Joe the Key."[53]

The new chief prosecutor enjoyed a host of powerful political contacts. Hence it is still difficult to prove who was the most instrumental in his appointment to Tokyo. President Truman remembered Keenan from his days as Senator Truman, chairman of the Senate Defense Appropriations Committee. Largely concerned with the appropriate financing of various World War II military operations, Senator Truman had admired Keenan's skillful lobbying "on a budget." Keenan took personal interest in the financing of the attorney general's office, and in an era of burgeoning deficits, he paid attention to balancing the books while at the same time proceeding with an ambitious agenda. Truman had moved forward with the plan to try Japanese war criminals with the assumption that there was plenty of available funding, and that from the Justice Department alone. This was not the case. Truman asked the War Department to shoulder the bill, although only a bare-bones budget would be available to the chief prosecutor.[54] Consequently, Keenan's talent in balancing budgets was especially important to Truman; the commander in chief also assumed that if Keenan's operational budget fell on hard times, perhaps he could appeal to another admirer, Douglas MacArthur.

Born in Pawtucket, Rhode Island, January 11, 1888, Keenan was a graduate of Brown University (1910) and the Harvard Law School (1913). During World War I he had served with the 137th Field Artillery and later with the Judge Advocate Generals Department. He always remembered his World War I service with fondness and at times regretted the decision to leave the military. This helped make him all the more an admirer of General MacArthur and his accomplishments. Keenan told him of his admiration, most likely influencing MacArthur to ask for him as chief prosecutor. The two men developed a lively correspondence before Keenan formally took up his duties in Japan. Although there was much heaping of praise upon each other in those many letters, issues of substance were also discussed. They ranged from staffing matters to reactions to the Yamashita case. This correspondence would continue for several years after Keenan left Tokyo and after MacArthur was relieved of command by President Truman during the Korean War.[55]

The War Department's orders to MacArthur in reference to "Joe the Key's" chief prosecutor duties had been straightforward. "The President has approved the appointment by you of Mister Joseph Baker Keenan as counsel on your staff to have full charge in your theater of the trial of persons charged with such war crimes as consist of planning, preparing, initiating or waging a war of aggression or in violation of international treaties and agreements or of participating in a common plan of conspiracy for any of the foregoing purposes."[56] Nevertheless, Keenan's task would always be part of a larger Allied effort. MacArthur's military tribunals would also continue, but the trials of so-called Class A war criminals, or the "Big Fish" as Keenan usually quipped, was the primary mission of the IMTFE. Yet, before the Allies could agree on the Class A list itself, agreement on the very definition of a Japanese war crime was required. In this basic but vital exercise, Keenan welcomed comparisons to the similar goals and objectives of the Allied-administered trials in Nuremberg; however, he especially wanted specific Far East distinctions made as well. At first Keenan believed that Allied agreement on a basic mission statement would symbolize Allied harmony as the trials moved along.[57] He was soon to discover that Allied harmony was elusive at times.

What is a Class A category Japanese war crime? Outside of gathering his staff of forty and building early working relationships with other IMTFE members, Keenan was most preoccupied with answering this basic question before his December 1945 arrival in Tokyo. It would be an answer in seventeen parts.

The first several subsections of the definition explained that war planning and the deliberate effort to break peace treaties constituted criminal behavior. The consequences of these plans and conspiracies were then addressed, such as murder, forced deportation, slave labor, or ill treatment of POWs, internees, or civilian populations and the "wanton destruction of cities, towns or villages or any devastation not justified by military necessity." Certain statutes of limitation were established, namely any involvement in the above issues near or after September 18, 1931 (the date of the "Mukden Incident," the Japanese invasion of Manchuria), was within the IMTFE's field of review. Other subsections even addressed the issue of Japanese reaction to the war crimes trials themselves, insisting that "fair play" must be a guiding factor in any IMTFE verdict. The "international character of the court," Keenan wrote, "and of the authority by which it is appointed should be properly recognized and emphasized, particularly in dealings with the Japanese people."[58]

Meanwhile, the United Nations organization could question any Class A list that was arranged, forcing the IMTFE to recreate that list if necessary. Even the execution of death sentences could be deferred if the testimony of the convicted "would be of value in the trial of other war criminals." At the same time, General MacArthur would be kept abreast of all trial developments. If he refused to turn over a suspect for trial in another country, the final decision to extradite or not would rest with President Truman.

But the final point, number 17, would raise the most controversy and opposition. Emperor Hirohito was not to be placed on any war criminals list. No explanation was given in the official Class A definition. That decision stimulated a variety of emotions in the Allied ranks. Keenan hoped it would all go away. It would not.[59] To some, such as the Philippine government, point 17 did not belong in the IMTFE mission statement/war crimes definition. It was a Class A listing matter, the Filipinos said. Keenan eventually agreed with them, and at least as the trials began, the Allies could claim a basic harmony on sixteen of the seventeen parts of their general working definition.[60]

The Allied debate over point 17 would still be raging when "Joe the Key" arrived in Tokyo. Building the Class A list was never as easy as Keenan hoped. Yet the American chief prosecutor set an optimistic tone in the weeks before the IMTFE trials began. When asked by an unusually candid Japanese press about the potential for "allied rifts" over Hirohito and other issues, Keenan insisted that Japanese worries in this regard were misplaced. The Japanese press should be concerned about the reaction of the Japanese people to the trials, Keenan said, and "not losing sleep over allied legal talk." The Allies had "come a long way," he noted, "just to set up trial procedure." The rest, he concluded, would "fly well."[61]

From the guilt of Yamashita to the fate of Hirohito, the World War II victors sometimes raised more questions than the answers they gave. In spite of controversy and argument, they never doubted the necessity of their mission. The cause of the "Good War" against fascism and militarism continued in the form of the war crimes trials. Given the record of Japanese mass murder and cruelty, there was, said Keenan, "little choice."[62] It remained to be seen whether the IMTFE and the military tribunals could truly contribute to the era of justice and reason that the new postwar world championed. By 1946 the stage, at least, had been set. "Evil" was about to be punished.

Chapter 2

The Trials Proceed

The IMTFE and Keenan's "Big Fish"

Japanese observers, at first skeptical, have been convinced of the genuine character of allied justice. The eminently reasonable and fair though strict sentence [*sic*] passed for charges which were proved, have convinced us of the fairness and judicious objectivity of the trial procedure.

Nippon Times, *September 16, 1947*

According to the Potsdam Declaration, issued on July 26, 1945, by the United States, Great Britain, and China, the Allies did not "intend that the Japanese shall be enslaved as a race or destroyed as a nation, but stern justice shall be meted out to all war criminals, including those who have visited cruelties on our prisoners."[1] Chief Prosecutor Keenan's first task, therefore, was to conclude who might be "the first war criminal." Some felt that there was no doubt. Emperor Hirohito, the symbol of Japanese life and culture, was that "first criminal." The lobbying effort to try him was intense, and it represented a cross-section of Allied opinion. Though the opening trial dates for Keenan's effort were long known to be in the spring of 1946, he had arrived early at his post, and one of the primary reasons involved the "studying" of the Hirohito matter. He wanted to make the Hirohito trial decision on site, he told the press. It was necessary, Keenan believed, to separate the major war criminals from those "who sinned more grievously in the matter of occupation tasks and the mistreatment of prisoners." The latter group, he concluded, was better dealt with in large U.S. military tribunals, such as the one that was handling the Pacific islands trials on Guam. For the moment, Hirohito would be his "primary personal concern."[2]

But organizing the war crimes trials effort would prove to be a mammoth task for Keenan. "This case is my primary personal concern" was uttered often by the chief prosecutor in reference to dozens of particular trials. He said it too many times. In the United States Keenan was known for threatening criminal suspects with "clearing his desk of all other cases" in the interest of making the life of that suspect a "living hell." Keenan made such statements when he wanted a given suspect to tell the truth or to supply additional information. The threat usually worked. The "my primary personal concern" comment was another favorite expression of the chief prosecutor, and it became a joke to the press corps covering the Tokyo trials. Fortunately for Keenan, no one took him to task for his repeated utterances of it.[3] Such things did add, however, to his reputation for showmanship and the 1940s version of the "sound bite."

The decision about trying Hirohito was not made by Keenan, although much of the world press assumed at one time that it was. General MacArthur, with President Truman's support, gave the final word on the subject. The Hirohito trial decision would always be intimately linked to the Occupation Government's larger endeavor to reform the entire political-economic infrastructure of defeated Japan. Various public hints of a "no trial" decision would come as early as December 1945. In that month MacArthur's headquarters released its "comprehensive list" of war criminals, without Hirohito's name on it. Quite a few Japanese, who assumed the "list" would include Hirohito and Tokyo-based wartime politicos only, were shocked to learn that it included members of nearly every profession from every corner of the country. Matsutaro Shoriki, for instance, the publisher of Tokyo's largest morning newspaper, *Yomiuri-Hochi,* read his indictment as a war criminal in his own newspaper. Shoriki's paper had enthusiastically supported the war effort; however, after the indictment his own employees seized *Yomiuri-Hochi* with the announcement that the newspaper now supported "democratic values." The former chief editorial writer for the paper, Michio Iwamura, even suggested that the employee revolution at *Yomiuri Hochi* should be emulated by other workers in other businesses. "Fascism has no place in the new Japan," Iwamura claimed, suggesting that MacArthur's war criminals list was meant to encourage antifascist purges across the country.[4] Iwamura was partially correct, for MacArthur's Occupation Government had a sweeping agenda. But there were limits to MacArthur's big sweep, especially if it might disturb Japan's delicate postwar stability.

Destroying the emperor would destroy Japan, MacArthur argued. Though once revered by many as a god, Hirohito had been little more than a figurehead, MacArthur said. Even if the emperor had been present during the Pearl Harbor decision-making process, for example, labeling that presence a criminal conspiracy would "weaken" the Japanese-American "co-operative spirit." That "spirit" also represented the new U.S.-Japan relationship. Horrible consequences, ranging from anti-American violence to procommunist agitation, would be the "real result" of a Hirohito trial. MacArthur based his conclusions more on personal assessment than on any hardcore intelligence information.[5] Keenan would later claim that "legally" his office had every right to try Hirohito and that MacArthur had exaggerated the possible Japanese reaction.[6] Yet Hirohito was never included on the war criminals lists throughout the trials period. For years to come, many Japanese thanked the American government for sparing him.

The "no trial" decision was not without controversy in U.S.-Allied relations. Washington's allies, namely the Filipinos, the Australians, and the Chinese, especially challenged the notion of Hirohito as a figurehead. Meanwhile, although often indirectly, several indicted Japanese war criminals helped argue the Allied case for a Hirohito trial. One of those defendants, Gen. Toshizo Nishio, remembered Hirohito's telling the September 6, 1941, meeting of the Supreme War Council that "Japan might have to fight if things didn't improve." Nishio's defense team attempted to point blame away from their client, and the emperor was not exempt in the effort. The September 6 conference had been called in response to growing military impatience with the deadlocked Washington-Tokyo peace talks during that period.

At this conference, Japanese army and navy leaders spoke of military plans to break the deadlock, Nishio remembered, and Hirohito listened to them all. Nishio had been the commander in chief of Japanese forces in China and a former inspector general of military education. His trial revealed great detail on Hirohito and early wartime policymaking. The emperor, he said, favored more negotiations with the Americans, but he did nothing at the September 6 meeting to halt military planning against them. As U.S.-Japan relations deteriorated, Hirohito called a second meeting of the Supreme War Council, consisting of fifteen or sixteen generals and admirals and lasting nearly three hours. The emperor sat silently throughout the meeting, but no one questioned the precise military plans to assault the Americans. Nishio insisted that these meetings were more informational than decision-making and that Hirohito was there to be informed. But he still had an opinion, and it was quietly but obviously exhibited. Hirohito's opinion, barely perceptible or not, Nishio's lawyers argued, carried great weight in the Supreme War Council. The emperor, Nishio said, "seemed" to take personal interest in the military plans through his "nodding approvals" of all of them. Again, Keenan believed this eyewitness testimony alone was good enough for a Hirohito indictment, but the

Koichi Kido, the former keeper of the privy seal, under cross-examination by the prosecution. (Courtesy of Douglas MacArthur Memorial)

MacArthur-championed political assessment of the emperor's postwar worth always prevailed.[7]

Although the emperor was protected from prosecution, his own royal household faced a long series of trials. Prince Fumimaro Konoye and Marquis Koichi Kido were arrested as early as December 1945. Konoye had been premier three times, and Kido, as the wartime lord keeper of the privy seal, had been the emperor's closest advisor. Under the three Konoye cabinets, the "China Incident" (the Japanese invasion of China) took place. All political parties with the exception of the totalitarian Imperial Rule Assistance Association had been prohibited, and the Japanese education system had been revamped along militarist lines.

Viscount Masatoshi Okochi and Count Tadamasa Sakai, also close to Hirohito, were jailed. Okochi had been a member of the House of Peers and president of the Riken Scientific Research Institute; he had once argued that the emperor "supported the eradication of the enemies of the Japanese Empire." Sakai, the former wartime agricultural minister, had once claimed that the Japanese farmers who in the summer of 1944 committed suicide on Saipan rather than surrendering to the invading Americans "were gods in the eyes of the Emperor."[8] Whether Hirohito himself offered encouragement to these wartime leaders, or whether his name was invoked only to justify their own policies, remained a mystery.

If there was a potentially powerful Allied argument in favor of a Hirohito trial that might sway MacArthur, it came from the Philippines. MacArthur's emotional attachment to Manila, his longtime home away from home, was well known. His friendship with J. Antonio Araneta, the national executive of the Philippines Lawyers Guild, was not so well known; Araneta was a tireless lobbyist in favor of a Hirohito trial. His efforts to persuade his friend were cordial and direct, but he combined this friendly persuasion with a lobby effort in Washington. Bearing a petition unanimously signed by his Lawyers Guild, Araneta urged President Truman to try Hirohito. The petition was submitted to the White House by both Araneta and sympathetic representatives from the American National Lawyers' Guild. A majority of the American guild's members had also previously endorsed a Hirohito trial.

Araneta's argument was a straightforward one. Comparing the emperor to Hitler and Mussolini, Araneta cited Japanese law, which confirmed that Hirohito was considered the head of state. He quoted members of Hirohito's own family who had proclaimed that the emperor was the "master" of that state. Hirohito had not denied that he was aware of a number of plans to wage aggressive war, including the Japanese invasion and occupation of the Philippines. According to Japanese law, only Hirohito had the authority to launch such a war. Hence, he "sanctioned" the resulting war crimes. "Hirohito," Araneta's petition read, "should be declared, together with his economic, political, and military associates in aggression, a war criminal, to be tried, and punished by the international tribunal." His trial, Araneta concluded, would assist General MacArthur in the effort to rid Japan of its "fascist past, clearing the way for a democratic progress and peace in the Far East and the entire world."[9] But MacArthur remained unmoved. Keenan later commented that he thought Araneta's trip to Washington and the appeal to Truman had been a "poor strategy which backfired."[10] His comments implied that Araneta's greatest sin was going over the head of his old friend and turning directly to Truman. Whether angered or not over Araneta's tactics, MacArthur never doubted his own

Hirohito decision. Truman welcomed Araneta and his petition with a smile and a firm Allied handshake for the cameras even as he continued to accept MacArthur's "no trial" reasoning.[11]

Although many in the Japanese political community thought it unwise to upset the victors and vocalize their opposition to any trial of the emperor, others made their position loud and clear. Known for his eloquence and skill at debate, Hiro Oyama, for example, a former Labor Party Diet member and a Waseda University professor, publicly urged MacArthur "to proceed with the trials of killers, proceed with the rejuvenation of Japan, and proceed with the protection of a sacred culture, our Emperor." His speeches were welcomed by Japanese of a variety of political persuasions, and his link of Japan's "peaceful future" to its "few symbols of a peaceful past" (Hirohito) was especially welcomed. He also warned that "a social peace" was not guaranteed unless these "full symbols" were kept intact. This type of comment implied that MacArthur's concerns over possible unrest were well justified. But there was no way of knowing for sure. Oyama's dramatic speeches came close to a call to arms to defend the emperor. At the same time he advocated the "swift trial" of Japan's other wartime leaders. "Fast action," he suggested, would bring about a "true postwar Japan much sooner."[12]

A forward-moving postwar Japan was especially desired throughout the country, according to the Japanese press accounts at the time. Even Oyama spoke of a "national impatience" with the trial procedure, as if the new, postmilitarist Japan could not be formally declared until the trials were over. MacArthur was always particularly aware of that "impatience," concerned that a bogged-down trial might in some way negatively influence the New Deal–style reforms that his government championed.[13] In the face of Japanese opinion favoring a quick trial, it was an irony that Chief Prosecutor Keenan and his staff worried about the appearance of an overly swift trial agenda that might convey to the Japanese people the improper impression that America was more interested in order than law. Nevertheless, years after the trials Keenan was still concerned, privately, that the trials "might have moved too quickly."[14] Publicly, he never spoke of the matter. He also wondered whether the Japanese had been kept locked in an unnecessarily long drama over the fate of their emperor. Not until the trials of Class A or senior wartime leaders began to wind down in favor of the trials of their immediate subordinates did the public concern over a possible Hirohito trial truly wane. This was in spite of Occupation Government pronouncements that such a trial was not on the agenda.

The Japanese doubt over what might or might not happen to their emperor was expressed in events later labeled weird and bizarre. Claiming to be a close relative of Hirohito who was kept from the prewar Imperial Palace because of his interest in world peace, Hiromichi Kumazawa claimed to be the "real" emperor in waiting. He crisscrossed his country on a speaking tour in 1947, suggesting that Japan need not worry about a possible upcoming trial of Hirohito. In fact, Japan should insist on the trial. Hirohito, he proclaimed, had been a tool of the militarists. Because of that "fact," the "old" emperor forfeited the right to rule a peaceful postwar Japan. Insisting that he also had the blessing of the Americans, Kumazawa urged his listeners to lobby the MacArthur government, support the quick trial and ouster of Hirohito, and thereby happily begin the era of the new Japan.

A good speaker, Kumazawa was the source of both awe and ridicule in Japanese public opinion. Wherever he went, a media circus followed. In some locales, such as Matsumoto City, Nagano, his speaking tour was canceled by local Japanese officials who were outraged by his claims. Elsewhere he drew large crowds, but he was never without hecklers and controversy. This self-proclaimed "Pretender to the Throne" appeared to be acting out a well-reported-upon fantasy. His claims could never be substantiated, and he faded from the headlines as quickly as he had made them. Nevertheless, the Kumazawa phenomenon might have been the stimulus behind a February 1947 MacArthur headquarters news conference dedicated to "clearing the air" over Hirohito trial rumors. "The role of the Emperor is most important and underscores the intelligence of the thinking embodied in the Potsdam Declaration," MacArthur told the Japanese press and a group of visiting American newspaper and magazine editors. Retaining the emperor, he concluded, "was one of the wisest decisions the Allies could have made." The benefits of that decision involved "the very cooperation of the Japanese people," he explained; and it was time to "move on."[15] MacArthur's final comment was his way of referencing the additional rumors of his own alleged wavering on the "no trial" decision. The tenor and tone of MacArthur's statement were firm, with a hint of annoyance that the Hirohito matter needed any further comment at all.

MacArthur's comments had been most reassuring to the concerned Japanese government. For instance, Katsuo Okazaki, the chief of the General Affairs Bureau of the Japanese Foreign Office, was appointed foreign vice minister shortly after MacArthur's news conference. A second secretary to the Japanese Embassy in Washington during the early 1930s, Okazaki noted in the acceptance of his new post that he was glad to learn that the emperor was "secure." He said he never doubted the "no trial" decision but that it was good to hear MacArthur's reiteration of it in the face of "foolish rumor." That reiteration lifted his spirits, he explained, and his predictions of a truly healthy Japan-U.S. relationship were now possible.[16]

Whether Okazaki had been one of those who had once accepted "foolish rumor" as fact was unclear. Whether because of simple distrust, misunderstanding, or the impact of seeing that many individuals from all walks of life, including those close to the emperor, were on the war criminals lists, it was difficult to kill rumor. MacArthur's stern, no-nonsense comments satisfied many, but concern still lingered throughout the remaining years of the 1940s.

A "no trial" decision did not necessarily mean, for instance, a "no abdication" decision. As the guilty verdicts began to be reached in the trials of the former regime, Hirohito became increasingly withdrawn and melancholy. A number of Japanese government visitors to the imperial household were convinced the emperor might commit suicide at the end of the trials, or at least abdicate the throne. MacArthur had similar worries. "The emotional effect of the sentences upon the Emperor," he told William S. Sebald, the U.S. political advisor for Japan, "might perhaps temporarily unbalance the latter's judgment." The conclusion of the trials, MacArthur said, "might be like blowing up a ton of dynamite—one cannot possibly foresee what might happen." Hirohito never told MacArthur personally that abdication was a consideration. It would be a "political disaster," MacArthur believed; the emperor, whether he wanted to make a "national atonement" statement or not, "would have to be stopped." Hirohito did make it clear to his staff that upon the conclusion of the trials, he wanted all appointments canceled and a "special" seclusion respected. With this in mind, MacArthur informed the emperor that if this seclusion led to abdication or suicide, no regent would be acceptable to both the American government and most of the Japanese citizenry. The postabdication or postsuicide chaos, he argued, would encourage "communist revolt," the end of Japan, and a "disservice to future generations of the Japanese people."[17]

Hirohito accepted MacArthur's argument for continuity. He always had, despite occasional soul-searching. Yet, according to Sebald, Hirohito was truly shocked by the number of guilty verdicts in the trials, and that shock might have led him to "ridiculous and preposterous" actions.[18] By late 1948 there were still those who believed in Hirohito's impending doom. As in the case of a possible Hirohito trial, the rumors of an impending

Hirohito suicide or abdication were strong ones. They faded as fast as "Emperor Kumazawa" when the trials ended without "national atonement" by Hirohito.

The emperor himself confused the historical record of the "no trials" and "no abdication" debate. In 1968, while privately discussing the twenty-year anniversary of the end of the trials, Hirohito told his grand chamberlain, Shuichi Inada, that he never seriously intended to abdicate and that suicide had never been an option. His statement was written down by long-time aide Yoshihiro Tokugawa, an offspring of the famous Tokugawa family of preindustrial Japan, who would also serve as a grand chamberlain in the mid-1980s. Hirohito's 1968 statement was kept secret by the imperial household until early 1999. It constituted the only written comment by the emperor on his possible trial or abdication. In it he noted that abdication would cause widespread "confusion" in Japan, "delaying reconstruction." He had a "duty to the nation" and to his own ancestors to remain in power. He also worried about who would rule if he left the throne. His then twelve-year-old son would inherit the job, but he would also need a regent. Hirohito was concerned that even the Americans might be involved in the regent selection. This was unacceptable, he said. Yet the question remained whether these comments and concerns were the products of 1968 hindsight or the faithful recording of his thoughts nearly a quarter of a century earlier. The debate continues.

Throughout the trials-period discussion over the emperor's fate, Keenan's public position, at least, remained the same. "We have real fish to fry" was his usual answer, suggesting that he had little time for high politics. Apparently, like Hirohito, Keenan reserved the right to have differing positions on the future of the imperial family. His explanation for the mission and objective of his chief prosecutor's office was more involved and better defined. "Nations alone don't keep or break treaties. It is the people within the nations, who have control, who force such acts. Our prosecution will be based on the theory that these persons are punishable for their crimes."[19]

Keenan's legal staff consisted of twenty-five lawyers, seven of whom were still in active military service. His personal staff included nineteen secretaries and twenty-one U.S. Army enlisted men. His investigative wing was run by Lt. Col. Ben Sackett, the former head of the FBI's New York office, and another FBI veteran, Harold "Pop" Nathan. Most of these assistants were handpicked by Keenan himself, but MacArthur appointed the staff for the rest of the IMTFE tribunal.

The tribunal bench consisted of a maximum of eleven judges in a given trial, including Sir William Webb, the presiding judge. A quorum was considered six judges, although defense lawyers always objected to this low number. If a judge was consistently absent from a trial, for whatever reason, his absence would "not necessarily" bar him from offering final judgment in a trial. This was a strange rule, written to cover any contingency in a fast-moving trial, and it was opposed by defense lawyers as symbolic of the tribunal's larger interest in "speed" over "justice." Both Webb and Keenan continually objected to complaints that the trials represented quick marches to the gallows. But they also had their own complaints. Their list accented basic infrastructure matters, such as the lack of adequate translators, poor air conditioning, and even homesick lawyers and staff members who, now that the war was over, would rather be in their home countries than in the former enemy's ruins. Nevertheless, Keenan and Webb drew distinctions between the challenges to their work and allegedly shoddy work. The latter, Keenan argued for years to come, did not take place in Tokyo.[20]

This did not mean that IMTFE trial procedure lacked controversies. The very way IMTFE lawyers introduced evidence, for instance, would raise eyebrows in any standard civil court. The tribunal's operating charter accented the "unique" character of war crimes trials, pointing out the horrible atrocities involved and the wartime confusion that often ruled in these matters. Because of these factors, the presentation of evidence would not follow the same guidelines as in a typical court of law within a democratic structure. Any information that could prove or disprove a crime against humanity or peace, if it "appeared" to be authentic, could be presented. Anything from a diary entry to the classic "hearsay argument" might be included. The tribunal would decide whether that evidence was "reasonable." "Fairness and justice" could still prevail in this approach, the IMTFE Charter concluded, suggesting that the tribunal was duty bound, before God and world opinion, to do the right thing.[21]

Doing the right thing was not necessarily defined by the tribunal alone. Japanese participation in preparing the war criminals lists was encouraged by the IMTFE, and the response went well beyond even Keenan's expectations. In early 1946 alone, over one thousand letters and reports were filed by Japanese nationals exposing fellow Japanese as war criminals. Very few of these reports represented jealous neighbors denouncing individuals for reasons far divorced from war crimes matters. The vast majority were quite genuine. Keenan established a special liaison office with the Legal Section of MacArthur's headquarters to handle the flow. Each report was investigated by the chief of that Legal Section, Col. Alva Carpenter, and his besieged staff. In one dramatic case, Carpenter personally received the teary-eyed and ashamed father of a young Japanese officer. That young officer was still a POW of the British in Burma. He had been responsible for the massacring of a small village there, and he wrote his father in detail about it. The father claimed that his son, Hideo Sato, had spoke gloriously and with pride of that military action, stating that the "determination" it took to kill Burmese men, women, and children was the type of "determination" required to rebuild a new, powerful Japan. His son was anxious to return home and begin this patriotic task, and that was what troubled the elder Sato. His son should have no place in a peaceful Japan, he insisted, unless that place was in a courtroom for war crimes. British authorities later confirmed Sato's tale, and Hideo Sato's letters to his father were used in evidence against him in the resulting war crimes trial. Like so many Japanese, the elder Sato insisted on a fast trial. It was time "to spring ahead," he said, although the personal tragedy was obvious.[22]

To those who still worried that the IMTFE was more interested in imposing quick death sentences on Japanese nationals than engaging in fair trials, Keenan's position was made clear in the opening trials of his "big fish": "The American people can rest assured that a procession of judicial lynching will not occur in the prosecution of any Japanese war criminals. The mere suggestion that such procedure can follow or that revengeful blood purges be permitted when Americans are charged with the prosecution and judgment is offensive to say the least. It can be safely assumed that those who upheld their country's honor during the active hostilities on the field of battle will not fail to sustain it when the hostilities cease."[23]

Former Japanese premier Hideki Tojo represented Keenan's top war criminal defendant. His trial began in an atmosphere of confusion and accusation. Tojo was one of the "infamous twenty-eight" wartime leaders under indictment. Two of the twenty-eight would die in captivity before the end of their own trials. Another would be proclaimed "mentally unstable." Because of his role in planning wartime offensives and his general championing of the militarist agenda, Tojo faced a number of damning charges. Shortly before his trial, both the Japanese and the American press headlined that "Tojo admitted guilt" from his cell in Yokohama's Sugamo Prison. The world press, which covered the Tojo trial as page 1 news, referred to Allied interrogation reports of the former premier. Those re-

Former prime minister Hideki Tojo in the docket. (Courtesy of Douglas MacArthur Memorial)

ports, allegedly leaked to the press by a "high-ranking officer in MacArthur's headquarters," were confusing, although Tojo could not deny that he had had a senior role in wartime planning. The reports did not note that Tojo and his counsel, Ichiro Kiyose, drew distinctions between the former premier's "guilt" as a onetime policymaker and his "guilt" as a conspirator and warmonger.

Given the press attention to the Tojo case, leaks were perhaps to be expected; however, Kiyose claimed that the leaks, combined with the general media fascination with Tojo's fate, made it impossible for his client to have a fair trial. Kiyose even questioned the adequate translation of the pretrial interrogation reports, insisting that they were "not worth the time and paper." Maintaining a decent reputation for thoroughness and no-nonsense argument, Kiyose faced a trial in which his client symbolized the "evil of Japan" in the eyes of much of the Allied world. In the face of this

The Class A war crimes defendants always received the greater share of world press attention. Each trial day began with the usual round of photographs and unsuccessful efforts to interview the defendants. (Courtesy of Douglas MacArthur Memorial)

pressure, Kiyose approached his difficult task with dogged determination, questioning the very nature of each indictment and the legality of the war crimes effort itself. More concerned with Tojo as a "criminal personality" and with the spectacular circumstances of the trial, the press and most later chroniclers paid little attention to Kiyose's efforts. Many considered Tojo the Hitler who was never tried in Europe. Hitler escaped trial via suicide. Tojo would not be so lucky. But in reality, Tojo was never a Hitler-style dictator; Kiyose's efforts symbolized a commitment to examine the origins and conduct of World War II, his client's role in this tale of complex decision making, and the definition of "crime" in the context of national leadership during times of war. Hence, Kiyose's contribution to the very basis of the war crimes trials in Japan was quite significant. His search for answers merited greater respect and appreciation than it won at the time or even in the later accounts.[24]

Questioning the accuracy of English-to-Japanese translations and vice versa was an important tactic for the defense counsel at the Tokyo trials. Here, San Francisco's George Kitagawa (*foreground, wearing earphones*) assists Japanese defense lawyers in translation strategies. (Courtesy of Douglas MacArthur Memorial)

The IMTFE thought Kiyose's probing interest in the proper conduct of wartime policymaking was better left to historians and philosophers. In the meantime, despite the tribunal's interest in a speedy trial, Kiyose's defense approach involved something of a Japanese history lesson, which extended the trial process much more than desired by Keenan, MacArthur, and Webb. Unwelcome or not, Kiyose's defense raised some intriguing questions. A crime against peace was not a matter of law, Kiyose argued. The illegality of war, he added, had never been established to the satisfaction of any international lawyer. With that in mind, he suggested that it was a little too easy to label one side in a war as "the aggressor state." Both sides were "the aggressors." Consequently, his client's role in waging "aggressive war" was identical to the leadership decisions made by Franklin Roosevelt or Winston Churchill. Kiyose rejected the conclusions of the

Yamashita case, whereby "criminal responsibility" was accorded to certain wartime leaders for the actions of subordinates. This conclusion went against certain historic "national traditions," he explained. The Yamashita decision therefore had been "arranged" to fit the victor's agenda in those emotional days so soon after World War II.

Kiyose also addressed alleged cultural differences, noting that "criminal conspiracy" was a matter of concern in Western law and culture alone and that his client should not be expected to welcome Western notions and legal conclusions. From that point he could argue that Japan saw itself in a defensive position in the days before World War II. Reacting to a European- and American-colonized Asian/Pacific world, Japanese international policy, although similar to nineteenth-century-style Western policies of expansion, was continually threatened and abused by Western leaders. During late 1941 America's insistence on a Japanese military withdrawal from China, coupled with resulting economic sanctions in "punishment" for Japan's China policy, was viewed in the Japanese government as an unnecessary assault on Japanese interests. America's demands on Japan also smacked of racism, Kiyose insisted, whereby the Roosevelt administration exhibited a callous disregard for Japanese arguments and concerns in contrast to the views of any Western government. Hence, he concluded, Japan's military decisions of the 1930s and early 1940s should be considered in the interest of national survival and international respect.

Kiyose even questioned the treatment of his client, suggesting that Japan had surrendered in recognition of the Potsdam Declaration and not under the "unconditional surrender" decision imposed by the Allies on the Axis powers at the Casablanca conference of early 1943. Nazi Germany's "unconditional surrender" in May 1945 came under Casablanca guidelines, and the Allies could therefore treat their Nazi prisoners "unconditionally," he said. But given the differing circumstances of Japan's surrender following two atomic bomb attacks, and given the existence of post-Casablanca legal statements, such as Potsdam, Tojo should not be charged with war crimes, Kiyose argued. Tojo was interrogated upon incarceration by the Allies, he noted, not knowing that he was not under any formal war criminal charge. Consequently, any interrogation statement, poorly translated or not, could be eliminated from the prosecution's alleged evidence on those grounds alone. Tojo's assigned American counsel, Maj. Ben Blakeney, especially echoed this point, but as an American he was particularly able to hammer away at the matter of America's own violations of prewar peace treaties, such as the Kellogg-Briand Pact. Negotiated at the height of

America's isolationist period, that treaty "outlawed war as an instrument of national policy."

In terms of character, Tojo's defense team depicted their client as an honorable man who actually prevented atrocities, at the same time leading his country during one of its most challenging moments since the Meiji Restoration of the 1870s. His entire career rejected extremism, they said, and that meant he had no use for a military that engaged in atrocities. The character portrait became the weakest position within the Kiyose argument. It drew attention to the many atrocities committed during Tojo's tenure as premier, and the IMTFE had little interest in what Tojo "might have done." But Kiyose challenged the court to produce specific Tojo-authorized orders to Imperial Army troops to commit atrocities, and he urged them to consider the "fine soldier's soldier" under indictment.

There were numerous governments in Japan throughout the 1930s and early 1940s, the defense reminded the tribunal in their summation. These governments were squabbling ones with divergent positions within their own cabinets. Tojo had been a part of this confusion. He had never been a Hitler. He had never been an architect of war crimes. With that final point, the defense team, after a brilliant display of hard work, asked the tribunal to recognize their client's innocence.

People charged with real crimes are also real people. This had been a message, sometimes subtle, sometime not, heard throughout Kiyose's argument. He wanted the IMTFE to ponder that fact as it deliberated over the fate of Tojo, his cabinet, and the wartime Japanese government in general. Claiming that World War II propaganda was hard to kill, he accused the IMTFE of demonizing his client. More to the point, the citizens of all the Allied countries, he said, had demonized Tojo and the entire Japanese leadership on trial. Throughout Kiyose's defense effort, the IMTFE learned of Tojo the grandfather, a kind man who dreamed of tending his garden and not taking over the world. He could often be found in that garden throughout his prime ministership, and he had been deeply concerned about its fate and that of his family even at the time of his arrest. He was not a monster, and neither was, for instance, Prince Konoye. In love with poetry, Konoye read it, wrote it, and found "inner peace" through it. This was not the type of person, Kiyose pointed out, who would deliberately order the massacre of civilians in China. Even Foreign Minister Togo was a decent sort who had worried about the future of karate training in Japan. An admirer of Shotokan Karate master and founder Giichin Funakoshi, who preached retreat before "striking in anger," Togo insisted that karate was a "fighting art and sport" wedded to Japanese culture; it was a "gentle pursuit," which, like Konoye's poetry, brought "inner peace" to all "karateka" (karate students). He was concerned that the victorious Allies might misunderstand those facts and discourage or even ban karate. This, in fact, almost happened, and Togo was not the only one in the former Japanese government and military who had deep concerns over the matter. As they made their judgment, Kiyose wanted the justices to remember these poets, grandfathers, gardeners, and aging karate students. Real people, in other words, deserved real justice.

Without question, Kiyose and his colleagues thought they had raised enough "reasonable doubt" to influence most courtroom situations. "Not guilty," they believed, should have been the only honest verdict. But this was never a typical courtroom scene. That fact was good news for Keenan, for in view of his own agenda, much of Kiyose's argument had been irrelevant. With his attention divided between this and other cases, and given a long bout with the flu and an unhealthy dose of overconfidence, Keenan had hoped the trial of Japan's most well-known "militarist" would be quite straightforward and workmanlike. This was not to be, and he stuck, in a sense, to an overly general script.

Tojo, the prosecution argued, was part of a fourteen-year conspiracy to wage aggressive war. Many spectacular atrocities took place during his days in the cabinet or as premier. His public statements at the time on behalf of "Japan's destiny" were especially damning. And his aloofness, as well as his off-and-on cynical smile, during the presentation of atrocity accounts at the trial itself, suggested to Keenan, at least, that the defendant was truly a cold-blooded killer.

As a defendant, Tojo did not offer too many ugly impressions to the Japanese. During the trial his eldest daughter, Mitsue, was a frequent visitor. Their warm relationship, always so visible to the Japanese press, suggested the loving father more than the mad killer. Through Mitsue the Japanese learned much about her father, including his concerns over the conditions of his bombed-out home, his true love of gardening, whether his youngest sister in Manchuria had survived the war, and his worries over a possible Hirohito trial or abdication. In saying that he would gladly give his life only to spare the emperor, Tojo's respect for Hirohito was very clear. Years later, these statements would be remembered above all others uttered by Tojo during the trial. They helped fuel a legend, first championed by Japanese ultranationalists and later by historical critics of the occupation period, that the Allies failed to "get" Hirohito and therefore "settled" for Tojo.

Alongside his pro-Hirohito statements, Tojo offered tips on how to tend garden vegetables or administer food rationing programs. He even expressed great joy over the early success for the new Japanese yen. Frankly, the Japanese had never seen this human side of its wartime leader before, and a debate soon raged over whether Tojo might have been "misunderstood." This was balanced by another debate. Was the new free press more interested in the ex-premier's family life than in his alleged crimes? The answer depended upon whom one read.

Especially for the prosecution, the most memorable, and most telling, Tojo public comment involved the ex-premier's "sympathy" statement to the family of Field Marshal Hermann Goering upon hearing of the latter's death sentence imposed by the Nuremberg tribunal. Goering cheated the gallows by committing suicide. Shortly before the field marshal's death, Tojo had much praise for the man once regarded as Hitler's closest colleague. Although he never met the man, Tojo allegedly felt a certain unexplained "kinship" to him, or so said Ichiro Kiyose. Moreover, Tojo took advantage of this occasion to express his views on the IMTFE's "weak" definition of "aggressive war."

Part of Goering's death sentence involved the indictment of "waging aggressive war," and Tojo wanted to set the record straight before the IMTFE handed down its final judgment on him. "I am unconcerned over the weight of the penalty—whether it is imprisonment or death. I wish only to know what the judge will term 'aggressive war' and under what circumstances the right of self defense is recognized and under what circumstances that right is denied."[25]

Perhaps anticipating the tribunal's distaste for Tojo's sympathies for one of the founders of Germany's Nazi Party, suffixed by a slap at IMTFE "aggressive war" indictments, Kiyose reminded the tribunal once again that his client was not a Nazi. Tojo's regime, Kiyose reiterated, had never been as "evil" as the Nazis. This did not jibe with a report in Keenan's possession that stated that Tojo even planned to wage nuclear war if his nuclear scientists had prevailed. Although the prosecution never found it necessary to enter it into evidence, the report, authored by David Snell, a former *Atlanta Constitution* reporter turned army intelligence officer with the Twenty-fourth Criminal Investigation Detachment in Korea, described the success of the Japanese atomic bomb project.

According to Snell's investigations, the Japanese project leaders had been captured by advancing Russian troops in Konan, Korea, three days after they had "almost" completed a working atomic bomb. Russian cooperation in finding out more details had not been forthcoming to Snell, but he concluded that the Russian downing of an American B-29 bomber over Konan on September 29, 1945, was due to the "fact" that the Russians had captured the atomic bomb test site. Whereas Snell's Russian attack was conjecture, the Japanese atomic bomb project was not.[26]

Buried in the records of the trials for years, and hardly a top secret, the Japanese wartime atomic bomb project was rarely mentioned by Western analysts after the war, and especially not by Japanese politicians and historians. The very reality of the project, some Japanese argued, would negate Japan's recognized postwar leadership in antinuclear causes because of its uniqueness as an atomic victim.[27] At the time of the fiftieth anniversary of World War II, America's CBS Evening News resurrected the general tale of the project's existence as well as Tokyo's plan to end the stalemated war in China with nuclear attacks. Their report suggested the unveiling of a deep, dark secret, thereby granting CBS something of a hot scoop.[28] This, of course, was not the case. In any event the 1990s rediscovery of Japan's atomic warfare endeavor stirred little discussion outside of certain academic circles. If few cared about the matter fifty years later under the guise of a CBS scoop, even fewer cared in the late 1940s. To Keenan, the atomic bomb project was part of the larger indictment, "waging aggressive war." The latter was the focus of much derision by the defense, and the last thing Keenan needed was a defense-led debate over the atomic "atrocities" of Hiroshima and Nagasaki.[29] The power of Keenan's prosecution effort came from specific battlefield atrocity accounts linked to Tojo himself, that is, actions so ghastly that the tribunal was physically disturbed by them. Linking Tojo to these horrible events was especially important, Keenan believed, in reaching a guilty verdict in the Tojo case.

A particular damning accusation for Tojo involved his friendship with Heitaro Kimura, including letters of encouragement intertwined with stern military orders. Kimura was a fellow defendant and the former commander of Japanese forces in Burma. During Tojo's leadership of the Japanese government, Kimura was ordered to destroy "the vestiges of British colonialism" in the British colony of Burma. More than one hundred thousand people were slaughtered in the process, Allied flyers there were often executed rather than being imprisoned, and 25 percent of the British who were taken as POWs were either killed or died in captivity. The story of "Japanese sadism," argued the prosecution, was not the result of independent command decisions in the field but a general policy championed by Tojo. The prosecution also attempted to link Burma atrocities to others across Japanese-occupied Southeast Asia. Specific, blow-by-blow accounts, such as the murdering of five thousand Chinese in Singapore, were offered as evidence by the prosecution.[30]

Graphic detail or not, the prosecution was often too quick to present a tale without available witnesses to confirm it. For instance, when describing atrocities in the Philippines committed during Tojo's leadership days, Philippines prosecutor Pedro Lopez ended his argument without providing a single witness. This led Webb, perhaps exhausted by the endless horror stories, to rebuke the prosecution's efforts. He wanted witness confirmation, and in the physical presence of the tribunal itself. Lopez complained that he had planned to have these witnesses. Sadly, they had been detained in the Philippines, he believed, "due to a lack of warm clothing" necessary for a winter's stay in Tokyo. Webb rejected this excuse, whereupon Lopez added to the tale. "More accurately," he said, the witnesses had been delayed by a typhoon that was battering the Philippines. Later checking the weather reports, Webb found clear and sunny skies from Guam to the Asian mainland. He told the tribunal that he doubted Lopez could be "accurate" about anything.[31] Eventually, Lopez flew six witnesses from Manila to Tokyo, but his star witness was already in Japan.

According to Tadakatsu Suzuki, a fifty-one-year-old ex–minister plenipotentiary to Egypt, Tojo and other members of the cabinet received appeals from both Allied governments and international humanitarian organizations to end the massacres and treat POWs and interned civilians with human decency. With scorn and contempt for "allied weakness," Tojo and the cabinet always rejected those appeals, Suzuki said. At one point, in front of Suzuki and other visiting Japanese diplomats, Tojo tore into little pieces a Red Cross–telegrammed appeal for "humanity." The very suggestion of "humanity," Suzuki remembered, had no place in the Tojo cabinet.[32]

Although the final words were spoken in the Tojo and twenty-four other senior or Class A war crimes trials during April 1948, it took seven months for the tribunal to pass its judgment at Tokyo. All were found guilty. Tojo was sentenced to death. Like Goering, he preferred suicide to the gallows, but the suicide effort failed, and he was not executed alone. Throughout these trials, the defense counsel complained that fairness remained elusive. The most damaging defense complaint noted that the Office of Defense Counsel had been established for propaganda purposes only and therefore had little practical significance. MacArthur paid close attention to this argument, for it led right to the heart of his reformist mission in Japan. If the Japanese concluded that the trials were, and always had been, a sham, the Occupation Government, he believed, would lose all sense of legitimacy. This view was well illustrated in MacArthur's reaction to the resignation of defense lawyer B.M. Coleman, a U.S. Navy captain. His resignation "threatened scandal of the highest order," MacArthur worried, and great pains were taken to explain to the Japanese people, once again, the good work of the defense teams.

Most of Coleman's complaint was personal. In short, the trials were dragging on too long for his satisfaction, and his impatience to return Stateside to family and friends would never benefit the tasks of the defense counsel. Despite its personal nature, fellow defense lawyers exaggerated Coleman's resignation request to pad their own arguments for a better hearing of evidence and other matters of concern. Coleman saw the dichotomy between the tribunal's mandate and a typical U.S. civil court as being much too wide, and he said so. It would be something else to denounce the trials as "shams," and Coleman, it appears, had no intention of leading such a cause. Nevertheless, news of Coleman's resignation prompted a flurry of complaints from defense lawyers to Keenan, Webb, and MacArthur. Some of the complaints, put in the form of a petition to MacArthur, were discussed openly and reported in the Japanese press. Hence, MacArthur's concern.

MacArthur took the offensive, with the blessings of the IMTFE. To his credit, he responded to each of the defense complaints individually. His response was linked to priority political concerns, however, and only tangentially connected to the daily procedure problems of the defense teams. In MacArthur's view there were "four precise matters of complaint" that needed to be addressed. First of all, there was the general makeup of the defense counsel itself. According to one common complaint, the defense teams were "composed of inexperienced, struggling lawyers." They were a pool of attorneys from which defendants would pick their particular favorite or favorites to work on their behalf. The one or more attorneys selected would, if necessary, work side by side with a Japanese lawyer or lawyers. Some said the latter were as incompetent as the former, and nothing would change the situation. The angry MacArthur responded that some of the best American and Japanese minds labored on behalf of the defense. Keenan echoed these comments. Even some defense attorneys, such as Lt. John Guider, disagreed with their colleagues over the belaboring of the so-called incompetence argument. It seemed quite counterproductive to Guider, and he worried that a potential Stateside employer might always consider him in the incompetent category because of it. The larger goal of the incompetence argument was also unclear: we must stop the trials because all defense lawyers are incompetent? To Guider, this was a bizarre cause to champion and especially a strange position for the defense counsel to take.

The second issue involved the role and influence of MacArthur himself. Coleman's resignation, the petition read, offered the supreme commander the opportunity to restate his role in trial procedure. Did MacArthur have the power to intervene in a defense argument if he did not approve of its direction? Did MacArthur's "authority" guarantee these interventions? Although MacArthur believed his role had been decently defined before the trials began, he reiterated his relationship to the defense counsels in the summer of 1946. Any intervention by his office in the work of the defense counsel, MacArthur claimed, "would be an unwarranted and highly irregular infringement upon the rights of the defendants." That was supposed to be his final word on the matter. It was clear to any observer of the trials that MacArthur was interested in guilty verdicts, but his noninterventionist statement suggested that he would be doing little to assure that interest. It was also clear that he did not feel such a statement had to be made at the outset of the trials, but again, the defense's raising of the "MacArthur issue" made a strongly worded response a matter of priority. This did not mean that MacArthur rejected the right, noted in the tribunal's original directives, to review a case upon its conclusion.

A third matter of concern involved the living conditions of the defense lawyers. According to the defense counsel petition submitted to MacArthur, certain unnamed lawyers would not have entertained abandoning their duties or resigning, like Coleman, if their Bachelor's Officers Quarters (BOQ) or Visiting Officers Quarters (VOQ) were not substandard. Considering MacArthur's own opulent lifestyle, even in a war-torn country, the defense suggested that basic guarantees, such as electricity and water, were essential to a successfully argued case. In short, a better infrastructure, closer in comfort to the living conditions of MacArthur, Keenan, Webb, and others, might convey to all concerned that the needs of the defense were as important as the needs of the prosecution. Returning the fire, MacArthur reminded the defense counsel that most of them had happily volunteered for their assignments. Most were aware of the war-ravaged ruin that had once been the great city of Tokyo. Essentially arguing that "all" Americans in Japan were divorced from the peacetime comforts of the United States, MacArthur urged the defense to carry on.

The defense counsel petition was not without some contradictions. The general implication of their list of complaints was that the tribunal was tilted toward the prosecution's arguments and that the defense counsel's commitment to a fair trial symbolized the best hope for justice. But their petition to MacArthur included a fourth complaint stating that some of them found their clients "repugnant." Attempting to point out "cultural differences" between the Japanese and the American approach to warfare was important, they said; however, those "differences" did not diminish the fact that their clients justified horrible acts of violence.

This section of the petition was meant to accent the strain and the challenges placed upon the defense counsel. Instead, it gave MacArthur the opportunity to wax poetic on the need for a healthy postwar American-Japanese relationship. The troubles faced by the defense counsel, he said, were representative of the troubles facing the general Washington-Tokyo dialogue. A terrible war had ended, and it was time to move forward. From worries over the competence of defense lawyers to the influence of substandard living conditions on good lawyering, MacArthur noted that the defense complaints were more imagined than real. The trials and U.S.-Japan relations in general were part of the same effort to reject the old Japan and bring in the new; both were plagued by misunderstandings and cultural clashes. There was no evidence, he concluded, that any of the defense counsel's complaints had negatively influenced the progress and outcome of a trial. He urged the defense to shed "all prejudice and conjecture," withdraw their list of complaints, and fight the good fight on behalf of their clients.

MacArthur called the defense counsel's complaints selfish and petty in light of the great mission of the IMTFE and the sought-after happy postwar U.S.-Japan relationship. He also made it clear that he would not be accepting the resignation of defense lawyers on the grounds of political or procedural opposition to ongoing trials. Better skilled at putting a positive spin on his own approach and policy than the squabbling defense counsel, MacArthur had little use for a contradictory list of complaints.

MacArthur's assault on the defense counsel petitioners was well done, yet the petition did have merit. There was reason behind the effort. In September 1947 the coalition of defense lawyers in Tokyo, sometimes referred to as the War Crimes Division, attempted to summarize its troubles in an official report to the White House. This was not a list of complaints by a handful of malcontents that could be easily dismissed or denigrated. Like the defense counsel petition to MacArthur, the report of the War Crimes Division pointed out obvious problems. Unlike the petition, the division's formal report to Washington did not constitute an emotional outburst or a potential en masse threat of resignation. Carefully crafted, informative, and persuasive, the War Crimes Defense Division attempted to acquaint President Truman with the "gaps in justice." What he was supposed to do about it, though, was as unclear as the same question was in the previous petition to MacArthur.

By 1947 the Tokyo defense teams had won a reputation in Washington for attempting to win their clients' freedom through the exploitation of tribunal procedures. This opinion, denounced even by Keenan, suggested to some, such as Gen. Albert C. Wedemeyer, the U.S. theater commander for China, that American defense lawyers were "obstructionists" in the effort to create a harmonious postwar Japan. That was an unfair opinion, implying that only prosecution victories were good for Japan. As a counter to this point of view, the War Crimes Defense Division reminded its observers that in Japan the judge had always been accorded more respect and consideration than the lawyer. In pre–Occupation Government Japan, in grand contrast to the situation in the United States, the lawyer was a minor figure in the courtroom drama. The Defense Division claimed credit for changing that approach, for elevating the Japanese lawyer to leading and responsible roles in Japanese trial procedure. Welcoming this change as an overdue democratic reform, Japanese supporters of more rather than less civil liberty hailed the imported U.S. concept of lawyer-based defense as a great achievement. The defense counsel won considerable praise from both the Japanese people and MacArthur for it.

With its patriotism, efficiency, and worthiness adequately touted, the defense could report to Truman their precise matters of concern. The first item in this bit of education for the president involved the language barrier. Instead of the usual complaint over improper word or phrase translations, the defense lawyers explained that the Japanese language was simply less direct than English. That meant that defendants attempted to "circumvent points" not in an effort to hide guilt but in the endeavor to answer questions that seemed to them strangely direct. The interpreters themselves would attempt to convey Japanese answers to the tribunal in the direct manner that the English-speaking lawyers expected. Consequently, the language issue went beyond the bad translation of a word or two. Perhaps, the defense counsel argued, "an entire testimony could be the interpretation of the interpreter."[33]

This problem was especially apparent when it came to affidavit testimony. The preponderance of the testimony admitted in evidence for the prosecution involved the affidavits of prisoners of war. The prosecution had unlimited time to determine which affidavits to select and translate, but the defense was rarely invited to review those documents in time to place a motion or argue their validity. Expediency demanded that the defense rely upon hastily translated Japanese testimony to counterbalance and deny some of the vague charges offered by the prisoners of war. Sometimes defense requests to review affidavits would be approved after the case was concluded. Furthermore, the gathering of prosecution witnesses was easy, the defense counsel claimed, compared with their own efforts to bring Japanese witnesses, lost in the confusion of the war-torn Asian/Pacific region, to the courtroom. A matter of fairness was involved, and President Truman was asked to appeal to the IMTFE and correct the imbalance. The president did ask for a "a show of fairness," and there was a response.[34]

By late 1947, for instance, if defense affidavits were received after a given case had been completed, they could be attached to the appeal brief. But the larger issue surrounding the affidavit/witness crisis involved willpower, politics, and prejudice. Few ex–Allied POWs, for example, had any interest in appearing at the tribunal on behalf of their former jailers and torturers. The prosecution would always have a longer list of witnesses and affidavits, and there was little the commander in chief might have done, if interested in the matter, to persuade potential defense witnesses and affidavit writers to assist in various trials.

Trying to set the record straight in reference to defense lawyers' complaints that their clients were "repugnant," the defense counsel explained to Truman that the recent petition to MacArthur had been the work of a minority in their ranks. Certain clients were seen as "repugnant," they said, because some of them used their trials as a sounding board for right-wing causes and anti-Allied sentiment. Sometimes this fact was found out a little too late, making the defense counsel, in the middle of a trial, either look foolish or appear to be part of an anti-American propaganda effort. That, the defense counsel concluded, was truly "repugnant." This kind of behavior (now labeled "disruptive" as opposed to "repugnant") was a rare occurrence within the daily work of the IMTFE, however. It was more common, although still fairly rare, in the military-run trials of former Japanese POW commandants and overseas occupation authorities. In any event, this was the best attempt to answer MacArthur's implication that a defense lawyer was not a defense lawyer if he thought his client was "repugnant."[35]

Even sentencing, said the defense counsel, was an unnecessarily difficult decision. In the United States, the court was limited by statutes in giving maximum sentences for specific crimes. In the Tokyo trials, the death sentence could be imposed for any offense for which the accused was found guilty. Since the maximum punishment was death for any offense, defense lawyers had been hesitant to recommend to the accused that he enter a plea of guilty for any offense, however slight. Most of the accused were charged with several offenses, varying in severity, and it was rare when the prosecution and the defense could even reach agreement on the plea of guilty. All of this made the determination of a fair sentence most difficult. The problem was compounded by the fact that there was little or no legal precedent available for consultation, making each decision a controversial one.[36]

Again, there was little President Truman might have done to answer these concerns, even if he had wanted to get involved in the daily workings of the trials. Outside of blanket support for the general effort and his call for "fairness," Truman would not be solving the problems of the Tokyo defense lawyers. In essence, the defense counsel's account of its struggles implied that the IMTFE never respected the complexity of a defense lawyer's tasks and that the justices ruling in these trials always spoke as one voice. That was not the case. There was dissent from the bench, and even confusion. The trial of Shigenori Togo especially proved that point.

Togo's principal association with the crimes charged against him was as foreign minister in the Tojo cabinet during an eleven-month period beginning in October 1941. He then resigned and returned to private life, but he joined the cabinet of Prime Minister Teiichi Suzuki during the final weeks of the war. Once again he served as foreign minister. From the date of his first appointment until the outbreak of World War II in the Pacific, Togo participated in the planning and preparation for war. He attended cabinet meetings and conferences, concurring in all the decisions made. As foreign minister, he played a leading role in the negotiations with the United States immediately before the outbreak of the war and supported the war plans relevant to both the China and the Pacific Islands campaigns.

All of Togo's fellow policymaking defendants spoke of their country's encirclement and economic strangulation by the Allies before World War II. Their war aims, they said, were defensive and required for national survival in the face of Western imperialism. Togo added a twist to the tale. He insisted that he joined the Tojo cabinet to negotiate a peace between the United States and Japan. When his negotiations failed and the war began, he stayed on in the Tojo cabinet. Although opposed to the war, he said it would have been cowardly and treasonous to resign over it. But by September 1942 he had had enough. His resignation came from a dispute with the cabinet over Tokyo's ill treatment of Japanese-occupied countries.

According to Ben Bruce Blakeney, the charismatic defense lawyer from the Hideki Tojo case, his new client was not a monster, a militarist, or even particularly conservative in his politics. Shigenori Togo's efforts to defend the rights of occupied peoples were daring ones, according to Blakeney. The several indictments against Togo, he said, were relevant to warmongers but not to a diplomat with an interest in peace. Blakeney provided evidence in the case that testified to Togo's interest in the rules of war: the foreign minister had urged his cabinet colleagues to treat prisoners of war, civilian internees, and, in general, "captive nations," with respect and consideration. He claimed to have no personal knowledge of specific atrocity accounts during his Tojo cabinet days. The IMTFE did not believe him, nor did they accept the argument that Togo had been a cautious peace activist throughout his tenure as foreign minister.

But the Togo case was a unique one for the tribunal. Blakeney's portrayal of Togo as a paper-pushing bureaucrat, not a busy, policymaking expansionist, impressed at least three justices. Of the three, Justices Radhabinod Pal of India and Henri Bernard of France credited Blakeney with an especially well-argued case, ruling that Togo had been detached from war-making policy. Although Bernard and especially Pal were not fans even of the concept of war crimes trials, it was the justice from the Netherlands, Bernard V.A. Roling, who offered the loudest dissent in the Togo case. Keenan regarded Roling as a loose cannon who approved "only" eleven of the sixteen life sentences imposed at Tokyo. He was also the best hope for the Togo defense, and he would later go on to edit the documentary history of the Tokyo War Crimes Trials.

Roling argued that Keenan had committed a number of procedural errors in the Togo case. First of all, the prosecution had included an atrocity on its list of Togo-supported war crimes that had taken place in 1939 while Togo was the Japanese ambassador to the Soviet Union. The original indictment against Togo was dated from his "entry into the Tojo cabinet" of 1941. Roling reminded both Keenan and the IMTFE that accuracy and fairness were still serious objectives in Tokyo and that Togo could not be found guilty for an atrocity outside of the tribunal's stated field of jurisdiction. Keenan, of course, insisted that he had only been trying to establish the pattern of Togo's commitment to policies that led to atrocities, for his career was attached to the militarist agenda as early as 1939.

Roling might have scored points in the jurisdiction debate, but his comments suggested that Togo's pre-1941 record must always remain outside the scope of the trial. Yet a large part of the defense's tactics involved the effort to portray Togo as a peaceful man trapped in a horrible war. The defense even had documents dated as far back as 1933 that demonstrated their client's commitment to peace. Togo had written letters in the early and mid-1930s to senior Japanese policymakers urging them to avoid militarist decisions. Roling's insistence, if successful, on the proper matching of jurisdiction with indictment would have rendered this evidence useless. In any event, Roling noted in his official dissent in this case that the defense's prewar evidence had been compelling. Keenan countered that the defense's evidence had been overly selective, for Togo had helped negotiate the Anti-Comintern Pact of 1937. The latter brought Italian fascists, German Nazis, and Japanese militarists together in order to denounce international Communist expansionism. To the chief prosecutor's office, and to the many Allies who remembered it, the Anti-Comintern Pact was an early symbol of fascist solidarity.

Roling found Togo an honorable man. He had remained in a cabinet that he despised largely because, if he left, there would be no one to fight the good fight for peace. Thanks to this "fact," Roling doubted that there really was a case against Togo. "Assuming that these are the facts, the question is whether a crime was committed under the mitigating circumstances, or whether no crime was committed at all. Comparison with situations under domestic criminal law would readily suggest the former conclusion. In view of the special nature of the crime against peace, and of the special nature and requirements of international relations, one is inevitably drawn to the latter. To join a cabinet, or, in general, to assume a function with the purpose of promoting opportunities for peace is an international duty if one is especially qualified to do so."[37]

Roling did not believe Togo ever had "aggressive intent." His championing of peace in a war cabinet was a heroic act. Keenan insisted that the facts presented a different Togo. There was also no evidence of Togo's peace agenda. In documented prewar conversations with the U.S. ambassador to Japan, Joseph Grew, Togo had argued various justifications for war in both official and social settings. His speeches to the Diet in December 1941 summarized those justifications, with enthusiastic predictions of inevitable victory. But Roling dismissed Keenan's documentation as testaments to Togo's "warlike talk." The issue at hand remained, he said, Togo's "warlike intent." With that in mind, Roling noted that he had been intrigued by the fact that Togo's late-1941 efforts to find a peaceful accord with the American secretary of state, Cordell Hull, had been rejected by Washington. That decision "forced" Togo into his lonely role as the Tojo cabinet's voice for reason and peace.

Keenan found Roling's argument to be based on rumor, conjecture, and perhaps wishful thinking. Roling's strongest position on Togo centered on Togo's reasoning behind his 1942 resignation. At that time Japan's Greater East Asia Co-Prosperity Sphere became the Greater East Asia Ministry. Theoretically, this meant that the nations in support of the Japanese war effort across the Asian/Pacific region were no longer left to administer their own fate. The new ministry now dictated policy to the Japanese allies. Togo opposed the shift, complaining that the "rules of righteousness" were being replaced by the "rules of might." Because of this position Prime Minister Kantaro Suzuki, near the end of the war, wanted Togo to be part of a cabinet that would soon be ending the war and making its peace with America. Suzuki claimed that Togo had opposed World War II "from the beginning." This made Togo, Suzuki said after the war, the perfect candidate for the job of foreign minister.

In Keenan's view, Togo's 1942 resignation was enshrouded in confusion and propaganda. There had never been free and independent nations within Japan's Co-Prosperity Sphere, he pointed out. There had been "occupied" ones influenced by collaborationist regimes or simply controlled by on-site Japanese administrators. The new ministry gave grander and direct administrative authority to the government in Tokyo, but it did not end an era of freedom and independence for noble allies. Statements to the contrary had been pure propaganda and little else.

Indirectly, Keenan accused Roling of accepting Japanese wartime propaganda as fact. Togo's resignation, the chief prosecutor argued, involved administrative and bureaucratic objections. It did not constitute a denunciation of Japanese brutality in the occupied territories. That brutality continued, Keenan said, whether it was labeled Co-Prosperity Sphere or Greater East Asia Ministry. Roling was unmoved and only reiterated his Togo, man of peace, position. "No one should be convicted for waging aggressive war if he entered a cabinet during war time solely with the intention of ending the war. He who undertakes this cannot be regarded as having committed an international crime under mitigating circumstances. On the contrary, he rather fulfilled an international duty."[38]

The Togo trial was often reduced to the "he said" versus "he said" argument. For every example of peacemaking touted by the defense counsel, there was an example of war-making touted by the chief prosecutor. Keenan saw Togo's defense as a convenient one, manufactured after the war to mask his role as chief foreign policymaker in a regime that conquered much of the Asian/Pacific region. Counsel Blakeney was more cautious with his rhetoric than Keenan or Roling. He never mentioned Keenan's push-button "naked" words, for example—in reference to Japanese policy— "naked power," "naked aggression," "naked conspiracy." He also avoided Roling's occasional acceptance of Japanese wartime terms, such as "Asian liberation," "Western tyranny," and "guided democracy." Instead, he always spoke of "peace" and his client's commitment to the concept. History was watching, he warned the IMTFE, and "persecuting" a peaceful Asian man would not win the allegiance of Asian/Pacific peoples to America's postwar anticommunist agenda. This charge apparently was meant to influence the Americans only, for there were few residents of the formerly Japanese-occupied Asian/Pacific region who would weep over a guilty verdict for Tojo's foreign minister.[39] At the least, Blakeney's unsuccessful appeal of that guilty verdict was a fine example of his gift for oratory, as well as an illustration of his ability to weave legal, historical, and international concerns into one eloquent commentary.

> Americans in time to come are unlikely to be proud of this verdict. Yet this Tribunal, and its verdict—like SCAP itself, under the aegis of which it came into being—however international in fact, is identified in the eyes of the world at large with the United States. Inevitably, it is to the United States that will inure, in great measure, the credit or discredit which history will attach to the proceedings of the International Military Tribunal for the Far East—and not history only, but contemporary opinion. That this verdict should stand, without an effort's being made to correct its glaring inequities, would constitute but poor tribute to our statesmanship, our attachment to justice and, in the end, our service to peace.[40]

Although Blakeney found a sympathetic ear in Roling, dissent was not a characteristic of the IMTFE justices. Bernard of France, for instance, complained of procedural infractions throughout the trials, but it was a general complaint as opposed to specific objections to the conduct of the Togo or any other case. A pretrial inquiry had not been held, he noted. The prosecution had greater resources at their command than the defense, he believed, and Keenan had been too selective in creating the Class A list. Bernard believed there was more than enough reason to try Hirohito, and he made that opinion clear. Nevertheless, these general complaints were prefaced by commendation. The IMTFE had a "natural" right to exist, he

Despite the life-and-death drama of the Tokyo trials, witness testimony was often a tedious affair. Here, Class A defendants fight to stay awake. (Courtesy of Douglas MacArthur Memorial)

argued, attacking anyone who believed the IMTFE's mission involved a cruel "victor's justice." He also had endless praise for MacArthur and the Occupation Government, echoing the American position that the trials of the old Japan made way for the new.[41]

In reality, Bernard, in his comments, took the lead from Webb himself. The latter just never regarded his concerns as formal, legal dissent. Although he enjoyed a warm relationship with MacArthur, Webb was sensitive to the always politically charged accusation that the IMTFE was a component of U.S. policy in Japan. He was more politically cautious than Bernard, but he also implied that Hirohito should have been put before the tribunal. He said further that he was "troubled" by the prosecution's efforts to convict on the offense of "naked conspiracy." The charge was "groundless," he complained. And he mused over a nation's "right" to make war, commenting that he wrestled with his conscience over how that "right" applied to Japanese wartime decision making. Webb considered these concerns to be philosophical ones as opposed to reasons for dissent. Whether or not this was a strong point of distinction for him remains unclear. Webb even admitted in his lively correspondence with MacArthur during the trials that he had a "serious philosophical side" and that he hoped his intellectual meanderings would not be interpreted as a bias toward either the defense or the prosecution. Forever conscious, at least in his discussions with MacArthur, of his "passion for intellectual hard ball," Webb enjoyed playing legal critic and devil's advocate.[42] But again, this did not mean dissent.

In view of Webb's health conditions and early arguments with MacArthur over them, it was amazing that he was able to proceed with his duties. Near the beginning of the trials, Webb had injured his shoulder. The pain, he told MacArthur, was "unbearable," and he anticipated a quick resignation from his role in the IMTFE. A special surgical unit was contacted in Australia, and Webb made travel plans. MacArthur considered Webb the anchor of the Allied effort on the tribunal and believed that resignation would be a "calamity" to the entire mission of the war crimes trials. MacArthur therefore offered his best medical staff to Webb but denied Webb's request to have his wife by his side as a personal nurse. Tokyo was not an accompanied tour of duty, MacArthur noted. Any exception would have a devastating impact on the homesick soldiers under his command. There could be no exceptions.

Webb disputed MacArthur's decision, reminding him that he was not a soldier in his command. Lady Webb, the chief justice promised, would maintain a low-key presence in their Imperial Hotel suite. Yet MacArthur continued to refuse Webb's requests, pointing out that Tokyo had plenty of fine nurses already. His no-exceptions rule also applied to foreign guests, he declared. The good general asked Webb to appeal to President Truman. With that unlikely suggestion, Webb finally retreated. Meanwhile, MacArthur kept his word. Tokyo's finest physicians were on call for Webb's every need, although the special surgery he required remained painfully delayed. Without question, the entire episode put an unusual strain on Webb's friendship with MacArthur, and it worsened when Lady Webb also took ill in Melbourne. Webb was caught between his duties in Tokyo and his family and personal priorities. His political friends in Australia even arranged for him to return home to lead various legal investigations, and he did, by the end of the trials, return to Australia before delivering his own lengthy judgment to the tribunal. At that time he commented that MacArthur had "conspired" to keep him in Tokyo no matter what his health and family situation. These personal concerns might have influenced Webb's critiques of the tribunal's approach to key issues. Webb had originally welcomed his assignment with enthusiasm, stating that the IMTFE "possessed the greatest mission in history." No one had expected him to raise doubts and concerns, especially not MacArthur.[43]

Justice Radhabinod Pal's views on the IMTFE, in contrast to Webb's, were well known before the trials and irreversible during them. Like Webb, he raised moral and philosophical issues. Unlike Webb, his moral and philosophical objections were the foundation for his formal dissent. Without question, Pal maintained a political agenda. Favoring a quick end to British rule over India, Pal doubted the moral authority of Great Britain, a colonial power, to pass judgment on the defeated colonial policies of Japan. Admitting a prewar attraction to Japan's "Asia for Asians" propaganda, Pal suggested that the Japanese might not have been liberators in the Pacific, but they did expose the folly of Western colonialism as well as to champion Asian "identity." These were positive attributes, he believed, making it impossible to label Japanese policy "evil." Racism, he worried, accounted for much of the prosecution's passion to punish Japan's wartime leaders. That issue, combined with emotions such as revenge, had no place in a court of law, he argued. No matter how loudly the IMTFE denied it, the war crimes trials were an exercise in "victor's justice," according to Pal. The expression "victor's justice" became a favorite one of the justice from India. It annoyed Webb, who once asked him to refrain from using it. Pal did not oblige him.

Pal's concerns over "race" were not confined to the work of the IMTFE. He had been a victim of racism himself, even in Japan. Upon the arrival of the IMTFE justices in Tokyo, the British Commonwealth delegation (Justices Webb, Patrick, McDougall, Northcroft, and Pal) were given suites at the elegant Imperial Hotel. Pal was expunged from that list by MacArthur's headquarters when it was learned that he was an Indian nationalist—also, perhaps, because he was not a fan of the IMTFE mission. "Other accommodations" were sought for him, and they were far from elegant. MacArthur's adjutant general's office gave a variety of official reasons for this decision, ranging from concern over Japanese reaction to an Indian (i.e., racial inferior) residing in the Imperial Hotel to the belief that Pal would be "uncomfortable" with pro–British Commonwealth justices as neighbors. To his credit, Webb did not care what the adjutant general's reasons were. He demanded that Pal be given the promised suite at the Imperial Hotel. MacArthur obliged after being personally approached by

Webb. But the damage had already been done, and Pal remained in an unforgiving mood.

Supporting the defense counsel's contention that there was no "binding" pre–World War II law that made war illegal, Pal's dissent needed little interpretation. He believed that the Kellogg-Briand Pact of the late 1920s had not been a sweeping, "binding" legal statement that assaulted war-making powers. Keenan argued otherwise, but Pal appealed to history. War, he noted simply, follows the collapse of the peace process. In the case of Japan, its complaint against the West developed "gradually," and its road to World War II had been a long one. The accusation of "naked conspiracy" and the follow-up of "naked aggression," he insisted, were irrelevant and inaccurate when describing Japan's "long fuse" to war. Rejecting the argument that Japan hatched conspiracies and launched evil offensives, Pal found the Rape of Nanking, the Bataan Death March, and other alleged symbols of Japanese-inflicted horror to be "stray incidents." Although awful events, they were little different, he said, from atomic bomb blasts in Hiroshima and Nagasaki. In the name of fairness, he asked that Allied leaders be tried as well, or at the least that all IMTFE defendants be found not guilty. The Japanese, Pal concluded, thought their very way of life had been threatened by the American and European colonials. They responded accordingly, and the resulting war crimes trials, as he always said, were still the "victor's justice." His colleagues failed to agree.

Pal reserved his comments for the twenty-eight senior wartime leaders at trial in Tokyo. Indeed, those twenty-eight always occupied the attention of the press, but more than twenty-two hundred trials were held throughout the Asian/Pacific region. Many of them were conducted on Guam alone, and by a military tribunal far less prestigious than Webb's group of elite justices. Since Pal found criminal behavior in alleged isolated incidents, he admitted that much of the postwar investigation into Japanese wartime actions was being pursued by these other tribunals. Although these tribunals had a similar Western colonial makeup, according to Pal, he saw no contradiction in his praise of their work. Echoing Keenan, although he probably did not mean to do so, Pal believed that the Allies had to do "the right thing" and try the underlings of the Japanese regime who unleashed their terror during specific battles, in tiny villages, big cities, and elsewhere. A "cleaner" war, in his view, had been possible, and he had little respect for the "lower classes who killed so many." Executing or jailing the losing government was never the answer. Punishing the soldier in the field was something else. Pal's interest in a class-based hierarchy of trials was barely known, even by his fellow justices. Largely denounced by the press and others as an apologist for Japanese tyranny, a lingering mouthpiece for Japanese propaganda, or as an Indian politico with a personal agenda, Pal's complexity won little appreciation.[44]

Given the controversial mission of the IMTFE, disputes and debate, even among the justices, were to be expected. In the long run, as Webb wrote in his two-volume judgment, the "evil" of the former Japanese regime had been addressed, the unfortunate past could be put to rest, and a "better world" was around the corner. It was an optimistic conclusion to the tribunal's difficult work, but the IMTFE had, indeed, accomplished its basic tasks.

In a rare reflective moment during November 1948, MacArthur commented on the challenging work of the IMTFE and its impact on history. Ranging from concerns over "victor's justice" to the trial procedure itself, MacArthur's observations recognized both the idealistic mission of the IMTFE and the many controversies associated with it. Perhaps he anticipated history's often critical view of his role as Occupation Government leader in general or as a staunch advocate of the IMTFE specifically. In any event he stated that his own review of the tribunal's judgment was a "lonely and forlorn assignment." Justice, he claimed, had been done. "No human decision is infallible but I can conceive of no judicial process where greater safeguard was made to evolve justice. It is inevitable that many will disagree with the verdict, even the learned justices who composed the Tribunal were not in complete unanimity, but no mortal agency in the present imperfect evolution of civilized society seems more entitled to confidence in the integrity of its solemn pronouncements. If we cannot trust such processes and such men we can trust nothing."[45]

Chapter 3

"Bonehead Diplomacy"
The Trials and the U.S.-Japan Relationship

Sometimes Washington saw Tojo. Sometimes they saw Red. They never saw a rebirth.

Mike Mansfield

It was generally accepted at the time that Chief Prosecutor Keenan welcomed MacArthur's political posturing. In precise reference to the war crimes trials, that meant that Keenan believed a new Japan could not emerge until the old Japan was found guilty and punished. The trials proved significant to the political goals of both Japan and America, although rumor, fear, and misunderstanding often typified the U.S.-Japan relationship in the Occupation Government years. While the Occupation Government planned Japan's future, the Tokyo trials punished its past. Since occupation authorities and the key leaders of the new Japanese government agreed with the concept that the nation could not move forward without moving away from its militarist extremism, the trials served as both a practical and a symbolic transition. Moving forward meant a decent, working relationship with Washington, and Washington would be in no mood to deal with a nation that refused or stalled its war crimes trials. General MacArthur was especially aware of the role that the trials played in the delicate Washington-Tokyo relationship, and he was quite the champion of purging the past in order to assure a progressive new era for Japan. Eventually, near the end of his tenure as the "American Caesar," MacArthur recognized Keenan's contributions to U.S.-Japan détente, but in the rush to acknowledge MacArthur's great role in that relationship, Keenan's efforts, like the trials themselves, have been largely ignored.

As early as 1946, Keenan courted a variety of Japanese reformists and remained at the ready to endorse their every move publicly. This, of course, brought him beyond his trials-related responsibilities. It did not necessarily match MacArthur's agenda. But it did connect the trials to a grand endeavor in American-Japanese rapprochement. That endeavor was a worthy cause to Keenan, and he was later thanked by Prime Minister Yoshida for his commitment to "Japanese and American understanding."[1]

The chief prosecutor's comments on the trials and their significance to Tokyo-Washington relations could be long-winded ones, such as his hour-long October 1946 speech on the subject before the annual meeting of the American Bar Association in Atlantic City, New Jersey. At that meeting, Keenan explained to his colleagues that U.S.-Japan relations were at a great crossroads. America faced two choices, he said. It could pursue the type of "racism and cultural misunderstanding" that marked prewar Washington's approach to Japanese affairs, or it could reject war-influenced hatreds and proceed with "respect and consideration."

Keenan's comments particularly reflected the concerns of numerous Tokyo trials defense attorneys, both Japanese and American, who explained in IMTFE cases that FDR's State Department had regarded prewar Japan with a certain racist disdain. A chief prosecutor quoting the arguments of a defense counsel was Keenan at his theatrical best, but he did succeed in winning the complete attention of his distinguished audience. Even echoing the then controversial arguments of Minneapolis mayor Hubert Humphrey, Keenan said America "could not move forward" unless it denounced its racist past.[2] Humphrey, of course, spoke of three hundred years of white versus black tension in American race relations, whereas Keenan referred to a world war that had only recently ended, in which the Japanese enemy was reduced to subhuman caricatures even in the American press. Shedding the "racist past" was easier said than done, and Keenan's influence on U.S.-Japan policy existed only as long as the trials did.

The Tokyo trials, Keenan said, were as much a "purging for America" as they were for the Japanese. So many defendants argued that the Americans had been as cruel and merciless as accused Japanese war criminals, in bloody encounters ranging from Guadalcanal to Nagasaki. Although at trial the prosecution often attacked this defense argument as an illegitimate and irrelevant one, Keenan was interested in its implications outside of the tribunal. The historical record emerging through the trial testimony was especially revealing and important. "There is much to be learned from the International War Crimes Trials in Tokyo of the American plan for getting along with other people," Keenan argued. "In contrast to the 1930s, America wants to work with Japan and not against it."   ·

Keenan was convinced that there were many "ordinary citizens" in Japan and the United States who saw the end of World War II as the beginning of a new era of Pacific cooperation. To those who believed this "new era required no war crimes trials at all," Keenan emphasized that there were "plenty more who saw the trials as essential." There might also be those, he worried, who would "take matters into their own hands" if the militarists were not prosecuted to the fullest extent of the law. The Japanese interest in purging the past was real, he insisted. If that interest was not answered, there could be Japanese-against-Japanese violence, and both real and imagined ex-militarists would be "exterminated." "These trials are neither blood purges nor judicial lynchings, but if they are not held, the people in impatience and disgust, will have their own lynchings and blood purgings. We are faced with one or the other choice and there can be little doubt as to which path we should follow."[3] Keenan may have exaggerated the matter of potential violence, but his general point on Japanese support for the trials was well put.

Brushing aside all modesty, and he sometimes found that very easy to do, the chief prosecutor claimed that his office was in the "business of making history." The "foundation" was being laid, he said, for a peaceful and cooperative relationship with Japan that would be "studied by historians for centuries." The alternative was "not to learn from the record of discord" and construct new barriers to Tokyo-Washington harmony.[4]

In his own way Keenan had also attempted to address the Truman administration's growing attraction to global anticommunist commitments and the role Japan might play as a new, noble ally in the effort. Officially, the Japanese ruling elite opposed any Cold War military role, for reasons ranging from domestic reconstruction priorities to a real interest in pacifism. There was also the strong possibility that Tokyo's Asian and Pacific neighbors would angrily oppose even the slightest gesture toward Japanese remobilization.[5]

In some unforeseen Asian/Pacific-based crisis, "could Washington demand Japanese military assistance?" Keenan asked his Bar Association colleagues. He answered his own hypothetical question. Indicating that MacArthur approved of Japanese pacifism and had no apologies for it, he suggested that President Truman doubted Tokyo's commitment to peace. Keenan believed that the president questioned Japan's timing of the peace commitment, for the Cold War was heating up. The deteriorating relationship between Washington and Moscow put Japan in a precarious position, Keenan noted. Japan, he said, rejected its fascistlike past. The IMTFE trial record even provided the detail to curious Japanese who had been unaware of the "evil" championed by many of their own leaders. With that in mind,

Keenan suggested that Japan had every right to sit out the Cold War "for the time being." America, he argued, had the resources to fend off Communist expansionism on its own. It "did not need commitments from the new Japan."[6]

Keenan's position was a bold one, urging that Washington maintain a "hands off policy" when it came to Japanese contributions to the Cold War. He was also guessing at what Truman thought or did not think. MacArthur shared some of Keenan's concerns over Japan's proper Cold War role, but it was Keenan, without consulting MacArthur, who demanded a "time of healing" for Japan once the trials were over. The transition from old to new Japan was tough enough. A transition from defeated enemy to active partner in the march to Cold War victory was truly asking too much, too soon.[7] Or so Keenan argued.

Since his comments also questioned the strident anticommunism of the day, Keenan might have won a rebuke from the Truman administration or at least an attack by certain members of Congress. Instead, Keenan appears to have been dismissed as an opinionated lawyer running amok. For instance, the American Bar Association thanked the chief prosecutor for his comments to their annual meeting but distanced themselves from him as well. Following Keenan's 1946 speech, the Bar Association issued a press release noting that Keenan had represented "himself" at their annual meeting and not the Bar Association. They also concluded that Keenan needed to focus on his "tasks at hand" and avoid "politicking."[8] Although politely worded in most cases, the Bar Association's official response to the Keenan address was less than flattering. The chief prosecutor had traveled far to speak his mind, and his effort was most appreciated in Tokyo.[9]

The Yoshida government's support for Keenan's speech was obvious. Muneo Makabe of the *Tokyo Shimbun,* one of the prime minister's closest contacts in the press, welcomed Keenan's assessment, urging the American political community to leave the chief prosecutor alone. Makabe informed his readers of Keenan's major themes in the Bar Association speech and other public comments, expressing his own concern that "some might worry" that the chief prosecutor was playing politics when he should be practicing law. Makabe, a respected editorial writer with political aspirations of his own, even added specifics to Keenan's general observations. Makabe saw the war crimes trials as connected not only to the vision of a new Japan but to foreign trade and economic recovery as well. After pointing out Japan's great potential as a giant in the export trade, Makabe insisted that few nations, including America, would ever conclude trade agreements with a country that refused to try and punish its war criminals.

Why would anyone "want to deal with their former tormentors," he asked? A Japan that removed all wartime leaders from society also removed post-war economic struggle. "Has Japan the qualifications necessary to be recognized as a peaceful, cultural, or democratic nation?" he also asked. "We would do well to consider our national strength, our international position, and push for more, never less, war crimes trials."[10]

Washington might not have fully accepted a Keenan-Makabe thesis, but that did not mean Keenan was in trouble because of it. His job was never in jeopardy because of speeches that were, essentially, on behalf of U.S.-Japan cooperation. Nevertheless, he failed to convince the Truman administration that healthy U.S.-Japan relations were connected to the number of guilty verdicts in the war crimes trials. In their own ways, Keenan and Makabe defined the political importance of the trials, suggesting that the U.S.-Japan relationship was better off because of them. How much better was a different story.[11]

Meanwhile, the question of Keenan's alleged "politicking" remained. Truman might not have cared, but others did. Retired general Robert E. Wood, who was close to MacArthur before leaving the military for a quiet life in Illinois, made headlines in Chicago through his complaint that Keenan had indeed become too powerful, too egotistical, and too involved in non-IMTFE matters. According to Wood, this was MacArthur's "fault." The next step, he argued, might be Keenan acting as a champion for Japanese trade interests. Was Keenan using his position, Wood asked, to develop a client list within the Japanese business community? Perhaps MacArthur encouraged this "unethical behavior?" And perhaps the ambitious Keenan would have too much of a hand in "determining postwar Japanese destiny." Truly, this was not the chief prosecutor's role, Wood concluded, warning that "amateurs" like Keenan hurt rather than helped U.S.-Japan relations.[12]

Wood's charges were wild and groundless. They also made juicy headlines. The chief prosecutor certainly had a right to his own ideas, recommendations, and good intentions. And he had little impact on the direction of the Occupation Government or on the agenda of Japanese economic planners. More to the point, even MacArthur resented Wood's implication that Keenan was a wrongdoer with shady ambitions. The Wood attack on Keenan, MacArthur concluded, was also an attack on the Occupation Government. As always, MacArthur and Keenan agreed that the trials, at least symbolically, represented the first step in the beginning of a new Japan. Wood had missed the point, and MacArthur told him so.[13]

In his private correspondence with Wood, MacArthur noted their "one time" friendship. He urged him to stay away from Keenan-bashing, from "all headlines," and from his own "foolish conclusions" about Japanese politics and economics. "The answer to Japan's economic ills lies not only in a redesign to make possible the emergence of an economic system based upon the principle of free competitive private enterprise, but even more, from an immediate and practical standpoint, on the reopening of the channels of trade and commerce to make available essential raw materials to feed the production lines, world markets to absorb the finished products, and food to sustain working energy."[14]

The American concern over the impact of the trials on U.S.-Japan relations went beyond an angry general or two. To California congressman Bertrand Gearhart, the trials had to do with "race, a delicate subject." If the Japanese perceived that the trials were about "white people punishing yellow people," Gearhart worried that U.S.-Japan relations might not ever recover. As a Californian, Gearhart was particularly sensitive to the issue of Japanese American internment there during World War II. That decision, he said, had been a mistake and had made a mockery of civil rights and civil liberties guarantees for an entire segment of the population. Could Japanese Americans trust their government anymore, he asked? Should American policymakers not be more sensitive to the issue of race in U.S.-Japan relations?

Gearhart offered his views in Congress and in personal correspondence with MacArthur during August 1947. Worried that the "Japanese were on trial" in Tokyo rather than specific individuals charged with war crimes, Gearhart wanted official assurances that the United States was not involved in the same type of "race baiting" that influenced the early 1940s Japanese American internment decision. He also wanted MacArthur's support in his personally sponsored congressional initiative to eliminate any immigration barriers to U.S. entry faced by Japanese in search of an American home. America's anti-Asian/Pacific immigration legislation dated back decades and had been a sore spot in U.S.-Japan relations for years. Given MacArthur's efforts at new directions in Japanese postwar life, Gearhart requested the general's public support in the effort to change America's approach toward Japanese immigration. But first Gearhart needed the general's guarantee that the Tokyo trials remained honest, legitimate, and divorced from any racist agenda. Then, according to Gearhart's interpretation, the U.S.-Japan relationship would happily move forward.[15]

In a way, Gearhart's request of MacArthur read more like an ultimatum than anything else. Gearhart implied that the general owed the Congress a full account with regard to the focus and direction of the trials. In reality, only Gearhart was requesting that account, and MacArthur never answered it. To Gearhart this meant the general had snubbed Congress and that the Occupation Government had something to hide regarding the trials. Because of MacArthur's silence, Gearhart waxed poetic on the arrogance of the general's command and his policy of trying the former Japanese government while constructing a new one. Meanwhile, he continued to claim that he "represented" the full U.S. Congress when he called for fair play in the trials. MacArthur, he insisted, must "come clean."[16]

Either Gearhart had not been paying attention to the progress of the trials or he was upset over the struggling position of his own legislation. Whatever it was, it added confusion to the Japanese examination of who might be in charge of the U.S. position in the U.S.-Japan relationship. The *Tokyo Shimbun* commented that it preferred the wisdom of a MacArthur over the confusion of the U.S. Congress.[17] Most likely, many Japanese, if they were aware of this minor public skirmish between Gearhart and MacArthur, agreed with *Tokyo Shimbun*'s conclusions. Dennis McEvoy of America's famous *Reader's Digest* did. McEvoy, a self-described Japan specialist, advocated clear directions and dedicated leadership within America's Japan policy. But he could not have cared less about Gearhart's concerns over race and MacArthur's alleged snubs to Congress. Most of the time, McEvoy accused MacArthur of going too slowly in the effort to reform Japan. He especially accused the general of "tortoise slow" war crimes trials, "lackluster leadership" in Japanese economic recovery, and "pompous showmanship" over adequate governing.

In "Japan's Problems Must Be Solved-Now!" McEvoy described an Asia on the verge of Communist takeover, a Japan not yet reconciled to World War II defeat, and war criminals defending themselves on the grounds of Allied misunderstanding of them. "Nonsense," he said. There was "no time" for Japan to be on the outskirts of the Cold War. The Americans in Japan, he insisted, were more interested in the trials of "yesterday's evil" than in preparing to meet the Communist version of that "evil" today.[18]

Reur G. Dashiell, managing editor of the *Reader's Digest,* thought this particular McEvoy article was his most virulent to date. It seemed to Dashiell that the article portrayed America as a "weak sister," struggling through its Japanese occupation duties. America's Cold War opponents, the Soviets, would enjoy reading it. McEvoy even suggested that the trials should be either stopped or finished quickly. This could mean that only a handful of "select war criminals" might go to the gallows, but it mattered little. To McEvoy, an effective, winning Cold War policy mattered.

Dashiell found McEvoy's conclusions rather disturbing. He sent the manuscript to MacArthur for prepublication review and comments. Since *Reader's Digest* enjoyed a high readership at that time, MacArthur worried that McEvoy's view of the Occupation Government would be the only one many Americans might ever know. He recommended against publication on the grounds that McEvoy's argument, on the whole, constituted a threat to U.S. security.[19]

If MacArthur had complained about various points within McEvoy's thesis, such as his view on the war crimes trials, his rejection decision might have been welcomed by Dashiell. But MacArthur's security concerns did not sit well with Dashiell and his editorial staff. Even though Dashiell had once noted that the McEvoy piece was too alarmist for *Reader's Digest,* he reserved the right to change his mind. In reality, MacArthur's argument in favor of national security protection was as wild as the McEvoy article itself. Yet Dashiell concluded that "first amendment rights" might be more important than MacArthur's interpretation of security. He prepared the piece for publication, but the battle had just begun.[20]

Col. Herbert Wheeler, MacArthur's aide and military secretary, handled the *Reader's Digest* matter for the general. His argument was clear. *Reader's Digest* had doubted McEvoy's work and sent it to MacArthur to confirm those doubts. Its decision to publish violated a certain trust with MacArthur. By doing so, it now welcomed dangerous propaganda and lies, giving comfort to America's potential foes in the Pacific.[21]

Wheeler might have exaggerated McEvoy's significance, but of the two McEvoy was a more accomplished master of exaggeration. In his original manuscript, for instance, McEvoy recommended certain "emergency measures." Some of the Japanese senior military officers charged with war crimes must be quickly released so that they, along with their American counterparts in Japan, could plan the defense of the Western Pacific against "inevitable Soviet attack." There could be no alternative to this decision, wrote McEvoy, unless both Tokyo and Washington preferred to reject the wisdom of Japan's wartime leadership, even hang them, and then most certainly lose World War III.[22]

McEvoy also complained that MacArthur's economic reforms did not go far enough. Even though it had long rejected capitalism, the Soviet Union, McEvoy claimed, would soon have the economic resources to tempt Japan with a reconstruction aid plan. He footnoted a study of successful Soviet financial planning in eastern Europe to demonstrate the point. With these data in mind, McEvoy predicted that a frustrated Japan might soon turn to a vigorous Soviet aid package unless MacArthur's government took swift action. Japan, McEvoy suspected, could be easily lured away from the American camp, and MacArthur was to blame.[23]

Throughout his analysis, McEvoy produced not a shred of evidence that Japan was wavering in the Cold War. Indeed, there was none. Lost in Red Scare–influenced conclusions, McEvoy's work, if published, promised unnecessary troubles to the U.S.-Japan relationship. MacArthur emphasized this point in his appeal to reject the piece. Apparently, Dashiell considered publishing it simply because a great general opposed it, for his defense of first amendment rights was short-lived. In the end Dashiell decided against publication, claiming that he rejected a lousy article as opposed to caving in to the charismatic general. Nevertheless, the episode helped to build a legend, especially among American reporters who covered the Japan beat, that MacArthur favored greater press freedoms in Japan than he did in the United States.

Without question, the politics of information was part of the U.S.-Japan relationship tale. Chief Prosecutor Keenan, for example, insisted that "the proper view" of the war crimes trials must be presented to the Japanese people. Like MacArthur, he was always interested in how policy-related information was gathered and offered to the Japanese. From the beginning of the IMTFE effort, Keenan set aside a budget to write a history of the trials. It was to be written in Japanese as the trials came to a conclusion. "Several hundred thousand copies" were then to be distributed to the general population. That was the plan.

At first, Keenan envisioned a small book, published on quality paper with decent graphics. The U.S. Army would assist in its distribution, for the logistics of this endeavor were immense. The Occupation Government would aid in the final costs of the entire project, including printing. As the Japanese attempted to lead peaceful, normal lives in their war-torn country, Keenan worried that many of them were fed up with World War II–related information, including the war crimes trials. This was most unfortunate in Keenan's view. A great record of Japanese wartime "evil," he believed, was required. "It was essential to Japan's full postwar development," Keenan once wrote, "that a clarification be given to the Japanese people of their war guilt and of the responsibility of the militarists for present and future Japanese suffering and privation."

Keenan believed he had President Truman and General MacArthur's full support in this grand project. He was wrong. For the Truman administration, the objection was largely a financial one. Throughout the IMTFE's existence, Keenan worked with a bare bones budget even though Washington favored quick trials in favor of moving forward with the postwar relationship. In spite of this situation, Keenan still hoped the White House would be flexible on operating costs, especially when it came to the publication and national distribution of his trials history. But Truman saw Keenan's book project as an overly expensive propaganda stunt, wasting the Occupation Government's time, paper, and resources.

Keenan argued cautiously for more funding in general reference to daily operations, but he became more emotional on the specific subject of the trials history. Quite simply, it was important to him, and he thought it important to U.S.-Japan relations. The verbatim testimony of some of the defendants had been most damning of the "old Japan," Keenan observed. Those Japanese interested in a postmilitarist Japan needed affirmation and confirmation of their beliefs. The trials record book, Keenan reasoned, would certainly help them. Truman disagreed, insisting that Keenan adjust to his budgetary realities and carry on. Although he never elaborated on this decision, it was apparent that the president did not find an easy connection between Keenan's legal responsibilities and his interest in posttrial propaganda.

And so Keenan turned directly to MacArthur for a financial commitment. He told the general that he was convinced his Chief Prosecutor's Office had become a victim of Washington's lack of understanding vis-à-vis Japan issues. But MacArthur proved not to be as sympathetic as Keenan had hoped. The Occupation Government was not in the business of providing fancy books to hundreds of thousands of Japanese citizens. Keenan was therefore forced to strike a deal, and he turned to Japanese newspaper owners and editors. Some of them even volunteered to excerpt "key passages" of Keenan's work in several consecutive issues of their papers, but Keenan preferred to have the full book serialized or nothing at all. And he wanted it done immediately. Sadly, for Keenan, he found no takers. By now Keenan had completed the writing of an account of the trials; the manuscript turned out to be much longer than he had first expected.

Keenan's best and only offer came from the editorial staff of *Asahi Shimbun,* one of Tokyo's most literate newspapers, which compared itself in quality to the *New York Times.* They offered to publish a first edition of fifty thousand copies on scrap paper. It would be an abridged version of the trials' history, and would sell for only ten yen. This was a very affordable price for most everyone, although Keenan had once envisioned no fee at all. A slightly larger version on better-quality paper would be sold at fifty-five yen apiece, although only ten thousand copies would be published. There was no guarantee that a second printing would be made, and *Asahi Shimbun* remained in charge of distribution.

It was a far cry from Keenan's original plan, but the *Asahi Shimbun* trials history was well written. It also included a decent summation of Keenan's final report on the general accomplishments of the trials. "This book," Keenan said, "closed a chapter in Japanese history"[24]; in hindsight, that appears to have been wishful thinking.

More often than not, the relation of the trials to other political or diplomatic developments was coincidental, purely symbolic, or just plain exaggerated to fit a certain complaint or need. Both American and Japanese leaders embraced this approach. During February 1947, for instance, MacArthur announced to the press that the war crimes trials were going so smoothly that it made little sense to "delay Japan's future." With that statement MacArthur connected the prosecution of the "old Japan" (the trials) to the slow-moving effort in Washington to sign a formal peace treaty with Japan. Japan was "shedding its past so quickly," MacArthur noted, that it "enjoyed grander potential for success as a democratic nation than Germany." Further delay of a final peace treaty, he argued, handicapped Japan's development, making it too dependent on the United States. For Japan to begin a working trade policy, for example, the peace treaty needed rapid approval, MacArthur told California congressman Norris Paulson. The trials, he said, spoke of a Japan where militarism was wrong and peace was now welcomed. According to MacArthur, the Japanese welcomed this assessment in the name of "peace and democracy." Hence, a less dependent Japan would quickly rescue the American taxpayer from unnecessary burdens. It was up to Congress and the White House, MacArthur concluded, to do the right thing.[25]

Paulson informed his best contact in the Truman administration, Julius Krug, the secretary of the interior, about MacArthur's personal appeal. Krug did not see the connections between war crimes trials, a peace treaty, and trade policy. He told this to MacArthur in a private meeting during the Interior Department's 1947 tour of Japan. Krug had been unimpressed with MacArthur long before he left Washington. Like his boss, Harry Truman, Krug believed that MacArthur "held court" in Tokyo rather than administering an Occupation Government. Meanwhile, the only State Department–mandated conditions in reference to a Japan peace treaty involved Japan's full acceptance of a democratic form of government. MacArthur insisted that a great Japanese democracy already existed. He offered the "evidence" of Japanese reaction to the trials and the antimilitarist purges. Krug still remained unimpressed. He doubted the "evidence" and returned to Washington with more questions than answers.[26]

Although far from connected to the Krug tour, Wataru Narahashi also disagreed with MacArthur's "evidence." Narahashi, a leading Democratic member of the House of Councillors, was accused of "dark politics" by the Yoshida government's Central Screening Committee. The latter consisted of nine individuals handpicked by the Yoshida cabinet. When they reviewed the wartime activities of Diet members, they accused Narahashi of "criminal behavior" while he served in North China during World War II. As MacArthur and Washington officials debated Japan's place in the world, many Japanese were fascinated by Narahashi's resulting counterattack on the Central Screening Committee.

Narahashi, who was running for reelection when he was charged by the committee, claimed that he was a victim of American tyranny. From the war crimes trials to the Central Screening Committee, Narahashi argued that MacArthur and Yoshida represented little more than a "new dictatorship" that planned to crush all dissent. His own "purging," he said, represented a "plot to contain Yoshida's political opposition."[27]

The Narahashi matter was a focus of a great deal of discussion in the Japanese press. Waging a campaign to clear his "good name," Narahashi always argued that a "real democracy" might not be possible so long as the Americans were present and while the Japanese government remained willing to act with them. "We will all be on trial," he predicted, as long as this "unholy alliance" continued.[28]

Narahashi's complaint was serious enough for Representative Paulson, an off-and-on Occupation Government critic, to ask for MacArthur's view on it for the U.S. House of Representatives Foreign Affairs Committee. The general responded that the Narahashi purging was solely the concern of the Yoshida government and that he supported their efforts. Narahashi, MacArthur explained, had exaggerated the purging issue to deflect attention away from his own case. He claimed that few Japanese supported Narahashi's assessment of things, although the press was "entertained," he admitted, by Narahashi's accusations. Indeed, later Japanese public opinion surveys suggested that MacArthur was right. Few Japanese saw legal assaults on ex-militarists as bad for the country. And Narahashi never did clear his "good name."[29]

To Dr. Soichi Sasaki, "troublemakers" like Narahashi could not be easily dismissed. People like him represented a certain "lingering militarism" that the war crimes trials would never be able to address or expunge. If one individual could make such a splash in the press, Sasaki warned, the Japanese-American relationship must expect further "embarrassments" in the years to come.

Sasaki picked his words carefully; he was used to doing so. As Japan's top authority on public law, he was a former professor at Kyoto Imperial University as well as the former dean of the Department of Law there. Also an advisor to the defense counsel in the war crimes trials, Sasaki played a major role in hammering out the specific legal language of the 1947 Japanese Constitution. He even wrote a book, *Nippon Kempo Yoron,* on how to interpret various constitutional principles (the English translation was titled *Fundamentals of the Japanese Constitution*). The book included a brief history of the making of that document and discussed the political challenges ahead.

Sasaki worried that future "outbreaks" of promilitarist sentiment would continue to be blown out of proportion by a fascinated press. That, in turn, might lead Japan's allies, namely America, to conclude that Japan had never truly renounced its militarist past. Consequently, the war crimes trials might soon be remembered as a token effort. He hoped that he was "mistaken."[30]

There was nothing legally wrong with the mechanics of the war crimes trials, Sasaki argued. Both Keenan and his defense counsel colleagues were doing "excellent work." The political implications were something else, but there was hope. According to Sasaki, the issue of what to do about lingering promilitarist sentiment was already addressed in the new constitution. Unfortunately, few nonlegal minds could understand it. In the press Sasaki attempted to act as constitutional interpreter, offering a pedestrian explanation of the law's answer to militarism. Within that explanation he drew a "distinction," for anyone who cared, between the "assault on past evils" (the war crimes trials) and a coming effort to "assault promilitarist opinions which still infect Japanese life." It was a complex "distinction."

Sasaki believed that the majority of the Japanese citizenry welcomed the end of the militarist era. Few, he hoped, were deeply troubled by Narahashi's complaints of MacArthur-Yoshida "plots" against dissent. But a healthy U.S.-Japan relationship, he also believed, hung in the balance of Narahashi or Narahashi-like political charges if those charges went unanswered. The onus was on the Yoshida government to demonstrate its commitment to peace and antimilitarism.

The vehicle was Article 9 of the new constitution. Sasaki had helped write it, but even before the document was officially put into effect, he admitted that the article had enforcement difficulties. Offering formal and polite apologies to both his countrymen and the world, Sasaki said he should have argued harder, during the early ratification process, for a stronger, tougher Article 9. The final version read as follows: "Aspiring sincerely to an international peace based on justice and order, the Japanese people, forever, renounce war as a sovereign right of the nation, or the threat or use of force as a means of settling disputes with other nations."[31] After the fact, Sasaki was now concerned over what the renunciation of war in a national law might mean.

Sasaki made it quite clear in an interview with NHK's Tetsuro Furukaki that, like most people, he hated war. However, he remained concerned over the lasting impact of the "renouncing war" clause. Eliminating it, of course, would make him and the government appear to be in favor of war, and that was "most misleading." He did recommend removing the clause before the full constitution reached its approaching enforcement date. Then, according to legal procedure, a new clause could be inserted. The new clause would reflect the success of the war crimes trials and the grander, more specific antiwar intentions of the new Japanese government. As it stood, the wording was too reminiscent of the old 1920s Kellogg-Briand Pact, which had become synonymous (in his view) with weakness and failure. The constitutional framers, Sasaki complained, had overreacted to Keenan's constant reminder throughout the trials that Japan had been a violator of the Kellogg-Briand Pact.[32]

Article 9 did not make exception for self-defense in case of attack. Given the growing Cold War tensions, this position now seemed as foolish as the Kellogg-Briand Pact. More to the point, the stripping of any defense responsibility on the part of Japan might encourage those militarists who escaped the justice of the war crimes trials, or those who received minimum sentencing in the trials, to resurface and advocate a full or partial return to the "old Japan." The justification, of course, would be "adequate defense." In the current constitutional approach, Sasaki warned, militarism could easily return.

Sasaki admitted that he had taken part in the creation of Article 9 largely out of shame for Japan's past wrongdoing. A decent antiwar statement needed to be made. But now he saw more harm than good in Article 9. He certainly did not want to be even partially responsible for a possible rise in neomilitarist activity. Indeed, he interpreted the Narahashi splash in the press, accompanied by the worsening Moscow-Washington tensions, as an "invitation" to that rise. Insisting that he was neither alarmist or exaggerating the facts, Sasaki urged Yoshida and MacArthur to listen to him before it was too late. The war crimes trials might have symbolized the effort to rid Japan of its militarist past, but, ironically, a pacifist constitution could bring it back.[33]

Sasaki's literate concern also gave MacArthur reason for concern. An architect of pacifism now doubted his own structure? MacArthur asked the professor what he proposed to do. Sasaki seemed to know what he was against, but he remained weak on precise alternatives. He spoke vaguely about a special UN-administered anti-militarism commission that could be set up in Japan but then confessed that he was worried about undue foreign influence in Japanese lawmaking. MacArthur still wanted answers, and he posed some straightforward questions. Did Sasaki truly advocate an emergency constitutional review? Since Sasaki often cited Cold War concerns, did he favor having the safeguard of Japan's defense, the U.S. military, take part in that review as well?

Sasaki had no replies for MacArthur. Although he succeeded in stimulating interesting discussions, Sasaki eventually admitted that he had no crystal ball to predict a new rise in militarism and a resulting strain in U.S. relations. In the long run, Sasaki's primary objective was to persuade the Japanese government to legislate propacifist initiatives once Article 9 was in effect. With "progressive antimilitarist legislation on the books," Sasaki predicted one last time, the government could demonstrate to its voters and to the world that "the old Japan was dead." Perhaps anticipating a request for more specifics about his views, Sasaki noted that he preferred to remain a "theorist and an academic" rather than a politician. He did not need to be specific. MacArthur resented Sasaki's public soul-searching. "Constitutional democracy always faces great challenges," he told the press in a backhanded slap at Sasaki.[34] Meanwhile, the war crimes trials continued, the constitution moved forward, and Sasaki's predictions of resurging militarism were never realized.

Whereas MacArthur might have found it easy to dismiss a Japanese debate on the possible resurrection of militarism, the Truman administration took a different view. Assistant Secretary of State Dean Rusk found the matter serious enough to launch a top secret investigation. To Rusk, the premise that the war crimes trials represented the end of militarism and the beginning of a new Japan was interesting symbolic politics and little else. U.S. security could not rest on symbols, and Rusk's office, along with the

Intelligence Research Division of the State Department, proceeded with its investigation. An angry MacArthur would learn of its existence only after its work was completed. His Occupation Government would then question Rusk's findings point by point.

Rusk labored under the assumption that MacArthur was too involved with the Japanese to see any trouble ahead. His team studied a variety of issues relevant to political/economic reform, MacArthur-Yoshida collaboration, and the reaction of the Japanese people. It was difficult work, and Rusk deliberately avoided asking anyone in the Department of the Army for records that might have assisted his investigation. It remained from start to finish a purely State Department endeavor.

Contrary to popular perception, the Rusk investigation discovered more struggle and confusion in occupied Japan than MacArthur-influenced success. First of all, they found plenty of Japanese who complained that MacArthur's "right" to have the final word in the war crimes trials verdicts equaled "imperial power" and a "contradiction to the democratic mission." This discovery did not mean that Japanese citizenry were angry enough over the matter to protest it or in any way ready to disturb the security of the U.S. bases. At least not yet, the Rusk team believed.

Second, Rusk arrived at different figures in reference to postwar economic growth in Japan. This was a major matter of concern for Rusk, making him wonder how quickly Japan was moving forward with a healthy democratic/capitalist outlook. MacArthur, using a 1932–1936 base index for Japanese industrial production, reported a 40.2 percent jump in productivity in 1947 and 58.1 percent in 1948. Rusk found no evidence of these great leaps and concluded that Japanese industrial growth was slow but constant. This conclusion raised questions about the accuracy of MacArthur's reporting techniques to the White House. How much was padded and doctored? Indeed, how firm were the Occupation Government's assurances that the militarist era was truly over in Japan? Rusk had no problem linking economic and security issues. Motivated by the development of the anticommunist Truman Doctrine as well as by the approaching collapse of Nationalist China, Rusk saw the Cold War going badly for America. Japan's support in the anticommunist cause was expected and required, but Rusk needed to know Tokyo's precise view on U.S.-Japan relationships. MacArthur, in the State Department's opinion, should not be consulted in the effort to find an answer.[35]

Again, the analyzing of facts and figures played an important role in the Rusk effort. More than a decade later, he would take this reputation for tireless information-gathering with him to John Kennedy's White House as Secretary of State. In the meantime, he looked closely at late-1940s Japanese unemployment, wondering whether an army of the unemployed might constitute an army of support for a freed war criminal, for instance, looking for a new base of promilitarist support. A pro-fascist success, Rusk reasoned, given Japan's attraction to capitalism, was more likely than a success for Communist agitators. Nevertheless, the assistant secretary of state ruled nothing out of his various scenarios.

Rusk found 430,000 persons permanently out of work in 1947, 260,000 in 1948, and in early 1949 he projected a jump to 340,000 before that year came to a close. MacArthur's data emphasized part-time versus full-time unemployment in key industries. From those data the general concluded that all was well and booming. Rusk disagreed, finding a "hidden unemployment" sector of the Japanese economy that MacArthur also "hid" in his reports to Washington.

Perhaps more damning to MacArthur's good and ethical image, Rusk found the general's command involved in "questionable politics" that would always benefit the Yoshida government to the detriment of its political opposition. A common tactic, explained Rusk, was for the Yoshida government to dispatch to Washington an important policymaker, such as Finance Minister Hayato Ikeda (who would later be prime minister during the early years of Rusk's role as secretary of state). Then Ikeda would confer, or not, with White House officials, and quickly report to the press that a new financial agreement with the Americans was at hand. In Japan this news had a devastating impact on Yoshida's opposition during any election period. And that, Rusk said, was the point of the exercise. The assistant secretary disapproved of this "fraudulent use of power," implying, of course, that MacArthur misused his office to benefit his favorite Japanese politicians.[36] Ironically, Rusk's argument echoed that of purged militarist Wataru Narahashi.

Digging even deeper, Rusk investigated the salary discrepancies of Japanese government workers and found them amazingly low in contrast to their mission to build and lead the new Japan. Given that situation, Rusk wondered why struggling civil servants would answer requests to work even harder on behalf of the anticommunist cause. Rusk especially blamed MacArthur's economic advisor, Joseph Dodge, who, according to Rusk, was more interested in obscure fiscal policies than in assuring loyalty in the effort to fight Communism or the resurgence of militarism, or both.

Given his mission, Rusk left few stones unturned. For example, in both the Japanese and the American press, one of the greatly touted successes of the Occupation Government was the stabilization of the Japanese economy, especially for the many small "ma and pa businesses" of the Japanese big city. In his study Rusk presented a grim picture of "unacceptable bankruptcies" on a month-to-month basis that made a mockery of the laudatory press accounts. Reality, Rusk suggested, was more important to the cause of economic stabilization than glowing praises in the press. Middle-class support for extremist causes, he warned, was essential to the success of those causes. Rusk saw no evidence of Japanese middle-class economic security; that lack of security made it difficult for the middle class of Japan, he emphasized, to resist old militarist temptations.[37]

Whether Rusk entered into his involved task with a determined anti-MacArthur agenda is a matter of speculation, but he certainly opened himself up to return fire from the Occupation Government on the same issues. Throughout Rusk's huge report, there were no words of praise for MacArthur or acknowledgment of jobs adequately done in any field of endeavor. To Rusk it appeared that MacArthur had done little that was right in the U.S. effort to help Japan through its reconstruction period. The war crimes trials had also accomplished little, according to Rusk's assessment. Consequently, his investigation suggested that it was impossible to kill an idea, and Japan's attraction to militarism had long historical roots. America and Japan could bet on bad days ahead.[38]

Maj. Gen. Carter Magruder, MacArthur's special assistant for occupied areas, led the counteroffensive against Rusk. His lengthy comments were sent to Rusk himself, with copies to the secretary of state and the president. Apparently, both Rusk and Magruder believed that their respective reports were watershed works that could determine the course of U.S.-Japan relations. This was not the case, but the Occupation Government–State Department debate did illustrate the confusion of purpose in Japan policy.

Magruder felt that the State Department was attempting to change America's Japan policy too late in the game. And if such a change was ordered, it would be based on mistaken assumptions and bad information, he claimed predictably. Rusk's work, said Magruder, was in "distinct contradiction" to Department of the Army information and to the reality of the Japanese political scene. Clearly arguing that he had the proper facts and Rusk did not, Magruder urged the White House, particularly, "to embrace the truth."[39]

Citing numerous press sources, personal interviews, and public comments by Japanese officials, Magruder pointed out that the war crimes trials had "exposed the evils of militarism" to a populace once humbled by that evil. They had "done the trick," he said, noting that the millions of supporters of a pacifist constitution could not all be closet militarists. Magruder declared the trials a great success within America's Japan policy. Japanese loyalty in the Cold War, he said, was assured, for there were no militarist or Communist threats to American interests in Japan. He also disputed Rusk's conclusions on issues ranging from industrial development to "hidden unemployment."

Seasonal variations in the economic data, including unemployment figures, were not considered by Rusk, Magruder complained. The temporary impact of fast-moving reforms across the Japanese economy was also absent from Rusk's assessment, which artificially linked alleged economic downturns to potential security risks for Americans in Japan. There were no risks, artificial links, or conspiracies, Magruder insisted. He challenged Rusk to produce evidence of the struggling, wavering Japan.

The Rusk suggestion that MacArthur manufactured phony Japanese diplomatic missions to Washington was especially hard hit by Magruder, who later insisted that the Yoshida government might soon need a formal U.S. apology for this "lie," if it became public knowledge. Any political benefit to the Yoshida government was of its own "honest doing," Magruder concluded. Quite simply, he said, Rusk's report "steered clear of logic."[40]

Urging the State Department and President Truman to accept his "realistic" study, Magruder admitted that the Occupation Government was nearing the end of its tasks. Its greatest contribution to postwar Japanese life, he noted, involved the effort to rid the country of its militarist attractions. That effort, he reminded his superiors, had been widely welcomed by the Japanese themselves. As both America and Japan were about to enter a new decade, arguments over data and labeling the Japanese militarists or Communists did nothing for the Washington-Tokyo dialogue. This was Magruder's final word on the subject.

Both Rusk and Magruder offered interesting arguments. Yet no one was really choosing between them. In simple terms, Rusk took a dim view of the decade to come and Magruder did not. MacArthur was amazed at both positions, finding Rusk foolish and Magruder too vague. Were these two men writing about the same country? he asked Keenan. Keenan had returned to the States immediately after the major war criminals had been tried, but MacArthur had kept him well informed, offering Keenan an opportunity to speak his mind on war crimes and militarism-related issues with a fairly secure source. Keenan's negative reaction to the Rusk report was predictable, but he also thought Magruder's response only encouraged the continuation of an unnecessary debate between the State Department and the U.S. Army. These difficult times, Keenan believed, required coop-eration and solidarity rather than confusion and debate. He wondered whether MacArthur shared this same conclusion.

Obviously, Keenan liked MacArthur personally, but he worried that his friend picked too many no-win fights with Washington. MacArthur never responded to Keenan's concern. Meanwhile, the chief prosecutor found it amazing that senior Washington policymakers had such little faith in the postmilitarist destiny of Japan.[41]

Washington's nervousness over whether Japan was truly rid of its militarist past or whether it was moving toward a new Communist future was not confined to the future secretary of state. As late as 1950 longtime Japanese journalist Isamu Suzukawa, a graduate of the UCLA School of Journalism, overheard a variety of Occupation Government officials in Ja-pan whispering the same concern. Suzukawa was amazed at this develop-ment, for there was no evidence to support it. He investigated the matter, looking into both the Japanese view and the origins of the American fear.[42]

Quite literally, Suzukawa had covered the Occupation Government beat from its very beginning. Suzukawa first met MacArthur when the general's plane arrived at Atsugi naval air station near the time of the Japa-nese surrender. That surrender saddened him, he admitted, but like many Japanese, Suzukawa was ready to move on. The resulting Occupation Gov-ernment and Yoshida cabinet did not disappoint him. Hence, his worry that foolish rumor and fear might disturb U.S.-Japan relations throughout the new decade of the 1950s.

Suzukawa's investigations found a Japan that was quite content with the outcome of the war crimes trials. The militarist past is truly behind us, both voters and their elected officials told him. His interviews with Yoshida and MacArthur produced similar assessments. Although he later admitted that his project was based more on personal than professional concern, he sent excerpts from his long series of articles on the subject to contacts in the U.S. press wire services and even to the White House. He never heard back from President Truman.

Japan had changed, Suzukawa argued. The war crimes trials under-lined the desire for change. Unfortunately, the press was not covering the issue as it should, he complained. He blamed *Asahi Shimbun* and other newspapers for not emphasizing the obvious: that warmongering was wrong and that the warmongers had paid the price.[43]

Years after the Occupation Government, the career diplomat and politician Tadakatsu Suzuki remembered the Suzukawa articles. He also remembered thinking how sad it would have been if U.S.-Japan relations had deteriorated because of "Washington's misunderstanding." Suzukawa claimed to have spoken to several senior U.S. policymakers who, even by the time of the Korean War, still referred to Japan as "the sneak attack" country where totalitarianism never died. As the official liaison between MacArthur's command and the Japanese government, it had been Suzuki who personally informed the emperor that the Allies would be definitely holding war crimes trials. Hirohito responded, "All the soldiers and officers were very devoted soldiers and officers and fought valiantly for the country. I feel very sorry." Suzuki remembered being afraid of mass suicides when the arrests of the war criminals began, but of course that did not happen. The Japanese people proved to be "above defeat," he said, and "marched forward into the new era."[44]

The most dangerous moment during the war crimes trials, Suzuki believed, was at the end when the Americans, for "unknown reasons," began to doubt Japan's commitment to remain a good, solid democratic ally. At that time Washington saw any Japanese labor unrest or any debate over the direction of reconstruction as a budding Communist plot, Suzuki noted. As the Cold War became a more and more frustrating experience for the White House, he theorized that it also became difficult for the Americans to accept a former diehard foe as the champion of a pacific foreign policy. Many of the same American policymakers who spoke highly of the "new Japan" in the late 1940s, Suzuki claimed, believed in 1950 that Japanese loyalty in the Cold War should not be taken for granted.

Although he gave no evidence of Japan's coming defection from the pro-Washington camp, Rep. Clement Zablocki (D-Wisc.), a member of the U.S. House of Representatives Foreign Affairs Committee, even told Suzuki that Japan had not gone far enough to demonstrate its anticommunist commitment. His previous statements in praise of Japan might have been premature. Zablocki would later go on to chair the House Foreign Affairs Committee, criticize the excesses of the Cold War, and become the House's leading champion of the 1970s War Powers Act. In 1950 he asked the Japanese government to provide written assurances to the House of Representatives that it shared America's mission to triumph over Communism. Answering on behalf of his government, Suzuki insisted that Japan had always been loyal in the American-led anticommunist cause. The request for these "assurances" was "insulting" to Japanese integrity, he believed.

Furthermore, Suzuki remained puzzled over what constituted an "assurance." The situation was not without irony. Perhaps a good way to demonstrate Japanese anticommunism, Suzuki once joked with his colleagues, was through the return of the wartime militarist government.[45] The Americans needed to make up their minds about what they feared the most, Suzuki observed: the possibility of a militarist revival or new Communist inroads. The alternative, he suggested, was to recognize the facts.

Sadao Ohtake, the director of the Kyoto News Service during the Occupation Government years and a highly respected expert on Japan-U.S. relations, considered those days just before the Korean War the "most difficult and unusual time" in the early postwar history of the Tokyo-Washington relationship. The war crimes trials had just ended, he once wrote, and the Truman administration never noticed. The White House had seemed more interested in the speed of the trials and keeping the budget low. Moreover, the American leadership outside of the Occupation Government, Ohtake complained, never understood the significance of the trials to the Japanese people. If they had, he insisted, they would not have been "still looking for fascists and communists under every roof."

To Ohtake, MacArthur and Yoshida's view that the trials represented the most important phase of a national rebirth was obviously accepted by a cross-section of Japanese opinion. The sadness over the wartime defeat, he noted, as well as concern over rapid postwar cultural and political change, was too easily confused by the Americans who never bothered to examine Japanese life. Echoing Keenan, Ohtake feared that lingering hatreds might always trouble the U.S.-Japan relationship. Yet Japan remained confident, Ohtake believed, in its "happy future." That future was never a threat to the Americans, he stressed, and it was truly unfortunate that the U.S. doubted Japanese intentions.[46]

The always-plain-speaking Mike Mansfield agreed 100 percent with Ohtake and told him so. The Truman administration's fear of a wavering Japan was "stupid," he once said. During the war crimes trials, Mansfield was a Montana congressman assigned to the House Subcommittee on Naval Affairs, so he was a frequent visitor to Japan throughout the late 1940s. He would take personal interest in U.S.-Japan relations issues throughout a distinguished career in the House and the Senate and as U.S. ambassador to Japan for Presidents Jimmy Carter and Ronald Reagan.

Mansfield believed the early postwar U.S.-Japan relationship was confused by the personal and policymaking disagreements between Truman and MacArthur. Truman, Mansfield said, had admitted to him personally that he doubted Japan could be "reconstructed." Truman later changed that position, but it was difficult, Mansfield noted, to determine what Truman's view of Japan might be on a given day.[47]

The future U.S. ambassador to Japan enjoyed his close relationship with Truman. The two had a distinctly feisty political style, and both believed that they knew each other's complexities quite well. For the most part, Japan was a subsidiary issue within America's Cold War confrontation with the Soviets. Truman did "not lose any sleep," Mansfield explained, over the future of U.S.-Japan relations. But he was definitely preoccupied with the issue of expanding Communism. If the latter collided with the former, then, Mansfield admitted, "the president might lose some sleep." Because Truman was often looking another way, the situation gave MacArthur and Yoshida more authority, Mansfield believed, to work and plan together. But Mansfield also agreed with Rusk that MacArthur was arrogant enough to pad arguments and data to benefit his own agenda. This activity fed White House fears that Japanese support in the Cold War also had to be "manufactured" by MacArthur, for there was no other evidence of that support. Also a member of the House Armed Services Committee during the Occupation Government period, Mansfield insisted that the CIA background reports that he received on Japanese political activity always praised Japan's prodemocracy position. Truman's decision to ignore these same reports, Mansfield noted, assured that, at a critical time, U.S.-Japan relations would be marked primarily by fear and rumor. It said a lot about Washington's postwar confusion over the direction of its world-power responsibilities. It also said a lot about Harry Truman. According to Mansfield, "Truman could be as bone-headed as MacArthur." In fact, to Mansfield, America's postwar Japan policy was best described as "bonehead diplomacy."[48]

It would take years for Americans to accept the fact that most Japanese welcomed the end of the militarist era and that they were happy to move forward with the U.S. as an ally rather than a foe. Upon his return to the United States, Joseph Keenan was amazed at the ignorance of the American people about the new Japan. America's wartime propaganda had been "too effective," he wrote MacArthur. The expression "once a Jap, always a Jap" was still heard, and it meant that Japan could never be trusted. Like Mansfield, Keenan found the prospect of poor U.S.-Japan relations a frustrating and unnecessary development. But whereas Mansfield was frustrated by Truman's behavior, Keenan was more concerned about the man on the street. One never heard "around town," Keenan observed, "once a

German, always a German." It saddened him that Americans reserved a special hatred for their former Japanese enemy.[49]

In the early 1950s, Keenan spoke his mind on this issue during a rare emotional speech before a group of New York businessmen and lawyers. His call for "tolerance and respect" for the emerging democracy of Japan received polite applause from his black-tie audience. He won a more sincere thank you from the ending Occupation Government. MacArthur compared Keenan's war crimes trials work to "unsung heroism."[50]

Whereas the early Truman administration would have agreed that the trials were important to the U.S.-Japan relationship, the later one, troubled by the burdens of the Cold War, doubted both the significance of the trials and its own relations with Tokyo. U.S.-Japan relations soldiered on, but they remained polluted by many of the fears and hatreds left over from World War II. MacArthur's Korean War firing, the folding of the Occupation Government, the final U.S.-Japan peace treaty, Harry Truman's retirement, and new security and economic cooperation arrangements were near-coinciding events in the early 1950s. Given these great developments, the role of the war crimes trials in the U.S.-Japan relationship was largely forgotten. They would never be forgotten by Keenan and by those Japanese who believed that the prosecution of militarism was the first step to the new Japan.

Chapter 4

Judgment on Guam

Justice under the Palms

In many cases now arising, good precedents do not exist and when decisions are made in these cases law is actually being made. It is important that such decisions be correct, otherwise they must inevitably result in later embarrassments and difficulties.

Adm. John D. Murphy

The IMTFE in Tokyo symbolized the Allied search for justice, but it did not constitute the entire effort. From China to Singapore, hundreds of postwar trials were held. Perhaps the most unique, spirited, and precedent-setting endeavor took place in what is today the U.S. Territory of Guam. Yet the tireless work of both the prosecution and the defense teams there went largely unnoticed outside of the Pacific islands. To Rear Adm. John D. Murphy, director of war crimes, USN, on Guam, the entire makeup of his trial commission, the great commitment to fair play, and the abundant resources at his command made the Tokyo trials "appear less than significant."[1] It was an irony, therefore, that few would remember the Tokyo effort shortly after it was over, and even fewer would remember Murphy's accomplishments on Guam.

To some historians, what happened on Guam would always be "lesser trials" and irrelevant to the larger, more significant effort in Tokyo. If the Guam trials were to be mentioned in a postwar discussion of the full trials period, then every trial everywhere would have to be examined in the name of "proper context." The implication of this generally held view was that the Guam trials might be worth a few sentences in an academic treatise that listed all Asian/Pacific region trials in a certain encyclopedic, blow-by-blow fashion, and that was all. This, of course, was not the view of Pacific islanders, many veterans of the Pacific islands campaigns, and Admiral Murphy. "Lesser" and "larger" definitions have become more the product of hindsight than of history. In fact, there was a time when many Americans could even find Guam on a map. As Admiral Murphy once quipped, the Tokyo trials made headlines and the Guam trials made law. Certainly some war crimes trials outside of Tokyo might have been considered more significant than others; however, in the categories of justice, fair play, and legacy, the Guam trials earned their label of significance early in the effort. They always served as fine examples of what could be accomplished far from the Tokyo spotlight.

Symbolically and politically, Guam made perfect sense as a war crimes trials headquarters. Located roughly one thousand miles due south of Japan, this thirty-two-mile-long island had been attacked at the same time as Pearl Harbor. As America's most far-flung Pacific outpost since it was won from the Spanish in 1898, Guam was outgunned and undermanned. Deemed expendable by the Franklin Roosevelt administration, Guam's U.S. Navy–run government, led by Capt. George McMillin, surrendered to the Japanese invaders within hours of the assault. This did not mean that Guam's defenders had refused to fight. Although largely unknown in the face of the coinciding, Alamo-like defense of Wake Island, soon transformed by Hollywood into myth and legend, the Guam defense had been a determined one. Guam's Insular Guard, consisting of U.S. Navy government–trained Chamorros, made their own legends in early December 1941.[2]

For the next two and a half years, Guam endured a ruthless Japanese military occupation. Renamed Omiya Jima (Great Shrine Island), Guam's fate alternated between Japanese Imperial Army and Navy administrations. As the Americans began to sweep across the Pacific, Japanese reprisals on Guam villages were common. To the Japanese, Guam constituted American soil, "more American" than the Philippines because of the politically volatile U.S.-Philippines relationship. Indeed, before the war the Guamanians had sought closer ties with the U.S., not independence. During 1936, as a timed response to Japan's announcement of a "Co-Prosperity Sphere" over much of the Western Pacific, President Roosevelt had met with two Guamanian activists, B.J. Bordallo and Francisco B. Leon Guerrero. They had traveled to the White House seeking U.S. territorial status and the resulting citizenship rights for fellow islanders. Roosevelt saw great propaganda value in their far-from-home mission, although he remained elusive with regard to a precise date for Guam's move from colonial to territorial status.

In Tokyo Roosevelt's action, vague or not, was viewed as a slap in the face to Japanese Pacific interests, especially given the fact that the island of Saipan, a showpiece Japanese colony since World War I, was only

150 miles north of Guam. Hence, the Guamanians were viewed as American citizens in the eyes of their occupiers during the war, and they paid a horrible price for their loyalty to the United States. This commitment would later assure them of President Truman's full support for the aging territorial/citizenship rights cause.[3] Liberated by America's Third Marine Division and other units in July 1944, the island became, on moral grounds alone, the headquarters for a war crimes trial effort whose jurisdiction included all of Micronesia (Mariana, Caroline, Marshall, Gilbert, Palau, and Bonin islands). Miniature versions of the Guam commission would be set up on site in certain islands or atolls, such as at Kwajalein in the Marshalls, but essentially the center of the Pacific islands effort remained Guam.

Throughout its long history, the U.S. Navy had never administered a war crimes trial. Concerned about what certain lawyers and the press might do or say about this "amateur operation," Rear Admiral Murphy vowed to set "great precedents" on Guam. He also believed that the IMTFE was too much in the world spotlight, too carefully watched by politicians, too broke, and too much in a hurry. "Real justice," he argued, would triumph on Guam. His criticism of the IMTFE was open although, as usual, little known outside of Guam. The big difference between himself and Chief Prosecutor Keenan, he said, was that he intended to practice "good law." Although he never elaborated on the point, Murphy worked from the assumption that his war crimes trial was more dedicated to "fairness" than Keenan's headline-making effort. The navy's "good name" was also at stake, he believed, and he hoped to link the navy's laudatory reputation in battle to a postwar commitment to peace and justice. On Guam soldiers would be trying soldiers, he said. Echoing Douglas MacArthur, Murphy pointed out that no one hates war more than the soldier. A certain respect for the soldier's plight in war, including difficult decisions made by commanding officers, should always be considered in both prosecution and defense arguments, he said. Meanwhile, his respect for the U.S. Army's war crimes tribunal in Tokyo was weak. The army, he suggested, had had the opportunity to leave a lasting legal legacy. Instead, they only laid a bare-bones foundation for Keenan's work.[4]

Although Murphy's commission never prosecuted the infamous wartime leaders of Japan, they did investigate horrible atrocities. The perpetrators of these crimes often took for granted their remoteness and isolation. The Guam commission would certainly make it clear that an atrocity far from the Big City and the press was still an atrocity. Meanwhile, much of this commission's mission reflected Murphy's own complex personality.

The rear admiral, in his own words, was never a "typical navy man." For instance, his later opposition to McCarthyism and the "excesses of the Cold War," as well as his often politically incorrect, for their day, defenses of America's Civil Liberties Union, made him something of a maverick in the eyes of his peers.[5] Consequently, his agenda for the Guam tribunal was not just the product of a spirited competition with Keenan or the army. He sought justice, and that in an atmosphere that encouraged the fairest war crimes trial of all time. It was a heady task. In fact, the navy had begun to plan its trials procedure as early as January 1945, over a year before the heyday of the IMTFE. Only hours before his death in April 1945, President Roosevelt even proclaimed Guam the war crimes administrative headquarters.

From the beginning the navy's effort was different from the efforts of the IMTFE and the army. Moreover, the procedures involving rules of evidence and jurisdiction were different. Whereas the IMTFE and army tribunals often relaxed the rules of evidence to admit affidavits, interrogation reports, and testimony that would be rejected as hearsay and irrelevant in a Stateside civilian court, the navy preferred to use the tough Stateside model, again in the name of "fairness." Of course there were exceptions to this approach, depending upon the specific case under review, but for the most part the Guam commission took its cue from existing navy courts, which had always been close to that Stateside model. This also meant that evidence-gathering required a stronger teamwork effort than it did in the IMTFE or army trials, and it was not unusual to see Australians, New Zealanders, and other Pacific region lawyers and evidence-gathering staffers working alongside their American counterparts in the Guam trials.

Procedurally, the navy effort maintained a stronger commitment to step-by-step decision making than the IMTFE or the army did. It was an approach loudly applauded by the defense counsel. Usually, seven senior officers represented an individual navy commission. If fewer than five were present, a mistrial could be declared. Anyone from a rear admiral to a navy captain or a Marine Corps colonel could act as the commission president. Their conclusions were reviewed by a number of others, beginning with Murphy, then the Marianas area commander, the Pacific Fleet commander in Hawaii or San Diego, the judge advocate general at the Pentagon, and finally the secretary of the navy. Surprisingly, there were more Japanese involved in Murphy's trials procedure than in Keenan's. Much of Murphy's budget was spent on shuttling to and from Japan Japanese witnesses, interpreters, defense counsel team members, and advisors.

In Murphy's tribunal the appealing of a death sentence was more than possible. Despite the conclusions of the Yamashita case, the navy frowned on death sentences for those who took blame for the actions of their subordinates. A certain onus therefore rested on the shoulders of the prosecution to prove without a doubt that offenses were committed by the defendant himself "without the influence of any higher authority." Thus, there were many more defense arguments here than in Tokyo stating that a particular defendant had been ignorant of the law, a victim of cultural misunderstanding, or both. Although this approach often led to defense counsel attacks on the "victor's justice" of the U.S. Navy, the prosecution usually countered that ignorance of the law, in anyone's culture, was not an adequate defense.[6]

The navy commission produced some spectacular trials, tackling issues that had not been considered in law before, such as the place of cannibalism and sadistic torture in war. To their credit the commissioners remained focused on the task at hand, preferring verdicts in individual cases to academic-like discussions on war and morality. Given his own tendency to wax poetic on moral issues, Murphy might have hoped for both verdicts and great discussions during the Guam trials, but he had to settle for the efficient, no-nonsense reputation of the commission.

A first-things-first approach ruled the day, especially for the prosecution. But, conservative tactics or not, the commission could not ignore its impact on the resulting legal debate over cannibalism and torture. By the end of the trials, Murphy had to arrange his priorities accordingly. Hence he admitted that if his own commission had become a sounding board on cannibalism and torture, those who engaged in these acts might have been found innocent on one technicality or another. By emphasizing the straightforward issues of the traditional murder case, guilty verdicts were found without the risk of testing new law and without courting defeat in an appeal.[7]

Murphy might have touted his commission's ability to raise new questions relevant to any future war crimes case, but defendants were indeed found guilty of murder and not, for instance, cannibalism. The case of Lt. Gen. Joshio Tachibana best illustrates this result. Tachibana, one of the last commanders of the Bonin Islands, was personally implicated in "eating the flesh" of an American POW on Chichi Jima. Tachibana had beheaded his victim before the feast. Human flesh, he had boasted to his men, toughened him up, making him "strong for battle."

With no airfield as late as the 1990s, tiny Chichi Jima was not a long sail from the main islands of Japan. But for its residents it might as well have been on the dark side of the moon. Near the end of the war, the deliv-

During the height of his spectacular trial on Guam, Lt. Gen. Joshio Tachibana poses with his nineteen-year-old U.S. Marine guard, Kenneth Maga. Although he attempted to charm his captors, Tachibana was the senior defendant in the infamous "Cannibal Case" of Chichi Jima. (Author's collection.)

ery of food supplies had halted and chaos reigned. These facts would not be accented by the Tachibana defense team, however, largely because their defendant had been cruel to POWs, and even to some islanders (fellow Japanese citizens), before the starvation crisis began. He was also described by his own men, and by the U.S. Marines who captured him, as "fat and healthy," thereby eliminating the defense strategy that he had resorted to cannibalism for survival.

The Tachibana trial was truly an amazing spectacle, although it never received the press attention of less disturbing cases in Tokyo.[8] The prosecution even charged that Tachibana's example influenced young officers in his command, creating a certain reign of horror on Chichi Jima throughout late 1944 and early 1945. Yet, finding "smoking gun" evidence against Tachibana was difficult for the prosecution, and Rear Adm. Arthur Robinson, who presided in this case, demanded evidence rather than damning tales. In August 1946 a prosecution evidence-gathering team went to Chichi Jima and scoured the island. They found the bodies of eight of Tachibana's victims. The torture, murder, and cannibalism accusations against Tachibana numbered in the hundreds, but there was little left to prove any of them. Fourteen of Tachibana's junior officers had been charged with similar horrors, but in the madness that was Chichi Jima, it was also difficult to assign specific murders to specific individuals.

Robert Shafer, a Marine Corps major, proved to be the prosecution's best witness in at least one POW beheading matter. The victim had been seen by both American POWs and Japanese troopers with one shiny, gold pencil at the time of Tachibana's murder of him. Stationed on Chichi Jima after the war, Shafer found what was left of a beheaded body in a shallow grave. In that grave was the pencil, with the name of the victim engraved on its sides. After weeks of sensational charges, the case had come down to one pencil and the few surviving witnesses who remembered seeing it shining in the hot sun.

On the day of Shafer's testimony (August 24, 1946), Arthur Herman of the International News Service, Dean Dittmer of the United Press, and William A. Arbogast of the Associated Press were with a House of Representatives Foreign Affairs Committee junket visiting Guam. They were unaware that the Tachibana trial had been going on. Their press reports back home changed that situation for the American public, albeit briefly. They now had front-page coverage of what they nicknamed the "Cannibal Case."[9]

Although the witness testimony was fascinating, it continued to be more hearsay than evidence. Capt. Hiro Kasuga, who was on Chichi Jima for a short period while en route to Tokyo near the end of the war, told the commission that one of the first things he saw upon arriving on the island was several American POWS tied to stakes near Tachibana's headquarters. All were starving, and at one point he dared to give one of the men a rice cake and water. The confusion of an American air raid had permitted him this action, for Tachibana, Kasuga learned, tortured all POWs who were left in his keeping. No precise orders from Tachibana existed in reference to it, but Kasuga assumed that helping a POW could mean death for whoever did so. The air raid, therefore, had come in handy for this Good Samaritan gesture. Kasuga saw only one American serviceman live longer than a couple of weeks on Chichi Jima. That soldier, Kasuga testified, had a decent command of the Japanese language, and Tachibana used him to translate American radio broadcasts. The wireless operator bayoneted him after "he was no longer of any use," and Tachibana commended this subordinate for his action. Kasuga claimed that Tachibana and his officers regarded "human life of no more value than an old post at a dusty crossroads." He said he "had been to hell," and it was Tachibana's Chichi Jima.[10]

Lt. Cmdr. D.H. Dickey of the defense counsel ripped apart the Kasuga testimony in cross-examination. Dickey accused Kasuga of being a deserter who had drifted into the Bonin Islands during the ending months of the war. He had been en route to nowhere, Dickey claimed, except to get as far away as possible from the battlefield. Dickey considered Kasuga a despicable and deceitful character who would say anything to anyone to improve his lot in life. Indeed, Kasuga was a mysterious figure who eluded all questions about his precise identity and his mission in the Bonins. His dodging of these simple questions raised more than enough reasonable doubt of both his integrity and his alleged witnessing of criminal activity. Few had survived Tachibana's "hell" unscathed. The prosecution struggled to produce better witnesses than Kasuga, but with much of Tachibana's command also under indictment, success remained far from certain.

The defense counsel had its troubles too. Given the dozens of translators as well as entire teams of Japanese legal consultants and experienced trial lawyers, any defense counsel attack on improper translation procedure and any request to debate U.S.-Japan cross-cultural differences in legal interpretation were quickly dismissed by the commission. The technical arguments that typified so many of the Tokyo trials were difficult to pursue on Guam.[11] For the defense counsel, that meant sticking to a grand, sweeping thesis. According to Dickey, Tachibana was not a "mad dog" but the victim of a "warrior culture." As one of Japan's youngest generals, he had been born and raised in a time of militarism and emperor worship. In his view the American enemy deserved nothing less than death for his very decision to surrender, and he could not understand how the American POW could live in a world of disgrace and dishonor. Dickey blamed the education system, the wartime leadership, Tachibana's older commanding officers, and Japanese political and cultural icons going back to the 1920s. He was also pleased to point out that these policymakers were on trial in Tokyo while, sadly, the "machines" they created, such as Tachibana, had been exiled to starvation "on rocks like Chichi Jima." In this larger story of national madness, was Tachibana truly responsible for his actions? Where did the chain of command begin and end? Dickey asked. Was the court to accept the wild accusations of the prosecution's alleged witnesses?[12]

Without question, the victimization argument had been well worn in the Tokyo trials, but it remained one of many avenues taken by the defense counsel. Victimization was at the very heart of the Dickey defense. By attacking the entire militarist system of Japan, the defense counsel truly placed the doctrine of command responsibility at a higher level than Tachibana. In the meantime, they assaulted the prosecution's witness list.

Deemed "impossible to locate" when the Tachibana trial began, Fumio Tamamuro gave the prosecution reason for hope. One of the few troopers in Tachibana's personal command to survive the war and remain unindicted, Tamamuro, the prosecution assumed, had been lost in the crowds of veterans who had returned to Japan. But they had been looking for him in the wrong place. Tamamuro was an American citizen, and he had been attempting to return to San Francisco when he was found.

Tamamuro's American roots made him something of a sensation at an already sensational trial. Visiting relatives in Japan at the time of the Pearl Harbor attack, Tamamuro had been drafted into Japanese military service. He spent most of the war as an Imperial Navy pay officer before becoming part of Tachibana's ragtag headquarters at the end of the war. His testimony, of course, was in flawless English, eliminating even the possibility of questioning the accuracy of translation reports. Tamamuro claimed that he had befriended the American POW who was used as a wireless operator translator. He also claimed to have witnessed the man's execution, describing in detail the leather jacket and scarf that the victim was wearing at the time. The clothing issue was critical, for prosecution evidence gatherers had found such a jacket and scarf near a road in Chichi Jima. They also found what was left of a body there, although identification was impossible. Tamamuro described the road and the grave site in detail, also noting that the victim had been ordered to dig his own shallow grave before the execution. When asked why he needed to be present during this murder, Tamamuro tearfully explained that he had promised his "friend" that he would be there to the end.

Comdr. Martin Carlson, along with Lieutenant Commander Dickey of the defense team, questioned Tamamuro's "treasonous behavior" during the war. They implied that he could not switch from being pro-Japanese to being pro-American at the drop of a hat, but Tamamuro's contention that he had been trapped by circumstances to serve in the Japanese military was well put. It was also irrelevant, Rear Admiral Robinson ruled.

Tamamuro even had a bombshell of his own. The island doctor—also under indictment as a close confidant of Tachibana—who had been more than aware of his friend's cannibalism activities, was accused by Tamamuro of actually preparing "meals" of dead American POWs for Tachibana. Tamamuro described where unwanted body parts from these "meals" had always been discarded, and prosecution evidence-gatherers once again demonstrated their skill at combing Chichi Jima. The "garbage dump" was found where Tamamuro said it would be, and it was apparent that surgical instruments had been used to sever the body parts. The prosecution now had much more than a monogrammed pencil. Tamamuro had become their star witness, and the evidence he produced was solid.[13]

Murphy believed that the trial had now entered a phase wherein the navy could make a difference and further define a soldier's conduct in war. Certainly a legal discussion on cannibalism and torture was now possible. But obvious dangers existed. No matter how well intended, this was still new legal ground. Given the drama of the Yamashita case, it was likely the Supreme Court would have the final say in the debate. Logic suggested that all decent men, no matter what their profession, would condemn cannibalism. But that condemnation could take years, unforeseen technicalities could emerge that might benefit the defendant, and Murphy, although his heart told him to pursue the matter, decided to stress the obvious.[14] Tachibana was guilty of murder.

In a last-ditch effort on behalf of their client, the defense counsel in the Tachibana case pointed a finger at Capt. Noburo Nakajima, a tough, hard-drinking army officer, as the instigator of the cannibalism craze on Chichi Jima. Already indicted for murdering POWs there, Nakajima had no apologies for his action. The soldier who surrenders, he proclaimed to the commission in a loud, defiant voice, deserves a horrible death. Nakajima, the defense counsel contended, introduced Tachibana to hard liquor and a doctrine of desperateness and evil. It was, in a sense, the command responsibility argument in reverse. Allegedly, for weeks on end Tachibana had no idea what he was doing because of Nakajima's impact upon him. Rear Admiral Robinson found this intriguing. He agreed with the defense that Nakajima was a rough character.[15] Yet the drunken Tachibana thesis seemed far removed from the earlier victimization argument. Was Tachibana influenced by his militarist upbringing or by Nakajima? In the long run, the commission found Tachibana guilty regardless of real or imagined influences.

In his final statement on the trial, Rear Admiral Robinson noted the Yamashita precedent of command responsibility, explaining that Tachibana was indeed responsible for the madness of Chichi Jima. But he stressed the point that Tachibana committed his own crimes. Linking his commission's work in the Tachibana case to "the very best" in the field of American law, Robinson concluded that more than anything else, Tachibana and much of his staff were guilty of specific murders.[16] Of course, Robinson could not truly compare a murder trial in his "home town" to the commission's work on Guam; but his points, like Murphy's, about "fair play," evidence, and fine lawyering were well taken.

There had been side benefits to the Tachibana trial, such as learning for the first time what had been the Japanese battle strategy with regard to their bloody, last-ditch defense of Iwo Jima. The commission also learned that others on Chichi Jima were perhaps more interested in cannibalism than even Tachibana. A former intelligence officer, Lt. Col. Kikuji Ito, was the source of these facts. He provided a detailed account of Japanese military preparedness and battle planning during the ending months of the war. His tale of commitment and self-sacrifice on the part of the Japanese soldier was already known, but his discussion of endless tactical disagreements between the Imperial Navy and Army and their negative impact on Japanese defense had not been known.

Ito had been charged with murder alongside his last commander, Tachibana. At first, the details and evidence in reference to that charge were sketchy, and the possibility loomed large that his revealing comments on Japanese defense issues might result in a release and a thank you. That changed quickly. Originally presenting himself as a bright and candid career officer concerned about the accurate historical recording of the battle of Iwo Jima and its aftermath, Ito's personality altered as the charges against him grew. Several young Japanese troopers who appeared on the witness stand in the Tachibana trial insisted that it had been Ito, more than anyone else, who encouraged Tachibana to execute American POWs. They also said cannibalism had been nonexistent on Chichi Jima before Ito's arrival. Ito, they said, bragged about various cannibal feasts throughout his wartime experiences, noting that he had a special taste for enemy flesh. He also preferred bayoneting American POWs to quick beheading exercises. The bayoneting would continue long after the American victims were dead, and the noncommissioned officers in Ito's command were afraid they would be next if they did not participate in these horrors. Even at the trial, those same young men, still afraid, made it a point to bow to Ito before and after taking the witness stand.[17]

The once academic-like Ito now looked and acted defiant. Angry outbursts, largely in denunciation of Allied weakness during the war, were not uncommon. Shortly before his capture by the marines, the commission learned, Ito had purposely destroyed documents, photographs, and other material that might have implicated him. Vowing revenge against those who would dare testify against him, his cover-up and extortion had almost worked.

Ito's behavior in the commission room became more and more bizarre as the trial wore on; it included laughing and scoffing at audience members who expressed their shock at various descriptions of cannibalism.[18] At best, Commander Carlson of the defense team was able to delay the verdict. Near the end of the trial testimony, Carlson objected to a comment from one of the commissioners that Ito had violated "the moral standards of society." Carlson complained that these "standards" were "undefinable, improper, illegal, and mere surplusage." This complaint was combined with the usual Tokyo trial–style effort to accuse sitting commissioners of biased, vengeful behavior because of their war records in the Pacific. Shizuo Morikawa, the lead Tokyo defense lawyer on the case, said that Ito was being set up as a commission scapegoat on cannibalism and that Japanese "moral standards" were different from Western ones. Robinson called a temporary recess in the trial to study the merits of these accusations, but they were rejected out of hand less than forty-eight hours later.[19]

On June 19, 1947, Ito had the honor of being in the first group of convicted war criminals on Guam to be executed. Of the six who were hanged that day near the Commander Marianas headquarters, Ito was the middle-ranking officer. Two navy admirals stood before him, and a captain, a private, and a seaman first class followed.[20]

For some, the hanging of one of these six men had been a horrible tragedy and perhaps even a mistake. Rear Adm. Shigematsu Sakaibara had enjoyed the reputation of "gentleman soldier" and protector of the common man. Hailing from a wealthy family near Misawa in Tohokhu province, some 450 miles north of Tokyo, Sakaibara never forgot his roots. Forever poking fun at the fast-paced Tokyo lifestyle, the rear admiral touted the value of rural living, the integrity and honesty of those who lived in Japan's rugged north country, and Tokyo's need to recognize their great contributions to the war effort. Contemplating a postwar political future, he would be following in the footsteps of his politically influential family in northern Japan. That future was linked to championing the rights of returning veterans and other have-nots. Misawa had indeed had a heroic reputation as an important navy town and base for years. Sakaibara had assisted in the training exercises held there for the Pearl Harbor attack plan in late 1941. His future seemed golden no matter who won the war. But what some in his command called "The 1943 Incident" changed all that.[21]

The commission found Sakaibara guilty of war crimes and sentenced him to death for the murder of ninety-eight American civilian POWs while he was commanding officer of Wake Island in 1943. Most of those killed had been contracted to Pan American Airways, which had maintained a prewar refueling and maintenance stopover on Wake for trans-Pacific flights. In 1941 a small contingent of U.S. Marines had protected the company's operation there and its effort to improve on stopover facilities. Although the marines held back a hugely superior Japanese invading force for days, they surrendered rather than face a massacre. The island defenders were shipped to Japan for incarceration, but most of the civilian workers, many of whom had come from Guam and had been wounded in the fighting, were left behind on an island with barely enough food for their captors.[22] Two years later, as the Americans came closer to the liberation of Wake, the food situation had worsened dramatically. There was also little chance that the now struggling Imperial Navy would sail the civilian internees to Japan.

Of the ninety-eight civilians killed, the first one was beheaded when he was caught stealing. Given Wake's barren isolation, Sakaibara thought the island had little strategic value to the approaching Americans. But the ninety-seven prisoners gave the Americans reason for invasion, rescue, and liberation. He eliminated that reason by shooting ninety-six prisoners. The ninety-seventh had escaped but was quickly recaptured and then beheaded by the admiral's own hand. These events, Sakaibara admitted in his trial, had taken place in an atmosphere of near starvation and impending doom. The defense counsel especially emphasized that point, asking the commission to understand and respect the pressures and strains on Sakaibara at the time of the incident. But the commission was not in a forgiving mood. In the chaos of retreat or not, innocent civilians had been murdered.

It was particularly significant to the commission, if not symbolic and tragic, that most of Sakaibara's victims were Guamanian workers. As on Guam itself, the Guamanians on Wake were killed in retaliation for the number of new American victories in the war. The people of Guam were especially interested in this case, and the commission room was usually filled to capacity with islanders during the Sakaibara trial. Unfortunately for Sakaibara, several members of his former command expressed surprise on the witness stand when asked about the desperate situation on Wake in 1943. These men insisted that Sakaibara and his defense team's description of a starving, chaotic Wake was an exaggerated one. There had been no unexpected miseries, confusion, or sense of peril, they said. Sakaibara's fate was sealed.

True to form, defendant Sakaibara offered a very literate final statement to the commission. In contrast to so many of his colleagues on trial in Tokyo, on Guam, or elsewhere, Sakaibara, albeit with carefully picked words, admitted he was guilty of rash and unfortunate actions. He appeared especially convincing when he noted that he wished he had never heard of Wake Island. But his most memorable comments involved his own view of morality in war. A nation that drops atom bombs on major cities, the rear admiral explained, did not have the moral authority to try so many of his countrymen. With Hiroshima and Nagasaki in mind, Sakaibara claimed there was little difference between himself and the victors over Japan.[23] With that statement a legend grew, particularly in his home town, of Sakaibara, the victim of American revenge.

Murphy considered Sakaibara a clever manipulator but still a murderer who shot and beheaded civilian POWs for no reason.[24] To some residents of Misawa, Japan, a very different man was hanged on Guam. As late as the 1990s, some people there, not necessarily of the World War II generation, still bowed in reverence to Sakaibara family members out of respect for the "sacrificed" gentleman soldier. To them, the good admiral would always be a hero and a modern-day samurai. The Americans had made a cruel mistake.[25]

Most Guamanians felt that Sakaibara had gotten what he deserved. A more sensitive issue for them involved the trials of islanders who had willingly collaborated with the Japanese occupation. Thanks to George Tweed, a former U.S. Navy radioman first class, most of the world viewed Guam as a proud, defiant bastion of resistance to the Japanese during World War II. In the face of horrible adversity, an entire people stood their ground against tyranny. His book, *Robinson Crusoe, USN: The Adventures of George Tweed, RM 1/C, U.S.N. on Jap-Held Guam,* was a best-seller across the United States in 1945. The strong patriotic image of Guam was well entrenched.[26] But reality was something different.

Tweed witnessed acts of great heroism. Refusing to surrender with his comrades in December 1941, he disappeared into the thick jungle. He hid in a cave near the northern end of the island, relying on sympathetic Guamanians to keep him safe. Discovering that he had a talent for writing, Tweed even published a resistance newsletter from his lair, and Japanese occupation officials dedicated themselves to finding him and his paper. They never did.

In the minds of the Japanese occupation authorities, the Tweed resistance, and the presumed Guamanian support for it, often justified beatings and reprisals throughout the island. Years later there would be debate on Guam over whether helping Tweed had been worth it. But no one had been more aware of the danger than Tweed, and two years after the liberation he returned to Guam to offer thanks. During his years in hiding, Tweed had jokingly promised one of his Guamanian contacts a brand new Chevrolet after the war was over. Courtesy of the Chevrolet Motor Company, Tweed returned with one of the first postwar Chevrolet coupes for his friend. It was in this atmosphere that Tweed commented on the collaboration issue, noting that it always had been a matter of concern but that it should not discount his praise for Guamanian heroism in the war.[27]

The politics of image had become intertwined with the search for justice. The worthiness of collaboration trials was now a new matter of concern for the reconvened Guam Legislature, largely an advisory corps to the reestablished navy government. The image of endless heroism and unanimous pro-Americanism was essential to the continuing territorial/citizenship rights cause, or so it was believed. President Truman in his Organic Act legislation for Guam in 1950 would, indeed, stress the Guamanian resistance record more than any other reason for the shift in political status.[28]

Whether it might disturb someone's political agenda or not, Murphy's commission did try known collaborators. The trials remained quite low-key, in contrast to the shocking cannibalism cases, and the verdicts were mostly limited jail terms. But the commission, as well as many Guamanians, agreed that something had to be done to address the horror of the occupation years.

The Japanese occupation of Guam had maintained a contradictory mission. On the one hand, all of the "Co-Prosperity Sphere" propaganda remained in place. The public pronouncements spoke of Japanese kindness to fellow Asian/Pacific peoples, the rescue from Western domination and racism, and the "partnership in Pacific peace." On the other hand, the locals had welcomed American rule. For this, they would have to pay a price. As early as December 11, 1941, those who had evacuated the major townships, such as Agana and Sumay, were ordered to return to their homes. Special identification badges were passed out, and strict discipline was required of all those waiting in the long lines to receive them. There was little toleration for the sick and elderly in those lines, and the latter represented the first casualties of the terror. To the close-knit Guamanian families, simple disrespect to the elderly was something of a crime. Military checkpoints proliferated and the Guamanians were required to bow even to lowly Imperial Army privates. If the bow was perceived to be inadequately performed, anything from beatings to on-the-spot executions were common.[29] Meanwhile, the small Japanese community on Guam found themselves courted and offered leadership roles in government and business that they had never had before. Many of these individuals were part Guamanian, part Japanese, and they usually had some family connection in the nearby Japanese colony of Saipan. Others, such as Samuel T. Shinohara, were born in Japan, drifted into the Japanese Mandate, and eventually settled on Guam.

The Shinohara case was an important one to those who had survived the Japanese occupation on Guam. Although little was known of his early life, Shinohara had maintained a low-profile existence on the island since his arrival in 1905. Because of his long, quiet residency there, his active collaboration with the Japanese, and his callous disregard for the property and the very lives of his neighbors, Shinohara's fate raised high emotions. The prosecution in his trial theorized that Shinohara, a restaurant owner, may have been a fugitive from premilitarist authorities in Japan before he came to Guam, but successful defense counsel objections made it impossible to pursue further into the man's past.[30]

Shinohara had declared his allegiance to the Japanese occupation government in mid-December 1941. He demonstrated his new loyalty to Japan by leading a raiding party on the small bank of the former Naval Government. He then confiscated the automobile perceived to be the finest on the island, owned by a certain J.E. Davis, and moved into the very visible and financially comfortable role of advisor and part-time "justice investigator" for the new government. The abuse of power came easy to him, as witnessed by his slapping of the captured American governor, Captain McMillin, the raping of two different Guamanian women in early 1942 alone, and the further raiding of homes and businesses to provide food and provisions for Japanese troops. To win even better favor, he formed the Dai Nisei organization to promote pro-Japanese Guamanian assistance, particularly from islanders who had some sort of Japanese background. The organization remained mostly on paper, but it had the desired effect on Shinohara's Japanese protectors. Threatening torture and death to islanders reluctant to attend, Shinohara managed to fill the few Dai Nisei meetings that were held. But even then, more government authorities than Guamanians showed up at Dai Nisei meetings. During the "happy hour" before one such meeting, Shinohara used the American flag that once flew over the U.S. Naval Government headquarters as a bar rag. At his trial, one of the many charges against him would be "defiling the flag of the United States."[31]

The collaboration trials were always emotional ones. Although the specific charges were minor in comparison to those faced by Tachibana or Ito, they were significant enough to fill the commission room beyond capacity with Guamanian spectators. "Formally," Shinohara was found guilty of treason against the United States, even though the defense insisted that their client was used as an unprecedented test case for collaboration. More to the point, the charge of treason was irrelevant, the defense claimed, for Shinohara was not an American citizen. Agreeing with the defense to a point, the commission ruled that Shinohara's behavior and the litany of charges that addressed his exploitation of fellow islanders was the "equivalent of treason." Consequently, Shinohara was found guilty on a number of specific charges. Politically, and in recognition of Shinohara's victims, the commission denounced Shinohara's "treasonous behavior." This was a curious distinction, but it once again kept the commission away from untried law and perhaps years of legal challenges. Because of these controversies, "death by hanging," a traditional sentence for treason, was commuted to eight years in Tokyo's Sugamo Prison, where most of Japan's infamous war criminals resided.[32]

In a sense Shinohara maintained a high profile as an "important" collaborator and eventually became more of a political animal than a daily tormentor. Less "important," yet more ruthless, were those islanders who willingly assisted the Japanese police. Most of them were Chamorro-speaking former residents of Saipan, complete with Guamanian-sounding names, who also spoke Japanese and had come to Guam to serve the new Japanese empire. For example, Juan Villagomez, Jose Villagomez, and Francisco Sablan, all police interpreters, served their masters well. Like Shinohara, they attempted to enrich themselves at the same time. They had little regard for the Guamanians who got in their way.

The job of police interpreter carried a number of responsibilities, including the interrogation of anti-Japanese resisters. In some cases the victim had been falsely accused, and the purpose of the interrogation was to extort money and possessions. Surviving an interrogation was never guaranteed. For instance, Vicente Babauta, an inhabitant of Guam, was beaten to death with a bullwhip by Juan Villagomez in late 1942. The bullwhip was Juan Villagomez's interrogation tool of choice. Three other Guamanians (Jose O. Guerrero, Jose M. Martinez, and Blas T. Taimanglo) faced similar beatings, but they survived the ordeal.

Jose Villagomez also used the bullwhip in his interrogations, but it was one of three weapons of choice. The others were a metal pipe and a baseball bat. His trial included seven counts of attempted murder by torture. Francisco Sablan had no favorite weapons. Twenty-four counts of attempted murder by torture were leveled against him, and he had used his fists and feet in most of the beatings. Sablan's higher number of charges was due to the simple fact that he sometimes interrogated the victims in their own homes. Hence, the beatings were witnessed by more people, whereas the charges against Juan and Jose Villagomez required witnesses from the jail itself.

Since some of the jailed witnesses had long histories of petty crime, it was easy for the defense counsel to question the integrity of their testimony or witness reports. The defense also suggested that the commission maintained an overly emotional reaction to the very term *collaborator* and that that fact was prejudicial to their clients. As in the Tokyo trials, former victims who described their tormentors as "gleefully" beating their charges were asked to define "gleeful" in the context of a beating. The answers were always struggling ones, proving the defense argument that such descriptions must be struck from the trial record. All the defendants claimed that they were colonial servants of an evil government. The real criminals were their Japanese overseers, they said, and most of them had died in the American liberation of July 1944.[33]

The collaborator trials were difficult ones for Murphy, but they did not define the larger mission of the navy commission. Since the collaboration cases were quickly heard in contrast to others, as well as put on an agenda tangential to the trials of Japanese military figures who had served in the islands, it was obvious that Murphy had certain priorities. Most of those found guilty in the collaboration trials were deported to Saipan or received short terms of hard labor on Guam. Jose Villagomez received ten years for the Vicente Babauta murder.

These verdicts did not mean that the surviving Japanese nationals, who had served as police officials on Guam, were destined to receive harsher sentences. The case of Akiyoshi Hosakawa, a sergeant major in the Japanese Occupation Police Force, which had supervised many interrogations, demonstrates this point. One beating victim told the commission that under Hosakawa's orders he had been beaten in his home and then dragged to the police headquarters to answer the charge that he had stolen a rifle. He told the sergeant major that he had no idea what he was talking about, and in response Hosakawa beat him with an automobile fan belt.

Under cross-examination, Hosakawa admitted to the fan belt matter and to other beatings. He said his lieutenant, killed in the American liberation, had ordered him to do the beatings and that in Japanese justice "physical intimidation" was common practice. Hosakawa's lawyer emphasized that in any interrogation procedure anywhere in Japan, the beating was a fact of life. Hosakawa received one year in prison.[34] Meanwhile, like Keenan, Murphy always had bigger fish to fry.

The case of Surgeon Capt. Hiroshi Iwanami permitted Murphy to charge most of the high officer corps associated with the Japanese administration of the Truk group in the Caroline Islands. Truk had been the home of Japan's most impressive and significant forward naval base during World War II, and Iwanami was the commanding officer of the Fourth Naval Hospital on Dublon Island within Truk Lagoon. Iwanami and much of his staff (one lieutenant commander, three lieutenants, one ensign, four warrant officers, and nine chief petty officers) were all charged with specific murders; however, it was the way the victims were murdered that made this case an important one to Murphy. Any surviving Japanese officer who played any leadership role at all in Truk now became a suspect, and the naval commission had no apologies for its decision.

Iwanami and his staff were charged with killing six American POWs on January 30, 1944, two more on February 1, 1944, and another two on July 20, 1944. In addition to murder, Iwanami was charged with "preventing the honorable burial" of bodies and with "dissection" and "mutilation" of them. Iwanami had used all ten of his victims for so-called medical experiments. Four of his January 1944 victims had tourniquets placed on their arms and legs by Iwanami for long periods. Two of the POWs had their tourniquets removed in two hours, and the other two at the end of seven hours. The latter two died immediately of shock, but the former survived. On the same day, four others were injected with streptococcus bacteria to cause blood poisoning. All four developed high fevers and soon died.

On February 1, 1944, the two survivors from the tourniquet experiment were marched to a hill in back of the hospital. Naked, with their legs stretched out as far as possible, the men were tied to stakes. Iwanami's staff then placed a small explosive charge three feet in front of each foot of each victim. The resulting explosion blew off the feet of the men, but both victims survived. Their amazing endurance was short-lived, because Iwanami ordered the men strangled; an aide accomplished the task with his bare hands. Their bodies were returned to the hospital, where they were dissected, and all vital organs were placed in specimen jars. Only some of the organs from the blood poisoning victims were kept, and their bodies were tossed off a nearby cliff.

During an evening meal near the end of July 1944, Iwanami asked his staff if they would assist him in experiments on two more POWs. Instead of answering quickly in the affirmative, the men asked about the value of such experiments. Refusing to discuss the issue, Iwanami ordered his men, instead, to participate in the execution of the two POWs. This time there was no opposition to the order. The two Americans were suspended from a bar placed between two trees. With the order to "stab with spirit," the hospital staff then began their bayonet practice. There was little left of the bodies after the practice was over, and those bodies, one of them headless, were buried near the scene of the execution. Shortly before his capture, Iwanami had the bodies exhumed and thrown into the sea.[35]

Once again, Rear Admiral Robinson presided. Noting that the Iwanami trial was the "most disturbing" to him of all the cases he had seen on Guam, Robinson favored harsh sentences for Iwanami and his staff. But the trial was as bizarre as the defendants. Three of Iwanami's old hospital staff members committed suicide, leaving word that they would rather die than testify against their commanding officer. Another, Lt. Shinji Sakagami, took great pride in the fact that he had strangled two POWs. A staunch advocate of the Japanese war effort and, like so many of his colleagues, convinced that death was better than surrender, he hoped his actions in Truk would serve as a warning to the future enemies of Japan. Iwanami was sentenced to death, although he attempted to cheat the hangman. Smuggling a small, sharpened pencil into his holding cell, Iwanami stood at one end of the tight quarters, shouted "Banzai," and vaulted against the opposite wall. The pencil was held close to his heart, but it did little damage. Both witnesses on the scene and the commission wondered why a surgeon would have failed to aim the pencil properly. Iwanami's hanging proceeded as planned, and the most generous verdict for a member of his staff was ten years in prison.[36]

A number of admirals would be held accountable for the horrors in Truk and the nearby Marshall Islands. At least one of them had taken part in POW executions; the others either approved of the killings or did nothing to halt them. Rear Adm. Shimpei Asano, the overall commander of Imperial Navy operations in Truk, was one of those charged. Specifically, he had authorized the murders of two American POWs there, as well as approving of the medical experiments. He was also charged with "violations of the law and customs of war" for failing to control members of his command in the ill-treatment of POWs. Since his administrative jurisdiction also included, for a time, part of the Marshall Islands, he was further charged with the torturing of two American POWs on Kwajalein. The latter was a difficult charge, for the torturers were described in the indictment as "persons unknown." In any event, the POWs had been victims of more medical experiments. Kept in small, unsanitary cells, the two men had been injected with coconut juice and their faces burnt beyond recognition by boiling water. Eventually, they were beaten to death. Asano's fellow administrators, Vice Adm. Masahi Kobayashi and Vice Adm. Seisaku Wakarayashi, also faced charges in the Kwajalein matter, including seven additional torture murders there. Again, with most of the perpetrators dead or missing, these were difficult cases for the prosecution. Murphy's reluctance to send anyone to the gallows based purely on the Yamashita precedent prevailed here.[37]

The most cut-and-dried trial of an Imperial Navy admiral was that of Vice Adm. Koso Abe. Proving most uncooperative with his own large defense team, Abe, like so many defendants, had no apologies for his wartime behavior. Arriving on Kwajalein in October 1942, he had personally supervised the beheading of nine U.S. Marines who had been taken prisoner on Makin Island. These marines had been part of a commando-style assault, and Abe considered them "spies." He had no regrets, and the commission included him on the first list of executions on Guam (along with Ito and Sakaibara).[38]

The Abe case might not have been the best one in which to raise the issue of what constituted a spy. Nevertheless, in cases that involved the killing of missionaries and other civilians throughout the Pacific islands by Japanese combat troops, the defense counsel pursued the "spy" matter vigorously. The justification given for the killing of missionaries, their families, and other native workers in Palau, the Marshalls, and tiny Rota near Guam was that the victims had been "spying" on Japanese military operations. In 1942 the U.S. Supreme Court had ruled that a spy, upon capture, did not need to be treated in the same fashion as the POW. Shizuo Morikawa of the defense counsel argued that the law was clear and that the charges against a variety of combat soldier defendants should be dropped. Murphy insisted that the merits of each case must still be considered, and the commissioners, after a lengthy debate, decided in Murphy's favor.[39]

The trial of Capt. Akira Tokunaga, Surgeon 2d Lt. Yoshio Takahashi, and Pvt. Shigeo Koyama was fairly typical of the "spy cases." All of these men had been stationed on Rota in 1944, and all were involved in executing several islanders as well as one Catholic missionary for "espionage activities." In spite of the defense counsel insistence that the men acted within the law and military traditions, the prosecution suggested that the killings had nothing to do with "spying." The executions took place in late June 1944, just three weeks before the successful American assault on Rota.

To the Japanese on this island, which is almost in sight of Guam, the arrival of the Americans meant certain defeat. They lived in constant fear of that invasion throughout the late spring and early summer of 1944. It was in this atmosphere that Captain Tokunaga, a battalion commander there, ordered the killing of a longtime Catholic missionary on the island. The elderly man was forced to drink coffee laced with potassium cyanide. When the priest did not die as fast as Tokunaga preferred, he ordered Private Koyama to bayonet him. Second Lieutenant Takahashi had prepared and personally administered the missionary's cyanide and then upped the dosage for several Rota islanders who were believed to be friends and colleagues of the man. Death came instantaneously for them, and no bayoneting was required. As the American invasion neared, other islanders were simply shot. Again, "espionage activities" was the charge against them, although few ever heard these charges. With all this in mind, the prosecution argued that retaliation, revenge, and desperation were involved in these murders. "Spying," they said, had nothing to do with it, particularly since there were never any trials of the accused or any serious investigation into espionage on Rota. Some Japanese survivors of the Rota command told the commissioners that the first time they had heard of "spies" on the island was in the commission room. Given these developments (and prosecution tactics), Murphy did not challenge the Supreme Court position on the treatment of captured spies. Instead, he questioned the espionage-based defense, and in most cases, such as in the Rota trial, he won stiff twenty-five-years-to-life prison sentences for the accused.[40]

Perhaps the most unique aspect of the Guam commission's work was its consideration of war crimes that took place after the war formally ended. The "straggler trials" were important to residents of the Pacific islands, especially Guam. Following the American liberation of Guam and other former Japanese strongholds, entire Imperial Army and Navy units preferred exile in the jungle to surrender. Third Marine Division personnel, who might have been better used for continuing military operations elsewhere in the Pacific, were required to root them out. Many Japanese still eluded capture, and islander homes and property were always in peril by raiding parties of these "stragglers." Given its then dense jungle, Guam suffered from a severe "straggler problem." As late as eighteen months after Guam's July 1944 liberation and several months following the end of World War II, these Japanese military holdouts continued to threaten the island's peace and postwar recovery.

Seaman 1st Class Koju Shoji and Imperial Army Pvt. Kiyoshi Takahashi were two of these "stragglers." At the time of the American liberation of Guam, the two men fled to an area near Mount Santa Rosa and created a jungle home for themselves. As time went by, various former Japanese military officers attempted to organize all jungle "stragglers" for purposes of both better survival techniques and possible renewed resistance against the Americans. Disagreements led to fighting among them, and the surviving "straggler" groups became more and more isolated from one another and civilization. One group might live a matter of feet or yards away from another, yet no communications or relationships were maintained. It was every man for himself.[41]

The typical "straggler" after 1945 was low in the Japanese military ranks, since most of the officers were killed in the reorganization struggles of late 1944 and early 1945. He was usually quite young, had little or no education, and came from a rural or rice-farming background. Although such men had little use for the officer corps, they accepted much of the propaganda that their officers and other elders had dished out to them over the years. Preferring survival to suicide, they reasoned that the best way to continue serving the emperor was through the life of the "straggler." To these young men, jungle survivalism was still noble resistance, patriotism, and the right thing to do. Shoji and Takahashi fit this profile perfectly.

Living only a matter of yards away from Shoji and Takahashi's Mount Santa Rosa hideout was a group of Okinawan civilian workers and their families. They had also accepted the propaganda about the evil of the Americans, and they had fled into the jungle. Doubting that any Okinawan allegiance to the emperor truly existed, Shoji and Takahashi did not trust them. They also considered the nearby Okinawans a risk to their own security. But the Okinawans refused to leave the area. At one point, one of the Okinawan elders was seen by his colleagues wandering toward the Shoji and Takahashi hideout. He never returned. The young son of the missing man went to Shoji and Takahashi to inquire about his father's whereabouts, and the two men, in a rare kindly gesture, offered what they described as "cooked lizard" to the boy. They were seen eating together by other Okinawans, but the boy also never returned.

When Shoji and Takahashi left for a hunting expedition, the Okinawan families descended upon the Shoji and Takahashi hideout. In that cave they found the clothes of both the boy and his father, along with the skulls and half-eaten remains of several other people who, it was soon learned, had been Guamanian civilians. Horrified by the cannibalism, and especially by the fact that Shoji and Takahashi had offered a meal of the father to his son, the Okinawans decided to betray their position to a marine patrol. Shoji and Takahashi were captured as well.

Of course, the Shoji and Takahashi trial was yet another spectacular event, particularly illustrating the seriousness of the "straggler problem." Both men were condemned to death and hanged, and additional antistraggler patrols were sent into the jungle.[42] That campaign was a highly successful one, although the last "straggler," amazingly, was not captured until 1972. In January of that year, Imperial Army Sgt. Shoichi Yokoi was captured by two Guamanian hunters near Talofofo, Guam.

Yokoi, who had lived off fish and shrimp for years, had made his own clothes from palm fibers. He had lived in a large hole (as opposed to a cave) in thick jungle. In contrast to other long-lasting "stragglers" in remote areas ranging from Saipan to the Philippines, Yokoi was mentally stable and in decent health when captured. He returned home to a hero's welcome, married, and wrote a best-seller (in Japan) about his experiences. Nevertheless, during his final "straggler" years, he had believed that the Japan Air Lines jumbo jets, complete with the large rising sun emblems on their tail and filled with sun-seeking Japanese tourists, were actually troop transports involved in a continuing war against the Americans on the northern end of the island. Admitting to his captors that there had been much violence among the early "stragglers" themselves and against the local population, Yokoi was always elusive in reference to his own role in the latter. In any event, few on Guam saw him as a potential war criminal. Time had healed quite a few wounds, and many islanders considered him something of a fascinating relic or ultimate survivalist.[43] Although both Japanese and American trackers participated in a massive "straggler" search as late as 1982, the helicopters, leaflet drops, search dogs, and even infrared photography and listening devices turned up nothing. Yokoi had claimed he was "the last man standing," and that appeared to be the case.

The "straggler problem" had also been one of the last matters reviewed by the commission. The navy commission on Guam had reviewed horrible atrocities. Most of the defendants were found guilty. But the defense counsel, in its closing statement to the commission, explained why their efforts had been so determined and vigorous. Four Japanese nationals made that statement, insisting that they had more of a "moral stake in the trial" than the Americans. Like his counterparts on the Tokyo defense counsel, longtime legal expert Kenro Ito stated that the Japanese participation in the Guam commission represented the "new Japan of democracy and enlightenment." Ito led the closing remarks for the defense, and he stressed the point that in the Japanese military an order was meant to be obeyed "absolutely." A good Japanese soldier, he said, had no choice but to follow orders. There were no exceptions. Understanding the selflessness and absolute commitment of the Japanese soldier was the key, he noted, to understanding the entire Japanese military. Ito said that he "appreciated the opportunity" to be a part of the war crimes effort, but he doubted that the commission, in turn, "appreciated" the differences between the Japanese and the Allied militaries.[44]

Nasanao Toda added to Ito's comments, complaining that the commission always viewed a given trial from a purely American view. It was both remarkable and ironic, he said, that yesterday's enemy would permit significant Japanese participation in the trials but refuse to consider the cultural and battlefield pressures on the many troopers under indictment. "True fairness" would not be a product of the Guam trials, he noted, unless the commission recognized obvious differences between the cultures. Quoting from the Bible, Toda ended his remarks by noting how important it was to "know thine enemy."[45]

Shigeatsu Ijichi continued with the cultural-differences theme. Worried about the impact of the trials on the upcoming generation of Japanese youth, Ijichi said the commissioners had a duty to history. The families of the accused will wonder years from now, he argued, why their loved ones paid the price for the madness of militarist Japan. Executing and jailing the foot soldiers for a "bad government" would do nothing to assist in the creation of a "good government." Japan was already moving forward, he pointed out, toward democracy and a total rejection of war. And finding scapegoats for Japanese militarism would anger many Japanese. In the long run, he warned, a great multitude of guilty verdicts would disturb the progress of a healthy postwar relationship between the people of Japan and the United States.[46]

But the best defense summation was saved for last. The elder and most respected of the four summation speakers, Shizuo Morikawa, stayed away from general themes. Instead, he stressed precise matters of law. His address went on for more than an hour and a half, but few noticed the time. The commission room was packed, once again, with spectators. A dramatic speaker, as well as a master of detail, Morikawa was the finest orator involved in the Guam trials. His argument was a straightforward one. First of all, he questioned the prosecution's evidence-gathering techniques. Its ability to produce, for instance, deteriorated clothing buried for months or years and link it to alleged murder victims was ridiculous, he said. Its efforts to negate defense witness testimony with other witnesses, usually from the same military unit, was more confusing than compelling. Given the navy's lack of experience in war crimes trials and the varying interpretations of the few war crimes–related statutes that existed, a fair trial had remained elusive on Guam, he concluded.[47]

The next logical step in Morikawa's argument might have been a request for dismissal, but apparently the defense team decided that request would be more effective coming from an American than from a Japanese national. As chief of the defense team, Comdr. M.E. Carlson thanked Morikawa for his "final word" on behalf of the defense. Explaining that the very future of a democratic justice system depended upon what took place in the navy commission room, Carlson proved that he had a flair for the dramatic as well. America and its allies could not expect a postwar democratic Japan if the alleged champions of fair play condemned the war heros of its new ally. The prosecution, he concluded, had grossly exaggerated and sensationalized its case. More to the point, they had no case.[48]

The presiding commissioner, Rear Admiral Robinson, responded by praising the Japanese participation in the defense effort. Echoing Kenro Ito and Nasanao Toda, Robinson found it remarkable that yesterday's enemy was indeed so much a part of the search for justice. In keeping with the dramatic tenor and tone of the defense summation, his "thank you" to the Japanese lawyers was quite moving. But Robinson had little use for their arguments, implying that they had missed the point. That point, stressed by Lt. Frederick Suss, who gave the prosecution's closing argument, was that solid evidence had been found to convict certain individuals of murder and other offenses. Suss made no allusions to history, cultural matters, politics, or diplomatic relations. Reminiscent of a closing statement by the prosecution in a traditional murder case, Suss accented the obvious. His team, he concluded, had proven that horrible crimes had been committed.[49]

Although the order formally closing the navy commission on Guam was issued in May 1949, much of its work had been accomplished long before that. Of the 148 Japanese nationals and Pacific islanders tried, 123 had been Japanese military personnel. Thirty of the 148 received death sentences, and several were commuted to life in prison. Hence, the total number of life imprisonments reached thirty-six by the end of the trials, and only ten men were hanged on Guam. There were also only ten acquittals. Admiral Murphy felt that his Quonset hut–housed commission had done its work with "dignity."[50] It would never receive the recognition he thought it was due. The executed war criminals were buried near where they were hanged. They are still there today.

Chapter 5

Rush to Judgment?

Ethics, Fairness, and the IMTFE

Let us not become so preoccupied with weapons that we lose
sight of the fact that war itself is the villain.

Harry Truman

Was justice served in the Tokyo trials? The answer depended upon a variety of factors, most of them political. For some, speed and justice had always been contradictory partners. For others, trial length was considered irrelevant. In 1948 even the Vatican had an opinion on the matter. The official Vatican position supported the view that "Japan was on trial" in the IMTFE and that the Allies had been too eager to convict a defeated enemy. For years to come, the Vatican statement read, the Americans and their allies would have to answer to the families of the condemned and jailed. Had their loved ones become the victims of a new, fast-moving Allied-led "political purge?"[1] Originally the Class A defense lawyers had sought moral support from a variety of quarters, including the Pope in Rome. But the Vatican's comment on the tribunal's alleged "rush to judgment" was an unexpected one. This position was especially surprising given the international criticism of what some believed to be the Vatican's minimal interest in the plight of European Jewry during World War II. But was there indeed a "rush to judgment?"

Standing in contrast to the concerns of its many critics, the Tokyo tribunal's commitment to justice and fair play continued to its ending days. And so did the controversies. As his office's work came to a close, Keenan attempted to footnote the prosecution's general thesis of Japanese "evil" during World War II. Much of the testimony on Japan's turn to this "evil" was deliberately meant for the trial record or history and was not solicited in the interest of breaking new ground in war crimes prosecution. Critics would be quick to point out that Keenan's priorities were misplaced and that his ending days in Tokyo were more connected to political showmanship than good lawyering. Yet in the opinion of Harvard University philosophy and legal ethics professor Michael Walzer, Keenan's approach was never misplaced. By accenting political and legal outrage over wartime atrocities, Keenan's style of "effective prosecution work" also set an ethical example for the decent, moral postwar government, which rejected atrocities. It was the type of example that Japan needed at the time, and a prosecutor without a moral code, Walzer said, had little business in a war crimes trial effort. In short, Keenan's specific methods and tactics were irrelevant to moralists like Walzer. Naturally, Walzer's larger points were that there was no working, moral alternative to the IMTFE setup and that its critics were more concerned with minutia and procedural matters than with offenses against humanity.

> It is sometimes said that the dilemma ought to be concealed, that we should draw the veil over the crimes that soldiers and statesmen cannot avoid. Or we should avert our eyes—for the sake of our innocence, I suppose, and the moral certainties. But, that is dangerous business; having looked away, how will we know when to look back? Soon we will avert our eyes from everything that happens in wars and battles, condemning nothing, like the second monkey in the Japanese statue, who sees no evil. And yet there is plenty to see. It doubles the crime to look away, for then we are not able to fix the limits of necessity, or remember the victims, or make our own (awkward) judgments of the people who kill in our name.[2]

Walzer wrote to an academic audience in the 1970s. He had not been part of Keenan's cheering section a quarter-century earlier, although the chief prosecutor could have used the boost. If Keenan wished to illustrate one last time the "evil" of Japanese wartime atrocities, he had, of course, plenty of material to use. He would not be, as Professor Walzer later worried, "averting his eyes." Indeed, one of the saddest and most memorable testimonies in the entire IMTFE trials record was made during its ending weeks. Master Sgt. Calvin R. Graef, U.S. Army, had spoken in front of an American army–administered war crimes trial before, but Keenan wanted his comments for the IMTFE record as well. As IMTFE staff literally began to pack up their belongings, Graef made his dramatic appearance before the justices.

Graef was a survivor, and an eloquent one, of the infamous "hell ships" of the Japanese military. He told an amazing story of suffering, struggle, and redemption.[3] A hushed IMTFE listened intently, and he was later congratulated by Sir William Webb for his "will to live." Graef also shed light on the chaos associated with the ending days of Japanese rule over the Philippines, the brutality of forced labor in Japan, and the horrible reasons why so few prisoners of the Japanese survived either short or long sea voyages. Keenan was especially interested in Graef's specific and descriptive "hell ships" tale, for it best illustrated the matter of "evil."

Just days before MacArthur's promised "return" to the Philippines, POW Graef was ordered transferred from his Japanese prison camp at Davao on the island of Mindanao to Luzon. From there he was destined for slave labor in a mine, mill, and factory in Japan. The Japanese POW camp commanders in the Philippines did not want to face the embarrassment of seeing their prisoners "liberated" by the Americans, and then in turn being made prisoners themselves. Their choices were clear. They could either murder the Americans or ship them off to the higher cause of assisting the war effort as slave laborers in Japan. Graef was fortunate enough, in a way, to be in the latter group.

Suffering from typhus at the time of his transfer, Graef was rerouted to Bilibid Prison in Manila He received minimal medical attention but did recover. He was lucky again. His original group of POWs were divided into two groups. The first group never reached Japan, for an American submarine sank the transport vessel that was carrying them. The second and larger group consisted of thirty-eight hundred POWs. Their transport was attacked by U.S. fighter planes before they left sight of the Philippines. Most of them escaped injury during the attack, but only eighty of them survived the following ordeal. Nearby Japanese gunboats machine-gunned the men as they attempted to swim to shore. Graef heard about the massacre from the few survivors. He theorized that the gunfire stopped only when the gunners ran out of ammunition, and his facts and figures were confirmed by affidavits from several of the eighty survivors.

Since his opening comments about the fate of other POWs could be easily dismissed as hearsay, the power of Graef's testimony always rested on his own experiences as a "hell ships" survivor. This was a painful memory for Graef, and on occasion he confused the tribunal by referring to "slave ships" instead of "hell ships." But they were one and the same. Graef's "hell ships" or "slave ships" were Japanese-built former cargo vessels outfitted to house between thirty-five hundred and four thousand POWs per ship destined for Japan. The POWs were stacked in what Graef called "book shelves," or wooden planks stacked one on top of another in the hold of each ship. A POW would be placed between two planks without concern for sufficient space, much less air to breathe in the oppressively hot tropical conditions. Graef compared his own eventual journey to Japan as a "marble in a bottle." In short, "when there are so many marbles in the bottle, you can't put any more in. This is the way the Japanese put their prisoners in the holds of these ships."[4]

Hold sections were divided in two with roughly fifteen hundred men to a section. Two five-gallon lard cans were used as latrines above each section. Since asking permission to use the lard cans could stimulate a beating from the Japanese guards, and since it was a logistical nightmare to "unstack" those who wanted to use them, human waste piled up inside each "book shelf." Many of the prisoners already had dysentery, and the grossly unsanitary conditions in the holds brought on a host of new diseases, which, Graef commented in a brief attempt at humor, he had "no idea how to pronounce."

With the average temperature in the holds estimated at 120 degrees Fahrenheit, the first days of the sail from the Philippines were, according to Graef, the most critical tests of survival. The majority of the POW deaths took place during those first few days. The men stacked in the bottom of the hold were always the first to die. The food ration was one-half cup of rice in the morning and one-half cup of water per man. Officers and enlisted men were "stacked" together, yet Graef insisted that military order and discipline prevailed throughout the journey. Confined and sealed, they found it impossible to discern the time of day. That, Graef noted, was especially maddening.

A remarkable fact about Graef's "hell ship," as well as several others he learned about while in Japan, was that no fistfights or angry confrontations broke out between the prisoners. The tension and desperation, Graef mused, should have caused this type of violence. But unruly behavior would have indicated collapse, and that would have equaled another surrender to the Japanese. Consequently, he remembered the "dignity" of his fellow "slaves" and how they refused to humble themselves in front of their captors.

Graef's testimony was weakest in terms of the precise dates of given events and their significance to Japanese military behavior. Because he was unable to answer questions intelligently about the precise condition of Japanese forces, as he and his group sailed from the Philippines, his account differed from U.S. military intelligence reports. He apologized for the "dating problem," explaining that time had blurred during his "slavery days." Nevertheless, his general account of the breakdown in Japanese discipline during the early stages of the American "liberation" of the Philippines did not differ from official reports. Indeed, his on-site observations served as good informational footnotes to those reports. Although the tribunal often asked Graef about conditions in the Philippines, Keenan did his best to redirect the questioning. The chief prosecutor kept the "hell ships" issue in focus, and the bulk of the Graef testimony continued to illustrate this particular horror.

Sadly for Graef, his journey to Japan took longer than most "slave ships" did. His transport, *Oryoko Maru,* left Manila during an American air raid. It was ordered south to escape American detection, and extra days were added to the full journey. There were not enough food rations for an extended trip. Because of the confusion of the Manila air raid, some of the ship's crew had not even made the sailing. Graef saw few seamen on board when he was sealed in the ship's hold. But a POW mutiny was unlikely, for a ladder, retracted to the deck, was the only means of getting to or from the hatches above. And the sealed hatches were protected with machine guns.

Oryoko Maru's primary mission involved the safe arrival of its slaves. Therefore, the hatches were sometimes opened above the holds to provide a better airflow to the trapped men. But in Graef's case, the hatches were not opened until several days into the voyage. By that time nearly half of Graef's fellow prisoners had already died. Food was scarce even for the Japanese on board, and the resourceful master sergeant doubted that the small crew had a cook in their midst. With that in mind, Graef volunteered himself to be the ship's cook. As a prewar "amateur chef," and particularly proud of his rice dishes, Graef knew it might be a simple task to prove himself to his captors. Succeeding in his lobbying effort, Graef won the right to leave the hold for a three-hour period each day to cook the ship's meals and prepare the ration for the hold prisoners. Graef credited his survival to this success, for it kept him, he said, from some of the worst diseases down below. It also gave him the opportunity to taste his own cooking and emerge, most likely, the healthiest of the POWs on board. At one point he was even able to sneak some extra food into the holds. But that made little difference. The death toll continued, and the Americans were denied permission to throw the rotting bodies overboard. Finally, not wanting to deliver a death ship, the Japanese separated what appeared to be the most able men from the less healthy, putting the former (only five hundred) in the forward coal hold. This decision permitted a little more breathing space for the men in the "book shelves," although the five hundred in the forward hold were forced to lie on top of the coal. During rough seas the coal shifted, and dozens at a time would be killed in the resulting avalanche.

Although he had no way to confirm it and there was no Japanese documentation to back his claim, Graef believed that the skippers of the Japanese "slave ships" always assumed that at least one-half of their "cargo" would never reach the final destination. This figure seemed to be borne out by the estimates of other "hell" or "slave ship" survivors that Graef met in Japan. But a specific study of POW ship arrivals in Japan had never been done by the IMTFE, and the lack of precise records did not help matters.

Oryoko Maru had served two additional purposes beyond its "slave ship" duties. As it finally began to turn north and head away from Philippine waters, a typhoon neared the islands. *Oryoko Maru* was ordered to return to a small Philippine harbor where two Japanese naval vessels were present and wait out the storm with them. The "slave ship" was placed near the mouth of the harbor to absorb some of the typhoon-generated waves that might damage the navy ships. Because of the possibility that all of the remaining men in the coal hold would be killed by shifting coal during the storm, those POWs were returned to the rest of their colleagues. But safety was not assured in the "book shelves" either, and collapsing shelves and men during the typhoon caused further casualties.[5]

Following the storm, *Oryoko Maru* took on its second role. It served as a shield for the two navy ships as they left harbor. *Oryoko Maru* was expected to sacrifice itself, should American submarines discover the tiny convoy and attempt to torpedo the naval vessels. In his testimony Graef noted that his POW colleagues had been aware that they were human decoys but that most were too sick and miserable to care.

The master sergeant estimated that they had been at sea for a total of fourteen days when the stern of the ship was hit with a tremendous force, and they heard a roar. An American submarine had, in fact, torpedoed *Oryoko Maru*. The Japanese skipper ordered an immediate abandonment of the ship, but he did not extend an escape ladder to the men in the holds. With the ship sinking fast, Graef and the healthiest of his fellow POWs made a human pyramid of the dead, roughly thirty feet high, to climb to the top of the hold. Then they broke through the two hatches that separated them from the main deck. The few remaining Japanese seamen were attacked and beaten to death while the ship sank. Several Americans went down with *Oroyko Maru* still pummeling their former captors.

The captain of *Oryoko Maru* and his senior staff had left for the navy destroyers in their vessel's only lifeboat. Both warships survived untouched by the submarine attack, and they were depth-charging the area as *Oryoko Maru* slipped beneath the waves. After their position had been secured, the destroyers began to pick up *Oroyko Maru* survivors, but they were looking for Japanese ones only. Any American POW who swam to one of the destroyers, and arrived before a Japanese seaman, was beaten back with what Graef described as long bamboo sticks. Since most of the Americans had been weakened long before the sinking, the energy expended to swim to the destroyers, only to be severely injured upon arrival, led to instant drowning. Graef and four other POWs never even attempted a rescue. Instead, they assembled their own makeshift raft of *Oryoko Maru* debris and decided to take their chances on the high seas. But they were not, they quickly discovered, on the high seas. Their "slave ship" had been torpedoed in Japanese home waters. Within minutes of the sinking, other Japanese vessels had joined the destroyers. It was Graef and his colleagues' good fortune that the new arrivals were in a humanitarian mood. They soon found themselves in the hold of a ship again, this time for only an hours-long sail to Japan.

Keenan ended Graef's testimony at this point. If he had been permitted to continue his tale at some length, Graef would have told the tribunal about his clever escape from a slave labor camp near a Tokyo Bay harbor facility and then about his amazing stowaway journey all the way to Vietnam. Most likely, he also would have told them about the nightmares that still haunted him and his fear that they might never end. Instead, the justices asked Graef a handful of follow-up questions in reference to "slave camp" life in Japan, while Chief Defense Counsel Ben Bruce Blakeney complained about Keenan's "theater" and "storytelling" witnesses. Since Graef's tale was always backed by additional witness testimony and numerous affidavits, he was recognized as a hero even by the controversial Justice Pal. The justices even thanked Chief Prosecutor Keenan for the effort to shed light on a matter that had remained somewhat vague and mysterious during the heart of the IMTFE's work, the transporting of POW slave labor.[6]

To Chief Defense Counsel Blakeney, "events" such as the Graef testimony would always be classic examples of the chief prosecutor's attraction to "bread and circuses." The trials, Blakeney argued in his own way, were not over until they were over. "Real" legal matters, rather than "theater," were at stake. The most significant matter, of course, was the very method of ending the trials. Blakeney charged that the defense had not been given enough time to close its case. He also charged that the death

sentences passed had been written in violation of the tribunal's own procedures. If not addressed to the defense counsel's satisfaction, this procedural violation, Blakeney said, would lead to the mass resignation of his
office. So much for Keenan's desire to leave the right impression to the
postwar Japanese, he implied. The mass resignation would prove the folly
of the trials, and the chief defense counsel's threat was not an idle one. If he
had not used this tactic previously, it might also have been a powerful one.[7]

In a dramatic show of solidarity, Blakeney's entire defense team signed
a petition backing up their leader's position. They emphasized the point
that they had the full support and cooperation of their clients as well and
that their effort was not linked to some last-ditch legal maneuver. Accenting this latter point, the defense counsel noted that the chief prosecutor did
not have a monopoly on ethics and doing the right thing. The defense team
insisted that war crimes trials following future wars would be determined
by how the IMTFE "responds today."

The Blakeney team's threat of resignation was accompanied by four
points of complaint. First of all, the defense counsel insisted that they had
had little time to prepare the "proper wording" of their concluding remarks.
Whereas the prosecution considered dramas, such as the Graef testimony,
an important part of its concluding efforts, Blakeney sought the tribunal's
support for his own, less flamboyant approach. A long defense summation
was to be that approach. Second, Blakeney noted that less than a majority
of the justices had favored death sentences for Class A crimes. How could
a minority overrule the majority, he asked? Blakeney claimed he had learned
of this violation of the charter of the tribunal from "a source of unquestionable reliability." Third, the position of those dissenting judges in the mysterious death-sentence decision had not been made available to the defense
counsel. Hence, the facts were being kept from their clients as well. This,
wrote Blakeney, specifically violated Article 4b of the charter of the tribunal, which guaranteed the justices' full cooperation with the defense
counsel's effort to "ascertain the facts." Finally, since the justices were
already in the process of packing out to their home countries, Blakeney
asked General MacArthur to hold them in Japan until the defense counsel's
concerns were answered. If some had already left by the time the petition
was formally delivered to their offices, then Blakeney and his colleagues
expected the justices to be recalled. More to the point, if this final request
was not granted, the defense counsel could assume that the tribunal had
something to hide and that the defense's demand for their clients' acquittal
would quickly follow.[8]

Blakeney's protest was the rough equivalent of a misconduct charge or, worse, a charge that the tribunal had led a conspiracy against the defendants. It was not an unusual accusation, but this time the "source of unquestionable reliability" had been wrong. A majority vote had been taken. Furthermore, the justices had no intention of sneaking out of Japan before their own final words were heard. Nevertheless, there was the appearance of a hasty shutdown, and Keenan and Blakeney could agree that a proper end to the trials was an important and delicate matter. But the figures spoke for themselves. Washington's budget allotment for trials work in 1948 remained weak. In the third quarter of 1948, the tribunal could expect a budget of roughly $742,000; but should the trials drag on into 1949, only $249,000 was available. Whether they were serious or not, representatives of the adjutant general's office in Washington even estimated that a bare $1,174 would be available by late 1949.[9]

Following the trials of the "major wartime leaders," there were still nineteen "less important" political and military figures awaiting trial under the Class A label. Yet Class A, by the very nature of its definition, always implied "major wartime leader." How could one be a "less important" Class A defendant? From deliberately poisoning the food supply of thousands of Chinese peasants to more cases of medical experiments performed on civilians and POWs, the crimes noted in the various indictments of the remaining nineteen defendants were shocking and horrible ones. The defense counsel needed to tread carefully. If a "rush to judgment" thesis was somehow accepted by the IMTFE and even the Truman administration, there might be more Class A trials. As it stood, the definition of "major war criminal" remained flexible and interpretive. Hence, the defense counsel sought further clarification from Washington, which in turn insisted that Class A prosecution decisions still remained in the hands of the chief prosecutor. Keenan took "major wartime leader" to mean a person in a senior policymaking role and consistently defined it that way. The Truman administration's answer to defense counsel queries, then, was a straightforward one: "Present responsibility for bringing charges against Class A suspects is vested in the Chief Prosecutor of the International Tribunal, and since he has determined that none of the nineteen persons now held as suspects can be considered in the category of major war criminals, the only recourse at present open to us is to try before a national military commission, as indictable B and C criminals, and to release the others in accordance with the recommendation of the Chief Prosecutor."[10]

Washington's final word was good news for the defense team, which had once attacked the very existence of the Class A definition and category as prejudicial to their clients. There was also the commonly held belief among IMTFE defense lawyers, bolstered by a certain public perception, that not guilty verdicts were much more possible in any other trial than a Class A one. This was not the case, but at least the prosecution would have a more difficult time accusing the non–Class A defendant of being an architect of "evil." Most military services–led trials, for instance, examined the enforcement of "evil." Quite simply, it was not in the interest of the defense counsel to see the IMTFE drag on much longer. But did their lingering clients have a better chance at acquittal without it?

In reality, there was little cause for jubilation here. Apparently, as suggested by Defense Counsel Blakeney to the IMTFE, the entire defense team assumed that some of the nineteen cases would be tried in another court in Japan and that many would be dismissed. They thought these Class A defendants could expect Class B or C treatment and that the chances of acquittal or short jail terms were high. This was pure nonsense. The chief prosecutor reserved the right to scatter the nineteen to tribunals in other countries if the defendant had been involved in a crime of "international proportions." Since World War II in the Pacific certainly carried "international proportions," there was no guarantee a given defendant would even remain in Japan. Nevertheless, Blakeney and others believed that a greater degree of justice would be present in the defendant's home country, Japan.[11] But Keenan did scatter several defendants to military tribunals in various Pacific locales, such as Australia and Singapore. Others remained in Japan. None were released simply because the larger IMTFE agenda had reached its end. None were assured an easy street to acquittal or a brief residence in the local jail.[12]

Having met both prosecution and defense team members during the ending weeks of the IMTFE, a visiting future U.S. ambassador to Japan, Mike Mansfield, remembered how exhausted everyone looked, how desperate many were for hearth and home, and how "decently" the IMTFE had conducted its work. They were not, he believed, at their "razor sharp" best in 1948, and his comments appeared to be borne out in the wild assumptions of the defense counsel and the more-than-usual pontificating by Chief Prosecutor Keenan.[13] Nerves were on edge. The New Zealand IMTFE staff even argued that the tribunal's work had, in effect, ended the year before. It was time to go home, they insisted. The weeks-long discussion over what to do with the remaining nineteen Class A defendants, if they were "real" Class A's at all, was utter folly, said the New Zealanders. They also threatened to bolt en masse, as well as to shut down the entire procedure, should the legal banter continue. But minor issues still delayed the desired end to it all, and the New Zealanders eventually admitted they had acted impatiently. There would be no bolting from the tribunal.[14]

Thanks largely to American press reports, the IMTFE was forced to deal with what some considered a minor scandal. Several executed war criminals had been buried in cemeteries where Allied military personnel had been buried. The matter stimulated a considerable amount of outrage from World War II veterans in America or from American families who had lost a loved one in the Pacific. Considering the fact that Japan had a national cemetery for its war dead, as did most of the Allied nations, this burial scandal seemed odd even to the press that created it. General MacArthur accented the point that the American burials were, in most cases, very temporary ones. Many were designated to be transported home to a new funeral and burial. The Japanese war criminal burials were also temporary, he said. Most had already been laid to rest in Japanese veterans' cemeteries. Unfortunately, MacArthur admitted, some of these men did not have families to arrange burial matters, and cemetery decisions had been made quickly at the time of the executions.[15]

But the good general was not the focus of attention in the burial scandal. The IMTFE was considered responsible and blamed accordingly. In the U.S. Congress, a bipartisan petition was written, whereby hundreds of American citizens joined their elected officials in an official protest of the IMTFE's "callous disregard for the sacrifice" of the American soldiers buried next to their "murderers." An apology was requested, and the IMTFE took weeks to decide whether to respond.[16] The discussion period only added to the tension. But the reasons for the delay were obvious. The burial scandal was an American press–generated issue important, apparently, to Americans only. A screaming headline or a U.S. congressman did not necessarily require a response. Similar arguments over burial matters or over solidarity behind the American apology request were not present in the other Allied nations. The IMTFE represented Allied interests. It was not in the business of calming American public opinion on one matter or another. The Truman administration, meanwhile, had no comment for the press.

Privately, the White House saw this bizarre, if not macabre, issue as truly unnecessary in the face of larger Cold War matters and the struggling campaign to reelect the president. That opinion was apparent in the commander in chief's "burials directive" to MacArthur, for Truman believed it was MacArthur's responsibility (and not the IMTFE's) to resolve the problem. "It is suggested that you make disposition of remains of war criminals as you believe local exigencies require with due regard to proclaimed directives of the War Crimes Program. It is desired however that whatever arrangement is made, IMTFE be relieved from continuing responsibility for upkeep of any area used for remains of executed war criminals."[17]

In reality, the U.S. Army had always been in charge of burial details. No IMTFE decision, money, or staff had ever been involved. For his part, MacArthur preferred that his command turn over the matter to Japanese officials and let them face any press assault over where the graves of war criminals should or should not be located. MacArthur even asked the Department of the Army for "guidance" in the matter and received orders in August 1948 to remove from his command, as he had hoped, responsibility for burying war criminals or maintaining their graves. Nevertheless, inaccurate and inflammatory press accounts continued a myth throughout the late summer of 1948 that the IMTFE, without thought or consideration, had buried "murderers" beside their victims. In fact it had always been U.S. Army burial details that had accomplished the task, and without foreseeing the brief political tempest it would cause.

During the Class A trials, a number of once mysterious and unknown Japanese wartime government bureaucrats and soldiers had been accused by both witnesses and defendants of war crimes. Consequently, a secondary list of previously uncharged individuals began to grow as the trials continued. What to do about these new accusations became a serious matter of concern as the original trials wound down. Yet the target date for final comments from the IMTFE justices was set at August 31, 1948. The many days of diversion by burial detail discussions, combined with the effort to agree on one final close-down date, kept the IMTFE from an official position on the secondary-list issue. A majority of the justices, along with the chief prosecutor's office, agreed that a dramatic statement about the list was required before it was too late.[18]

The IMTFE believed it important to offer a formal statement of support to the Japanese courts, and to the continuing Allied military tribunals across the Pacific, who would soon be investigating the secondary list. This did not mean the IMTFE could agree on the statement's specific objective and wording, or whether suspects should be mentioned in it. Some felt that formally acknowledging that a new list had been gathered suggested that the IMTFE had not accomplished much of anything at all. It also implied a certain finality, whereby only those on the list should be captured, charged, and brought to trial. Others wanted this growing, new list categorized in specific A, B, and C classes again. Once that was accomplished, the outgoing IMTFE might offer procedural recommendations to the next court or tribunal. Emphasizing their own trial experiences, the IMTFE could offer advice on how to succeed with the new round of trials.[19]

Chief Prosecutor Keenan saw great historical significance to this latter suggestion, whereby the mission of the IMTFE would formally live on in future war crimes trials. Defense Counsel Blakeney believed that Keenan missed the point. The IMTFE, he said, had no authority to create and pass along a new list. Blakeney argued that the war crimes trial must not become a revolving door of countless defendants. When would the "purge" in Japan end, he asked? If the IMTFE wished to avoid the damning charge of putting "Japan on trial," it would do well, he warned, to stay away from list gathering.[20]

In this matter of lists and legacies, Defense Counsel Blakeney's view prevailed. As always, the IMTFE was most sensitive to the charge of trying the entire nation of Japan versus the placing of "evil" militarists on trial in Japan. Consequently, in their closing statements, the IMTFE justices noted the continued existence of unapprehended war criminals. Simply expressing that these individuals must be brought to justice, the IMTFE as a whole mentioned no specific list or the precise crimes involved. Instead, the statements noted that "residual work" still existed and that "variable factors" would influence any post-IMTFE war crimes trial. Such careful word selection was not what Keenan had in mind for the IMTFE's final commentary, but his views and successful prosecution record were obvious. Indeed, Keenan and every justice would soon claim that their last written judgment constituted something of the final word of the IMTFE. They were correct; however, there was also a grand or senior statement that represented the group. Sir William Webb's summation was generally regarded as that statement, even though he observed that no final word on the horror of Japanese war crimes could ever be written.[21]

The New Zealand staff even suggested that, considering that the justices came from differing legal backgrounds and systems, an intelligent summary of the IMTFE's work and legacy for the future might be "impossible to write." They recommended against it, insisting that a general summary statement cheapened the process and reduced their hard work to oversimplified conclusions. The record, combined with Keenan's official trials history, they said, was certainly good enough, and the individual justices could write their memoirs later. For the moment, enough paper, they concluded, had been wasted already. This did not mean they opposed

Keenan's post-trials history project, for that was supposed to be an IMTFE contribution to Japan's healing process. They just considered the extra days spent on statement writing "an unnecessary drama."[22]

A final closing down of the IMTFE always seemed out of reach to the impatient and homesick foreign lawyers in Tokyo. One delay followed another. For instance, at one point, President Manuel Roxas of the Philippines insisted that the IMTFE could not end its work until it answered one of his official requests. Roxas estimated that there were "at least twenty" Japanese war criminals now serving jail terms in Japan who had had some role in a Philippines-based atrocity. Regardless of any previous decision made in reference to proper jurisdiction, Roxas wanted those twenty or so individuals identified and transferred to jails in the Philippines. The Japanese jail, he also implied, was too comfortable for these men. A less generous prison life awaited them in the Philippines, he promised, and he asked the IMTFE to consider his request "of the highest order" and on behalf of the "people of the Philippines."

The IMTFE took weeks to discuss this request, which read more like a demand than anything else. Both General MacArthur and the Truman administration were consulted during the discussion period. All of the discussants agreed, although not easily, that existing arrangements were to be maintained. The impact in Japan of a possible prisoner transfer was especially considered. The Japanese, now committed to democratic justice, might be insulted by the request. Bowing to a foreign leader's apparent interest in anti-Japanese revenge might also strain the Allied-Japanese dialogue at a critical time in the new postwar relationship. Because of these concerns, Roxas's request was denied. General MacArthur issued the denial, upon receiving a recommendation from Washington to "go easy" on the Philippines president. Given MacArthur's longtime association with the Philippines, he was, both the IMTFE and the U.S. State Department reasoned, the only one who could accomplish the "go easy" task. Indeed, Roxas backed away from his transfer request, particularly after being assured by MacArthur that the U.S. government would comb the earth to capture hiding Japanese war criminals who had committed atrocities in the Philippines.[23]

Although it was never informed about the Roxas request and MacArthur's answer, the American press did have an opinion on the issue of apprehending war criminals at large. Their view was an aging one, that War Criminal No. 1 still lived in Tokyo's Imperial Palace. As the IMTFE folded, U.S. press accounts of the event included a flurry of editorials denouncing the tribunal for never having tried Emperor Hirohito. This decision, most of these editorials noted or implied, was criminal in itself. Their point of view was sweetened by a summer 1948 report from "unknown sources" that said Hirohito's freedom was the product of a "secret deal" personally arranged by President Truman. The details of this "deal" were unclear and speculative, but the press was quick to condemn it. Whether or not the report had been arranged to smear Truman somehow during his tough reelection bid of that year also remained unknown. But it certainly was not the type of testimonial that Keenan and others had hoped for from the press.[24]

If there was a testimonial to the Tokyo trials, it was always in reference to the twenty-eight senior defendants whom most trials watchers could identify easily. Of those twenty-eight, Yosuke Matsuoka and Osami Nagano had died of natural causes during the trials. Another defendant, Shumei Okawa, had suffered a mental breakdown on the very first day of the trials. He spent nearly three years in a mental institution and was released a free man in late 1948. The twenty-five others were all found guilty, most of them on multiple counts. Seven were hanged, including Hideki Tojo, of course, along with Kenji Doihara, POW camps supervisor and former Kwantung Army chief; Koki Hirota, former foreign minister and prime minister; Gen. Seishiro Itagaki, the chief of staff and war minister; Gen. Akira Muto, the vice chief of staff and veteran of Japanese army campaigns in both China and the Philippines; and Gen. Heitaro Kimura.

Ironically, Heitaro Kimura had once been known as the "peace general." He had been the personal appointee of the emperor and in charge of the "peace-making" delegation at the mid-1930s Geneva Disarmament Conference. He went on to be the overall commander of Japanese troops in the Nanking area during the time of the massacre there. His retirement from military affairs shortly after the Nanking madness did not spare him from the trials of a decade later. Following his execution, his body was secretly interred by supporters as a "martyr" in the Yasakuni Shrine, a spot reserved for Japan's honored war dead.

Several of the sixteen "greatest" war criminals given life sentences received early paroles. Gen. Sadao Araki, a former war minister and education minister who had rebuilt the Japanese education system along strong militarist lines, was paroled in 1955. Col. Kingoro Hashimoto, a propaganda spokesman and a participant in controversial military actions ranging from Mukden in Manchuria to the Nanking massacre, received parole in 1954. Field Marshal Shunroku Hata of the Supreme War Council, found guilty of committing atrocities against Chinese civilians, was also paroled in 1954. Naoki Hoshino, the chief cabinet secretary throughout World War II and the former chief of financial affairs in Japanese-occupied Manchuria (Manchukuo) won parole in 1955. Hoshino's boss, Okinori Kaya, the minister of finance and an advocate of selling narcotics to Chinese civilians, was paroled in 1955. The lord keeper of the privy seal, Marquis Koichi Kido, whose own detailed diary (later published) helped convict him and others, was paroled in 1955. Adm. Takasumi Oka, who once ordered the shooting of both military and civilian survivors of torpedoed Allied ships, was paroled in 1954. Gen. Hiroshi Oshima, the military representative to Berlin who helped author the military alliance with Germany, was paroled in 1955 along with the policymaker behind the use of "hell ships," Adm. Shigetaro Shimada. The following year, Gen. Kenryo Sato, chief of the Military Affairs Bureau and former commander of occupied Indochina, won parole, as did the architect of slave-labor policies in China, Gen. Teiichi Suzuki.

One defendant, Mamoru Shigemitsu, had helped sign the surrender document to the Allies in 1945. A former ambassador to China and vice minister of foreign affairs, Shigemitsu was sentenced to seven years in prison but was released in 1950. He returned to the diplomacy game and was appointed foreign minister in 1954. The prize for the quickest parole would have to go to Gen. Jiro Minami, an early leader of the army clique that controlled Japan in the early 1930s and a former "supervisor" of the Korean colony. He was paroled in 1945 and died ten years later.

War criminal suspects were captured even in the days immediately following the folding of the IMTFE. To both American and Japanese observers, these post-IMTFE trials appeared to test the new era of Japanese justice and fair play. The post-IMTFE trials were supposed to be continued by existing U.S. military tribunals but turned over to the Japanese courts, if necessary, within one year. The turnover could come sooner if the American Occupation was terminated or if a clause in the soon-to-be-concluded peace treaty between the U.S. and Japan mentioned Japan's responsibility to continue all trials. Hence, the post-IMTFE trials were conducted under the strange circumstance of watchful waiting. Theoretically, a trial could begin under American jurisdiction but end under Japanese jurisdiction.[25] No matter who was in charge, of course, both American and Japanese officials claimed that justice would be served.

The most spectacular case of 1949, and therefore the most observed, was that of Norimi Otosu. Captured only three days after the exit of the IMTFE, Otosu had been hiding for nearly four years in the hills near

Fukuoka, one of southern Japan's largest cities. Otosu's name had surfaced for the first time in an earlier IMTFE case, and for a while he was presumed dead. Although only a first lieutenant, Otosu had been the last commander of the so-called Guerrilla Squad in Japan's Western Army headquarters at Fukuoka. He was also a fanatical supporter of his emperor and government; he had volunteered to lead a special unit largely dedicated to defending Japan at all cost, should the Allies invade. Planning to fight on even after the ammunition was gone, Otosu and his men also trained in the use of traditional Japanese archery (kyudo). Under Otosu's orders, the Guerrilla Squad used American POWs for archery practice. They also honed their tracking skills by releasing other American POWs and forming "hunting parties" that pursued them. None of the "hunted" survived. Samurai sword drills included POW beheadings, personally demonstrated by Otosu. During one such exercise, Otosu beheaded eight Americans in a matter of seconds.[26]

The Otosu case shed a considerable amount of light on Japanese fanaticism at the end of the war. The defendant was known for his hatred of those fellow countrymen who might prefer surrender to a heroic battle against an Allied landing. He claimed, even at his trial, that he thought his young generation of army officers represented the "good future" of Japan. The trial stimulated a considerable amount of discussion in Japan over "what might have happened" had there been no atomic bombs and no emperor's request to accept defeat. The alternative might have been a successful military coup led by young fanatics who would have insisted on a disastrous last stand as the Allies fought their way across Japan. In a fit of disgust and shame, Otosu admitted to killing several American airmen immediately after he had heard the emperor's appeal to stop the fighting. He had also urged the young family men in his command to execute their own children, for no one should grow up in a "Japan without honor."[27]

The revelations from the Otosu trial were shocking, but that was nothing new. In 1949 Japanese thought and reflection on wartime-related matters did not foster the type of debate typified by the early trials of the IMTFE. As their country neared the new decade of the 1950s, most Japanese favored discussions on the democratic future and not the militarist past.[28] The "what might have happened" discussions in the Japanese press were interesting, but reality was a new Japan with a new democratic constitution in a new era of cooperation with the West. Otosu was found guilty on multiple counts, and the story did not even make page 1 news.

While MacArthur's government waited for the final order to fold and the diplomats finalized the formal peace between Japan and the United States, the one year of military tribunal jurisdiction expired. For weeks, bureaucratic and procedural matters delayed the actual transfer of jurisdiction and responsibility from the military tribunals to the Japanese courts, but the official U.S. Eighth Army history would record the time from IMTFE closure to Japanese leadership as one year. There was no fanfare, no senior Japanese politician waxing poetic on the significance of the transfer, and, again, little attention by the press. The war crimes trials were over and, for the time being, were yesterday's news. Japan had inherited the role of jailer and caretaker rather than that of continuing trial lawyer.

Joseph Keenan took on a new role as well. Back in the states, his health faded as fast as his name in the headlines. Suffering from heart disease, he was under doctors orders to maintain a low profile. There would be no more tales for the press of Keenan's alleged boozing and womanizing. The ex–chief prosecutor always claimed that those tales were spread by his political enemies anyway. He returned to private practice with offices in Cleveland and Washington but despite his ill health did not stay away from controversy very long. Keenan was not a low-profile kind of guy. In July 1949 Georgia congressman Carl Vinson of the House Armed Services Committee appointed Keenan to a special prosecutor assignment. Charged to investigate corruption, mismanagement, and "general improprieties" in the government's new B-36 Bomber program, Keenan wrapped up the investigation in a matter of days. The B-36 informant who had prompted the House Armed Services Committee investigation tearfully admitted during a Keenan-led interrogation that he had made the whole thing up. It was the last time the American public was to see the determined, dogged ex–chief prosecutor in action. In December 1954 Joseph Keenan died at his home in Asheboro, North Carolina. To his dying day, he never agreed with those who said his greatest lifework, the Tokyo trials, had constituted a "rush to judgment."

Since more than twenty war crimes trials had experienced the unique situation of straddling three jurisdiction changes from IMTFE to U.S. military tribunal to Japanese courts, the general argument of "rush to judgment" could have been best applied to the IMTFE's last weeks on the job. The implication of the argument, as suggested by the Vatican, was that justice had never been served during this period. This was an exaggeration of the facts, making "rush to judgment" the most overused platitude next to "Japan on trial." Without question, a tired IMTFE retreated into divisive and sometimes bizarre debates during 1948, but none of them involved the abuse of a defendant's rights as defined at the time. All the way to their conclusion, the Allied-administered trials continued to enjoy the blessings and participation of the postwar Japanese legal system. The trials ended as they began, struggling, controversial, and flawed as hell. Insisting that "evil" must not be ignored, they continued the pursuit of justice and the punishment of horrible crimes. Sadly, this latter commitment was too quickly forgotten.

The Case for a "Proper Legacy"

From Tokyo to Cambodia

But why should Americans care about these murderers? Americans should care because our country stands for certain principles, chief among them liberty, justice, and equality.

Bob Dole

In January 1999 Susumu Yokota strolled quietly into the office of publisher Aoki Shoten. He then withdrew a baseball bat, which had been concealed beneath his long coat, and began swinging at everyone and everything in that office. Shoten had just published *Our Nanking Platoon,* a Japanese-authored exposé of the "facts" of the 1937–1938 Nanking massacre. The book was the first of its kind by a Japanese national. Yokota, only twenty-three years old, was arrested on site, and no one was seriously injured in the assault. Appearing quite calm and rational after his arrest, Yokota claimed that he was not a right-wing extremist. Someone, he said, had to "speak up for Japan." Tokyo's NHK television news found significance in that statement, wondering if Yokota's action should be considered the last word on Japanese war crimes–related matters of the twentieth century or the opening argument of the new century.[1] Certainly a legacy beyond baseball bat attacks and endless arguing was possible for the issue of Japanese war crimes.

Although they had no crystal ball, and no means to predict new atrocities or debates over old ones, the IMTFE justices had hoped for a decent sequel to their work. Their ending comments at the trials suggested that future war crimes investigations should learn from the mistakes of the Tokyo trials. A permanent, internationally supported, well-staffed, and always-at-the-ready IMTFE-like organization must be established, they said. The justices envisioned this new tribunal's having an impact on warfare for the rest of the century. It could become the living legacy of their hard work in Tokyo. But it was not to be. More than a generation later, after more atrocities in an Asian/Pacific setting (the Cambodian holocaust), many would regret having rejected the IMTFE's vision when there had been time to act.

The IMTFE justices had raised the issue of what they termed a "Proper Legacy" during the summation period of 1948. Whereas Keenan thought of legacy more in terms of a decent historical record and its important antimilitarist message, the justices were thinking about a permanent legal apparatus (more powerful and influential than "anything created in history") that would always be poised to try and convict war criminals.[2] It was an unpopular suggestion in 1948. First of all, calling for a permanent war crimes tribunal implied that more horrible wars were around the corner. Allied propaganda assumed that that would not be the case. Second, while it waited for the next war, the proposed new tribunal would only try more and more Japanese as the years went by. Since the late-1940s war crimes trials were meant to represent the formal death of militarist Japan and the birth of the new democracy there, the establishment of a permanent tribunal would disturb this important symbolism. America, meanwhile, moved on to its role of policing the world against the spread of Communism. With the Truman Doctrine promising wide-ranging global obligations, America seemed to be inheriting a world of violence. A permanent war crimes tribunal therefore might soon be spending most of its time investigating American military actions in the brushfire wars of the anticommunist crusade. This interfered with America's larger national self-interests, so the IMTFE's recommendations for a permanent tribunal disappeared as fast as they were expressed.

The original IMTFE recommendation went beyond simple generalities. Sir William Webb even drew distinctions between potential war crimes in the Asian/Pacific region and those that had occurred at other places. Webb thought the Allies were too Eurocentric. When they thought of war crimes trials, he complained, Nuremberg and not Tokyo came to mind. A minimum of press and world political attention had been paid to the Tokyo effort as compared to that in Nuremberg. He worried that this pattern of neglect would continue in a permanent tribunal and therefore argued for a specific court within the permanent tribunal that would keep close watch on Asian/Pacific conflicts and events "alone." A crime was a crime, he implied, whether it was observed by a European or not. At the time, Webb was particularly concerned about the role of France and brother European colonials in a permanent tribunal. As the IMTFE ended its mission, the French had dedicated themselves to a new postwar era of colonialism in Vietnam, Laos, and Cambodia. A bloody decolonization period was more than possible, Webb worried, and America most likely would support the side whose anticommunist position was the strongest. It was an irony, he noted, that the Allied judges of Japanese military behavior in Southeast Asia and elsewhere preferred to be exempt, themselves, from a similar possible scrutiny.[3]

Webb's general and specific concerns went unheeded, although debates over whether an IMTFE-style effort should be resurrected surfaced now and then throughout both the French and the American versions of the Vietnam War. Indeed, that debate went on for half a century, reaching a fever pitch as the fiftieth anniversary of the end of the IMTFE arrived and as Japan's "atrocity issue" debate was going on. It was a fitting tribute to the late Sir William Webb that Australia argued the loudest for that permanent tribunal and a specific Asian/Pacific section within it. This new, long-in-coming tribunal constituted one of the only obvious legacies of the Tokyo War Crimes Trials era.

Sir Ninian Stephen, a judge and former governor general of Australia, led the 1990s fight. As a member of The Hague-based tribunal on crimes against humanity committed in the former Yugoslavia, Stephen argued that this specific investigation had been hastily arranged. Too many war criminals, he worried, would slip through the cracks. He advocated a larger, sweeping operation, namely a permanent international war crimes court attached to the United Nations. The world, he complained, had been quick to investigate war crimes associated with postcommunist Yugoslavia, but so many other crimes went unpunished. His most glaring example of the problem was the Cambodian holocaust of the late 1970s. Although Hollywood had made Academy Award–winning films about the Khmer Rouge terror in Cambodia, such as the 1984 *Killing Fields,* the international community had done nothing to bring the "killers" to justice. Fifty years ago, Sir Ninian exclaimed, "the IMTFE had been correct. The best 'legacy' was a new, permanent court." That court, with its own Asian/Pacific wing, would not have permitted the neglect of the Cambodian holocaust, Stephen suggested. But it was never too late to make amends and to accept the aging challenge of the IMTFE.

Without question, the "ethnic cleansing" violence in the former Yugoslavia put a 1990s Western media spotlight on the issue of war crimes and war crimes punishment. Stephen's concern was that the spotlight would remain narrowly focused and that Asian/Pacific-based issues would always take the backseat.[4] Meanwhile, political change in Cambodia, especially following the UN-supervised elections there in 1993, made successful war crimes investigations in that country more than possible. Interestingly, it had been a Japanese overseas peacekeeping mission, the first of its kind in Japan's postwar history, that had made that success possible. The launching of the expedition had caused considerable debate throughout Japan, for many worried that their pacific constitution had just been compromised. But to Prime Minister Kiichi Miyazawa, assisting the UN in Cambodia demonstrated Japan's new moral authority in the Asian/Pacific region. It also answered years-long Western criticism that Japanese foreign policy consisted exclusively of selfish financial interests.

Stephen found the irony of Japanese humanitarianism in once Japanese-occupied Indochina most revealing, for it was now the old World War II Allies who seemed to have little use for humanitarian gesturing. Stephen thought that prosecuting war criminals was a government's finest statement in favor of humanity.[5] There were many who disagreed.

The Khmer Rouge effort to purge Cambodia of its real and imagined opponents had been so complete that few records existed and few survived to shed light on the precise policies of this genocide. Although the death toll varied widely from source to source, the UN accepted the conservative figure of 1.7 million victims of the Khmer Rouge violence. For years, the international community was divided over whether a productive war crimes trial could be held. The best chance for success, Stephen always argued (echoing Sir William Webb), would come from a well-financed, well-staffed permanent tribunal. In July 1998 that possibility came down to one vote at a huge international summit in Rome. The summit arguments were bitter and emotional ones, and the problems of Cambodia were lost in the big-picture debate over the new tribunal's jurisdiction and whether it should enjoy the power to investigate any country at any time.

Exactly 160 nations sent negotiators to the Rome war crimes summit. It was the first seriously focused meeting of its kind since the days of the Nuremberg and the Tokyo trials. The goal was the creation of the permanent tribunal and a specific Asian/Pacific court within it. The latter was the only subcourt proposed in the permanent tribunal plan; it received scant attention in the face of the angry American opposition to much of the Rome summit proceedings.

Although he had kind words for the good work accomplished at Nuremberg and at Tokyo, David Scheffer, the chief American delegate to the summit, saw more harm than good in a new tribunal. "If the court seeks to overreach established customary international law, or to shove aside national judicial principles, or to create a single supranational investigative mechanism, then we will have created an institution with limited membership and dubious credibility."[6] In short, the United States sought strict restrictions on any permanent tribunal's ability to survey American military operations and their implementation. President Bill Clinton was concerned that the tribunal might even become a political tool by various UN member nations to harass, injure, or simply embarrass the American government. Given this interpretation, the tribunal would possess the opportunity to denounce any U.S. military operation in the world as a criminal act. Both civilian U.S. policymakers and U.S. military personnel could fall victim to endless trials and inquiries, for the American military's post–Cold War commitments continued the pattern of worldwide involvement that had typified the Cold War era.

While the U.S. endorsement of a permanent tribunal remained troubled by possible political nightmares to come, the majority of the delegates to the summit agreed that the Americans were hung up on "picky" points. The bottom line, said the summit chairman, Canada's Philippe Kirsch, was that the tribunal "had been needed for fifty years and will be needed for the next fifty as well." Kirsch sided with the majority, urging the Clinton administration to detail its precise grievances with the tribunal proposal. If America's basic objection was based on the fear of the unknown, he did not believe that "emotion" remained an adequate reason for the defeat of a "noble proposal."[7]

Particularly from the perspective of the 250 human rights and humanitarian organizations who were permitted delegates to the summit, the Americans were obsessed with near-paranoid scenarios and contingencies that were not very flattering to the UN membership. But the United States did make serious concessions at the summit. For instance, Delegate Scheffer had once complained that the proposed charter for the tribunal was too "vague." According to Scheffer's interpretation, the charter granted the tribunal full authority to intervene in a country's domestic troubles if crimes against humanity were suspected there. After some heated debate, Scheffer finally bowed to the general language already in place. More precise language leaned too heavily toward a blanket right of intervention.[8] Furthermore, in the original draft of "tribunal objectives," the UN Security Council would have the right to halt the work of a war crimes prosecutor anytime, in any place (especially if the prosecutor's work interfered with an ongoing UN peacekeeping mission). It was the prosecutor's role and not Security Council action that disturbed the U.S. delegation. To the Americans, this original draft statement implied wide, sweeping authority on the part of the prosecutor that went far beyond the powers of a Joseph Keenan, for example. Why would the prosecutor even think of interfering with a UN peace-keeping mission? With this question in mind, the summit agreed to an American compromise whereby the prosecutor's office would need a special request from the Security Council to begin and end his or her work. But even with the compromise, the United States still noted its "displeasure" over the prosecutor's "mysterious" responsibilities.

Bill Richardson, the U.S. ambassador to the United Nations, visited Rome during the summit and asked to address the delegates. He gave little encouragement to those who sought the permanent tribunal. The United States, he said, "simply does not like the interventionist powers" of the proposed tribunal and its chief prosecutor. "We are not here to create a court," he proclaimed, "that exists to sit in judgment on national systems."[9] Declaring their solidarity behind the American opposition, the delegates from only two nations, China and India, applauded Richardson's speech. Considering the sword-rattling and human rights violations present in both of those countries, the Clinton administration recognized the strange-bed-fellows character of this alliance. But the White House offered no apologies for its position. By the end of this landmark, five-week summit, Indonesia, Pakistan, Iraq, Libya, Iran, Cuba, and the Sudan joined China, India, and the United States in opposition to the tribunal. For the Americans, this was indeed odd company to keep on a matter of international justice and democratic fair play.

Strong support for the permanent tribunal would have won the president few friends in the U.S. Congress. Senator Jesse Helms (R-N.C.), the chairman of the powerful Senate Foreign Relations Committee, made his opposition to a permanent tribunal loud and clear even before the delegates had gathered in Rome. Since any arrangement in Rome promised to be put in treaty form, and since his committee would be the first to recommend or not recommend Senate ratification, Helms denounced any international court that had the power to question U.S. national self-interest.[10]

Historically, the Rome summit provided a rerun of Wilson at Versailles, where a noble internationalist agenda was undercut by selfish national interests and then eventually defeated in the U.S. Congress. The difference, of course, was that the U.S. president had championed the democratic cause at Versailles. He was not the champion in Rome, and a Rome treaty would never reach the U.S. Senate. The Versailles parallel, although flawed, was a favorite one for international human rights groups and war crimes trials lobbyists during the Rome summit. Finally, as the summit debates came to a close, the primary issue became crystal clear. Like the League of Nations of old, a product of the Versailles conference, the war crimes tribunal, a product of the Rome summit, would be little more than a debating society if the United States was not an active participant. Quite aware of this dilemma, the Rome delegates turned their attentions away from possible jurisdiction-related problems and accented the daily working machinery of the new court that they were determined to create. Through discussions of precise operating matters, it was hoped, the Americans would be won to the cause. Naturally, it was difficult to plan budgets, staff, and other bureaucratic functions if the basic concepts behind the tribunal were not yet fully understood or accepted. Hence, a rather bizarre atmosphere dominated those final days of the Rome summit. While certain delegates argued over possible court staff appointments, the Americans and others still worried that the new tribunal championed the right to review a member nation's security policy at a moment's notice.[11] To make matters worse, Chairman Kirsch usually referred to the proposed chief prosecutor's office as the "Special Prosecutor's Office," a term with special, unpleasant significance to the Clinton administration during its involvement with the Whitewater and Monica Lewinsky investigations.

On July 17, 1998, the Rome summit voted in favor of a permanent International Criminal Court. The United States was one of seven nations to vote against it. In his long-winded explanation of the "no" vote, Delegate Scheffer referred to historic precedent, the 1948 dreams of the IMTFE, and America's long-standing opposition to crimes against humanity. It was sad, he concluded, that the new tribunal was more interested in political maneuvering than in justice.

To the casual observer who had not been paying attention to the complexities of the Rome summit debates, Scheffer's comments were strange and contradictory. In an effort to clarify America's position at Rome, the U.S. State Department spokesperson, James Rubin, issued a concise, no-nonsense final word from the Clinton administration. He accused the Rome delegates of a new "rush to judgment." "The United States has been a leader in trying to bring war criminals to justice for their crimes. But the instrument that is being created in Rome will not be an effective instrument. It is being created in a rush to judgment that does not adequately reflect the important role that America and our armed forces play around the world. It opens up the possibility of politically motivated and unjustified prosecution, which is unacceptable to us."[12]

Shortly before the July 17 vote, Scheffer had attempted to build one last compromise that could assure U.S. participation in the new court. Only "sovereign states or the UN Security Council," he insisted, must be authorized to refer war crimes cases for prosecution. The majority delegates favored a court where cases would originate from three sources: any country, the Security Council, or an independent chief prosecutor. Winning no one to the compromise effort, the United States cast its opposing vote. The representatives from the human rights and war crimes trials advocacy groups were especially shocked. Despite America's arguments at the summit, many believed the United States would never vote against the new court. Richard Dicker, chief monitor at the summit for the New York–based Human Rights Watch group, commented that July 17, 1998, was the saddest day of his life. "It was a disgusting thing to see," he said, "after the United States played such a crucial role in establishing the principle of responsibility for war crimes and genocide."[13]

The Rome summit's creation, the International Criminal Court, was supposed to set up shop in The Hague. Eighteen judges from an equal number of countries, each appointed to a nine-year term, were required. A full-time chief prosecutor's office would initiate the new cases, and the maximum penalty for the convicted war criminal would be life in prison. Sixty nations would have to ratify this arrangement, and years, if not decades, could pass before that happened. The key to an International Criminal Court that could be up and running quickly was U.S. participation; however, the Clinton administration noted that it would not be having a change of heart. America, the White House predicted, would "never" support a court that, under certain circumstances, claimed international jurisdiction over the U.S. armed forces and all U.S. civilians.[14] Although they always preferred to distance themselves from the ultraconservative from North Carolina (Senator Helms), the Democratic Party–controlled White House objected to Rome on the same grounds as the Republican-controlled Senate Foreign Relations Committee. Thus, the American government's rejection of the new court was a product of bipartisan consensus.

To Stephen and other war crimes trials advocates, the creation of the International Criminal Court also meant the death of the old IMTFE dream. The IMTFE had wanted a court, but a court that truly worked and made an immediate difference. Time, some believed, was running out for a thorough investigation of one of the most horrible crimes of the twentieth century, the Cambodian holocaust. Nevertheless, further developments in Cambodian politics paved the way for a new, specific Cambodian war crimes tribunal. An American-supported International Criminal Court might have made this entire effort much easier, but another and obvious key to success depended upon the level of Cambodian participation and assistance. The latter was never easily assured.

Kofi Annan, the UN secretary general, agreed with the majority of the former Rome delegates that "Cambodia must be the top priority of the International Criminal Court." But he also admitted that the court was not yet in position and that special measures were needed for the Cambodia investigation. Annan considered the court a "gift of hope," although he worried about the future. The possibility that many Cambodian war criminals might go free disturbed him, he said, even though he still "hoped" the UN's new focus on bringing all war criminals to justice would lead to success in the Khmer Rouge case. "No doubt many of us would have liked a court vested with even more far-reaching powers, but that should not lead us to minimize the breakthrough we have achieved. The establishment of the court is still a gift of hope to future generations and a giant step forward in the march toward universal human rights and the rule of law."[15]

In November 1998 Stephen, along with Rajsoomer Lallah, a judge from Mauritius, and Stephen Ratner, an international law professor from the United States, arrived in Cambodia for their preliminary investigation. Pol Pot, the former Khmer Rouge chief, had died in a rebel village on the Thai-Cambodia border seven months earlier. Most of his "lieutenants" were still alive and surviving in the dwindling number of Khmer Rouge hideouts throughout the northern section of the country. Others had been welcomed into the post-1993 government. Although the ailing King Norodom Sihanouk and the full Cambodian government had backed the creation of the International Criminal Court, it was unclear whether they would support any action from that court or a special tribunal.

Stephen's preliminary work met limited success. The Cambodian government said it would assist in the trials of Ta Mok, the former Khmer Rouge military chief, and two of Pol Pot's closest political aides and advisors, Khieu Samphan and Nuon Chea. Stephen wanted Ieng Sary, the former Khmer Rouge foreign minister, placed on this Class A list as well, but Sary had defected to the new government. The Cambodian government insisted that the official encouragement of Khmer Rouge defection, along with writs of amnesty to hundreds of former Khmer Rouge operatives, also encouraged peace, unification, and national reconciliation. Stephen disagreed, urging the Cambodian government to separate political goals from war crimes prosecution. King Sihanouk, already annoyed, answered that he and his fellow countrymen, and not the international community, had the right to judge what was best for Cambodia's future.[16]

Sir Ninian Stephen had walked into a political hornets' nest. Two men had ruled Cambodia since 1993, Prince Norodom Ranariddh and Hun Sen. The former had once been considered a rank political amateur with little interest in the mechanics of policymaking. The latter had once served the Vietnamese occupation after the Khmer Rouge genocide. The men were copremiers in a government characterized by squabbles over power-sharing, a situation that led to Hun Sen's violent 1997 ousting of Ranariddh. In late 1998 King Sihanouk brokered a deal to bring Ranariddh back into the government. Political peace was the goal, and the government especially demonstrated its commitment to that objective through a generous amnesty policy for former Khmer Rouge disciples. Since the Pol Pot regime had once looked to China for ideological guidance, particularly in the area of forced collectivization, the Chinese government praised the Cambodian amnesty policy. They also urged the UN to go easy on Cambodia in regard to dragging up old war crimes "stories." The new, yet delicate Cambodian government, the Chinese said, "was dealing well with its past." Meanwhile, Cambodia's policies of domestic peace and cooperation had the extra benefit of aiding that country's application to join the Association of Southeast Asian Nations (ASEAN). Cambodia was the last of the ten nations in Southeast Asia to join this important economic alliance, and its membership symbolized Cambodia's return to economic potential and international significance.[17]

In this Cambodian government–generated atmosphere of the exciting, up-and-coming nation, the UN's new interest in war crimes trials was a frustrating development to some Cambodians. From the official Cambodian government view, a sweeping investigation into twenty-year-old war crimes only resurrected the ugly past at a time when the country was finally looking ahead. This did not mean Cambodia would refuse all UN requests. From the beginning of the Stephen inquiries, the Cambodian government made it clear that "some" suspects might always be made available for trial (particularly if Cambodian opposition to war crimes trials would lead to an economic boycott of Cambodia in the West).

Without question, Cambodia presented a confusing picture to much of the world. The American and European press even reported on Khmer Rouge victims living next to their former oppressors and not minding it a bit. Could it be possible, Reuters news service reporter Robert Birsel asked, that Cambodia had "healed" without war crimes trials? Would it be cruel to insist on those trials now?[18]

To Dith Pran, the world's leading advocate for both war crimes trials and democracy in Cambodia, the answer to these questions was simple:

Cambodia could never move forward unless a full round of trials took place. The fact that the current Cambodian government always hedged on that commitment symbolized its rejection of what could be a democratic future. Echoing the arguments of the IMTFE, Pran suggested that a nation's future remained intimately tied to its past. The past would have to be addressed, and given the horror of the Cambodian holocaust, it would also have to be a thorough and complete effort.[19]

Pran was fairly well known in the West and adored by many in Cambodia. The subject of a North American and European best-seller in nonfiction during the mid-1980s (*The Death and Life of Dith Pran* by Sydney Schanberg), Pran's epic story of survival during the Cambodian holocaust was also highlighted in the blockbuster film *The Killing Fields,* which won multiple awards. Pran eventually settled in the United States and became the founding director of the Dith Pran Holocaust Awareness Project. As a tireless lobbyist and activist on behalf of Cambodian democracy and war crimes trials, he was also well respected in the UN. In 1997 he was awarded the UN's highest honor, the Medal of Freedom.

From high-profile speeches in cities across the United States and Canada to his daily reports on Cambodian political and war crimes developments at his organization's well-visited Internet website, Pran continued the good fight. A common theme in his many public addresses was the role of history in the Cambodian struggle. Comparing late-1990s Cambodia to late-1940s Japan, Pran said the need to "purge" the past was the first step to "greatness." Indeed, he always compared, rather than contrasting, his country's economic potential to the Japan of fifty years earlier. With a striding confidence and optimism, he predicted that Cambodia could soon become a major, influential power in the twenty-first century. Standing in the way of this great takeoff, he insisted, were fellow Cambodians who supported order over law and who worried that national progress would be delayed by the shame and embarrassment of the war crimes trials. They were wrong, he said; they were as wrong as those Japanese who had once brutalized the Pacific. "Face the past, honor the dead, offer hope to the children."[20]

January 1999 marked the twentieth anniversary of the fall of the Khmer Rouge. A French polling agency discovered that 81.1 percent of the Cambodian people supported the Pran view of a full, sweeping set of trials (as opposed to one or two symbolic trials). Responding to these results, the *New York Times,* Dith Pran's former employer, urged the Clinton administration to lead this particular "human rights" fight and make up for its awkward defense of nationalism in Rome. Former president Jimmy Carter, remembered for his own commitment to "human rights" during the time of the Khmer Rouge madness, echoed this sentiment. Although Clinton admitted that his government was working behind the scenes to persuade the Cambodian government to hold war crimes trials, it soon became apparent that that persuasion was in reference to a show trial or two. The State Department's official position proved the point: "The United States has consistently attached great importance to bringing senior Khmer Rouge leaders such as Khieu Samphan to justice for their actions during the 1975 to 1979 period. We are now consulting with the Cambodians and other interested governments on how to accomplish this."[21]

To Dith Pran it seemed that the United States had squandered the opportunity to lead a noble "human rights" effort. But the Clinton administration remained unmoved. There were a number of reasons for this decision. First of all, as the assistant secretary of state for East Asian and Pacific affairs, Stanley Roth, once noted coldly, the U.S. government's first foreign policy commitment was to economic national self-interest, not to Carter-like "human rights" crusading.[22] Second, the Clinton administration had already made the mistake of making post–Cold War foreign policy appear too ambitious and far-reaching during its announcement of a new policy of "African engagement" in 1997. After years of neglecting African policy, the White House had tried to suggest that the post–Cold War era required America to reassess its position in Africa. Many misinterpreted this statement to mean the United States would now be "resolving" problems, ranging from famine relief in East Africa to refugee rescue in Rwanda. That was not the case.

In Southeast Asia the United States had maintained a hands-off policy since the end of the Vietnam War, winning popular approval at home and applause from opponents to American interventionism abroad. Did the United States truly wish to abandon this approach, embrace a policy of Southeast Asian "engagement," resurrect the folly of its "engagement" elsewhere, and test this fresh commitment through the vehicle of a new IMTFE-style effort in Cambodia? Besieged by scandal, yet enjoying the support of an electorate who welcomed his focus on domestic economic issues, Clinton had no good political reason to saddle his Democratic Party with a controversial commitment to punishing Cambodian war criminals by the hundreds or thousands. Few Americans, for that matter, had ever heard of the Rome summit and their government's position there. Furthermore, it had been the 1970 U.S.-led invasion of Cambodia that, indirectly, helped bring the Khmer Rouge to power. The countless trials would most certainly further expose America's darkest days of the Vietnam War. Did a comfortable twenty-first-century America need this reassessment of past sins? The UN, meanwhile, moved forward with a special tribunal of limited power and scope.

It is not known whether Sir William Webb and the IMTFE justices of 1948 ever expected the Allies to act quickly on their "Proper Legacy" recommendation for the permanent tribunal. It is known that none of them went on to lobby for it after the recommendation was ignored by their respective governments. Cold War solidarity superseded such concerns. Nevertheless, given the reasoning behind their "Proper Legacy" comments, it could be speculated that the former justices would have disapproved of America's behavior in Rome. And most likely they would have welcomed the arguments of Sir Ninian Stephen and Dith Pran. These speculations can be made simply because little, in fact, had changed over the years. The Rome and Cambodia-centered argument over the right thing to do was the same general debate of the late 1940s. War crimes trials also remained intensely controversial. Political priorities never seemed to include grand efforts in war crimes prosecution. Decent people fought for justice, and well-intentioned as well as ill-intentioned politicians questioned their fight. The argument that "evil" must be punished before embarking on the road to "greatness" remained as powerful as always. And many preferred to forget the past when faced with reliving it. The question of what constituted "proper" accountability still had no answer. More than mechanisms like the International Criminal Court, that fact was the real legacy of the Japanese war crimes trials era.

Notes

Preface

1. "Statement of Individual Responsibility for Crimes Set Out in the Indictment" (1946), RG 5, box 118/4, IMTFE Indictment, Archives of the Douglas MacArthur Memorial, Norfolk, Va. (hereafter cited as MacArthur Archives).

1. The Stage Is Set

1. The Tsuchiya case was covered extensively and on a daily basis by the U.S. military–administered *Pacific Stars and Stripes* newspaper. This paper is often derided by scholars as a mouthpiece for U.S. military policy, suffering from poor writers and limited resources. Nonetheless, it covered the Tsuchiya trial (as well as other trials) quite well, offering detail not found in the official trial record or in another English language newspaper also published in Tokyo, the *Nippon Times*. See especially the December 19–29, 1945, editions. For official trial transcripts and personal recollections, see the "Little Glass Eye" case folders in the papers of Louis Geffen, the chief prosecutor in the case, and the papers of John Dickinson, chief defense counsel, both in the MacArthur Archives.

2. "Trials Set for Tokyo."

3. "Little Glass Eye" case folder, Geffen papers.

4. Compared to the great wealth of material on Nazi war crimes trials, the body of work on Asian/Pacific region war crimes trials is scant. Nevertheless, some of this latter material is more useful to interested readers and scholars than others. On the Internet alone, one can find various anti-Japanese sources seeking retribution for the massacre of Nanking, the Japanese occupation of Korea or Taiwan, the torturing of Australian POWs, and so forth. The following works are divorced from an anti-Japanese agenda. This select bibliography represents an analytical framework (although some of the authors had a personal role in the trials themselves): Brackman, *The Other Nuremberg;* Ginn, *Sugamo Prison;* Roling, *The Tokyo Judgment;* Feis, *Japan Subdued;* Hanayama, *The Way of Deliverance;* Kodama, *Sugamo Diary;* Taylor, *A Trial of Generals;* Glueck, *War Criminals;* Keenan and Brown, *Crimes against International Law;* Piccigallo, *The Japanese on Trial;* Willoughby, *Shanghai Conspiracy;* Smith, "Justice under the Sun"; Bergamini, *Japan's Imperial Conspiracy;* Russell, *The Knights of Bushido;* Shiroyama, *War Criminal.* Additional works are discussed in this chapter.

5. Hiro Nishikawa, "Race and Justice: The Sad Case of the Tokyo War Crimes

Trials," lecture, University of Maryland, Asian Division seminar, New Sanno Hotel, Tokyo, Apr. 1989; Hiro Nishikawa, guest lecture before author's class in modern U.S.-Asian/Pacific Relations, Bentley College, Waltham, Mass., May 1994.

6. See *Publishers Weekly*'s December 1997 on-line review of Tanaka's book, <http://www.bookwire.com/PW/Nonfiction/read.Review$2634>. *Hidden Horrors* was published by Westview Press in Boulder, Colorado, in 1996. Especially see Tanaka's final chapter, "Conclusion: Understanding Japanese Brutality in the Asia-Pacific War." Tanaka's tales of horror are what most readers remember. Author Iris Chang wrote a best-seller (in the United States) on the Nanking topic two years later, and even Princeton University got involved in the Nanking discussion. In 1997, Princeton hosted a conference "Commemorating the 60th Anniversary of the Nanking Massacre." The event, and the resulting publications, received widespread press coverage in the United States and across Asia. Focusing on information and horror, the conference organizers assumed that there were many undergraduate-aged students at Princeton and other universities who had never heard of the Nanking atrocity. Their top priority remained "to inform the video generation" of this horrible event. Hence, the conference's photo and film gallery, highlighting the snapshots and home movies taken by Japanese soldiers at Nanking, was especially powerful and effective in that task.

7. Ienega's limited success in his long struggle received page 1 coverage by the *Japan Times,* for instance, throughout October 1997. A good summary of these reports appears in Nishikawa, "Japanese History in the Dock"; memo on the "Ienega Case," Hiro Nishikawa to author, Dec. 10, 1997.

8. See, for example, "Race, Language and War in Two Cultures"; "The Useful War"; "Fear and Prejudice in U.S.-Japan Relations," all in Dower, *Japan in War and Peace,* pp. 9–32, 257–85, 301–35. Dower, *War without Mercy.*

9. Minear, *Victors' Justice.*

10. Various notes and handout material from this spring 1995 seminar are available from the author.

11. Maga, *Hands across the Sea?*

12. See the Geffen and Dickinson papers (the "Little Glass Eye" case folder and postwar observations on the trial, via recorded oral interview, are included). See also the mid-to-late December 1945 daily accounts of the Tsuchiya case by the *Pacific Stars and Stripes* (available in the MacArthur Archives).

13. Geffen and Dickinson papers; *Pacific Stars and Stripes,* Dec. 1945. "Kagawa Affair" press clippings and press analyses were included in background material preparation for both the defense and the prosecution in the Tsuchiya trial.

14. Geffen and Dickinson papers; *Pacific Stars and Stripes,* Dec. 1945.

15. Geffen and Dickinson papers; staff report, "Drama Continues," *Pacific Stars and Stripes* 1, no. 83 (Dec. 22, 1945), 1; "The Pearl Harbor Conspiracy," depositions and testimony by Sen. Scott D. Lucas, Illinois at War Collection; oral interview with Louis Geffen (available in written transcript), "Little Glass Eye" case folder, Geffen papers.

16. "Little Glass Eye" case folder, Geffen papers; "'Little Glass Eye' Awaits Life or Death: Grim Drama Reigns at Crimes Trial," *Pacific Stars and Stripes,* Dec. 24, 1945, p. 2; for Tsuchiya's final remarks at his trial, see "'Eye' Awaits Verdict as Trial Ends," *Pacific Stars and Stripes,* Dec. 27, 1945, pp. 1, 2.

17. "Little Glass Eye" case folder, Geffen papers; "'Little Glass Eye' Awaits Life or Death: Grim Drama Reigns at Crimes Trial," *Pacific Stars and Stripes,* Dec. 24, 1945, p. 2; "'Eye' Awaits Verdict as Trial Ends," *Pacific Stars and Stripes,* Dec. 27, 1945, pp. 1, 2.

18. "Guard Is Found Guilty, Gets Life"; "Lawyer Lauds Fairness of Hearing for 'Glass Eye,'" both in *Pacific Stars and Stripes,* Dec. 28, 1945, p. 1.

19. "Tribunal Hears Reports of Torture, Starvation against Accused," *Pacific Stars and Stripes,* Dec. 29, 1945, p. 1; International Prosecution Section, General Headquarters, Supreme Commander for the Allied Powers to President Truman, memo, "U.S. Military Tribunals," Dec. 22, 1945, RG 9, box 159, folder "WC 1-110, 12 Sep. 45–12 June 46," MacArthur Archives.

20. General Headquarters, U.S. Army Forces, Pacific, Adjutant General's Office to Gen. MacArthur, memo, "The Yamashita Case," Dec. 18, 1945, RG 9, box 159, folder "WC 1–110, 12 Sep. 45–12 June 46"; for Yamashita's last words, see "Yamashita Hanged near Los Banos Where Americans Were Tortured," *New York Times,* Feb. 23, 1946, pp. 1, 4, press clippings file, Yamashita Case, both in MacArthur Archives.

21. "Yamashita Order Shocks Japanese," *New York Times,* Feb. 2, 1946, p. 13; "Shanghaied," *Newsweek,* Mar. 11, 1946, p. 48, both in press clippings file, Yamashita Case, MacArthur Archives.

22. Hanson W. Baldwin, "Nuremberg Trial Upholds Our Justice," staff editorial, *New York Times,* Oct. 2, 1946, p. 20, press clippings file: Yamashita Case, MacArthur Archives.

23. Fuqua, "Judicial Review."

24. General Headquarters, U.S. Army Forces, Pacific, Adjutant General's Office, to MacArthur, memo, "The U.S. Supreme Court and Yamashita," Dec. 22, 1945, RG 9, box 159, folder "WC 1–110, 12 Sep. 45–12 June 46," MacArthur Archives. Written directly from the court transcripts, a nearly definitive account, and one of the more straightforward, of both the Yamashita and the Homma trials is Kenworthy, *The Tiger of Malaya.*

25. "Homma Faces 43 Charges," *Pacific Stars and Stripes,* Dec. 18, 1945, pp. 1, 2.

26. "Wainwright to Accuse Homma," *Pacific Stars and Stripes,* Dec. 21, 1945, pp. 1, 2.

27. General Headquarters, U.S. Army Forces, Pacific, Adjutant General's Office, to MacArthur, memo, "The Yamashita Verdict," Feb. 7, 1946, RG 9, box 159, folder "WC 1–110, 12 Sep. 45–12 June 1946," MacArthur Archives. "Petition Seeks Easier 'Out' for Yamashita," *Pacific Stars and Stripes,* Dec. 22, 1945, pp. 1, 2.

28. "Petition Seeks Easier 'Out' for Yamashita," pp. 1, 2; MacArthur to Adjutant General's Office, memo, "The Araki Drive," Jan. 9, 1946, RG 9, box 159, folder "WC 1–110, 12 Sep. 45–12 June 1946," MacArthur Archives.

29. Although the "MacArthur Period" in Japanese history remains a popular topic for postwar historians, few emphasize any connection between war crimes trials decisions and Occupation Government goals and objectives. The following text, written by a former member of MacArthur's headquarters staff in Tokyo, sees the war crimes trials as part of a FDR-style agenda of reformist policymaking. Hence, according to this account, Douglas MacArthur sought to "punish the past" before proceeding with "the new era." Cohen and Passin, *Remaking Japan,* pp. 41, 154, 157, 168.

30. Appleman, *Military Tribunals and International Crimes;* Rovere and Schlesinger, *MacArthur Controversy and Foreign Policy;* Fairman, "Supreme Court on Military Jurisdiction."

31. The debate between Truman and MacArthur over the "proper" rehabilitation of postwar Japan is a major focus of Hans Baerwald, another former MacArthur staffer turned post–Occupation Government analyst. According to Baerwald, Truman and MacArthur shared the same ambition to purge Japan from its militarist past, but their "similar personalities" and "conflicting responsibilities" led to disagreements over "tactics and strategy." This is not a unique thesis; however, it is researched and argued well. Baerwald, *Purge of Japanese Leaders.* A similar analysis is offered by Hadley, *Anti-Trust in Japan.* Hadley also had a minor role in MacArthur's Tokyo command.

32. "The Yamashita Case: Transcripts and Review," General Headquarters Command Report, Feb. 1946, RG 5, VIP File, "MacArthur," MacArthur Archives. Although MacArthur's extensive unpublished (and once "top secret") report and personal review of the Yamashita case is invaluable to the historian, the complete record, including dissenting opinions, can be found in Lawyers Co-Operative, *"In Re Yamashita, 327 U.S. 1,"* in *United States Supreme Court Reports,* book 90.

33. Reel, *Case of General Yamashita,* pp. 47–48.

34. *"In Re Yamashita, 327 U.S. 1,"* pp. 99–100.

35. MacArthur to Adjutant General's Office, Feb. 7, 1946, RG 9, box 159, folder "WC 1–110, 12 Sep 45–12 June 46," MacArthur Archives.

36. Command and General Staff School, *Principles of Staff Organization,* p. 1.

37. Attorney General Tom C. Clark to Truman, Oct. 29, 1945, Truman papers. Falk, Kolko, and Lifton, *Crimes of War,* p. 68; *Law of Land Warfare.*

38. Bilbo to MacArthur, Sept. 14, 1945, RG 9, box 159, folder "WC 1–110, 12 Sep 45–12 June 46," MacArthur Archives.

39. "McNutt for Erasing the Japanese," *New York Times,* Apr. 6, 1946, p. 1.

40. *"In Re Yamashita, 327 U.S. 1,"* p. 517.

41. L.H. Redford, a master's degree student in history at Virginia's Old Do-

minion University, interviewed Kerr for his thesis. A copy of that thesis is available in the MacArthur Archives. Redford, "Trial of Yamashita," pp. 144–45.

42. "The Yamashita Case: Transcripts and Review" (MacArthur observations and trial data), Feb. 1946, RG 5, VIP File, "MacArthur," MacArthur Archives.

43. Feldhaus, "Trial of Yamashita," p. 243.

44. "General Yamashita's Sentence," staff editorial, Feb. 10, 1946, *Nippon Times*, p. 4.

45. Tokutaro Kimura, *Justice and Peace*, pp. 1–34. The author is not to be confused with Heitaro Kimura, a Japanese Imperial Army general who was convicted of war crimes at the Tokyo trials.

46. Horwitz, "The Tokyo Trial," pp. 477–78.

47. Pell to Secretary of State Cordell Hull, Feb. 16, Apr. 26, 1944; memo, "The Chinese Proposal," all in Pell papers.

48. Pell to Hull, Feb. 16, Apr. 26, May 8, 1944; memo, "The Chinese Proposal"; memo, "General Discussion by Committee on the Far East and Pacific," all in Pell papers.

49. Webb to Pell, Dec. 22, 1944, Pell papers.

50. Ibid.

51. "General Discussion by Committee on the Far East and Pacific," May 8, 1944, Pell papers. Piccigallo, *The Japanese on Trial*, pp. 3–4.

52. War Department, Bureau of Public Relations, to MacArthur, background report, "Joseph Baker Keenan," Nov. 29, 1945, RG 5, box 2/2, "O.C., July–Dec. '45," MacArthur Archives.

53. See Brackman, *The Other Nuremberg*, pp. 54–56. Especially to critics of the Tokyo prosecutions, Keenan's own "flawed personality" helped explain the "flawed trials." From tales of womanizing, heavy drinking, and endless partying to concerns over his moralizing and elitism, Keenan stories were legend. Brackman, who was present at the trials, sought to debunk most of these unflattering stories and succeeded quite well in the effort.

54. Keenan to MacArthur, Dec. 26, 1945; John McCloy, Office of the Assistant Secretary of War, to MacArthur, Nov. 19, 1945; memo, "The President and the Trials," all in RG 5, box 2/2, "O.C., July–Dec. '45," MacArthur Archives. Bureau of the Budget to Truman, memo for the president, "Financing War Crimes Trials," Jan. 23, 1946, Truman papers.

55. A file of the MacArthur-Keenan correspondence from December 1945 into the 1950s is kept at the MacArthur Archives. For Keenan's appointment to Tokyo, early duties, and warm relationship with MacArthur, see the MacArthur-Keenan correspondence in the file folder "December 1945–September 1946," RG 5, box 2.

56. Adjutant General's Office, General Headquarters, U.S. Army Forces, Pacific, to MacArthur, Nov. 2, 1945, RG 9, box 159, "WC 1–110, 12 Sep. 45–12 June 46," MacArthur Archives.

57. International Prosecution Section, General Headquarters, Supreme Commander for the Allied Powers, to Truman, Dec. 22, 1945; Keenan to Joint Chiefs of Staff, Dec. 22, 1945; Secretary of State James Byrnes to George Atcheson, political advisor to MacArthur, Jan. 7, 1946, all in RG 9, box 159, "WC 1–110, 12 Sep. 45–12 June 46," MacArthur Archives.

58. Joint Chiefs of Staff to MacArthur, Apr. 25, 1946; lengthy memo/report, "The Apprehension, Trial and Punishment of War Criminals in the Far East," (Keenan quote) both in RG 9, box 159, "WC 1–110, 12 Sep.–12 June 46," MacArthur Archives.

59. Joint Chiefs of Staff to MacArthur, Apr. 25, 1946; "The Apprehension, Trial and Punishment of War Criminals in the Far East," both in RG 9, box 159, "WC 1–110, 12 Sep.–12 June 46"; Keenan to MacArthur, Sept. 3, 1946, RG 5, box 2/2 "O.C., July–Dec 45," MacArthur Archives. The Hirohito issue is discussed in chap. 2.

60. The Philippines Lawyers Guild, as early as December 1945, had unanimously called for a Hirohito trial. Calling him Japan's "despotic master," the guild insisted that Hirohito was no different from Hitler or Mussolini. "Try Hirohito, Philippines Lawyers Urge," *Pacific Stars and Stripes,* Dec. 23, 1945, pp. 1, 2. "Apprehension, Trial and Punishment of War Criminals in the Far East," Apr. 25, 1946, RG 5, box 2/2 "O.C., July–Dec 45," MacArthur Archives.

61. "Try Hirohito, Philippines Lawyers Urge," p. 1.

62. "Emperor's Case to Receive Study," *Pacific Stars and Stripes,* Dec. 1, 1945, pp. 1, 2.

2. The Trials Proceed

1. "Statement of Individual Responsibility for Crimes Set Out in the Indictment," appendix E, MacArthur Archives.

2. William May, "Keenan Sketches Crimes Trial Aims," *Pacific Stars and Stripes,* Jan. 10, 1946, pp. 1, 2.

3. Author interview with George Reeves, former *Pacific Stars and Stripes* reporter, Apr. 1996.

4. Reeves interview, Apr. 1996; "War Criminal Indictments Nearly Ready," *Pacific Stars and Stripes,* Apr. 12, 1946, p. 1.

5. MacArthur's precise position over the future of Emperor Hirohito has stimulated plenty of speculation. See, for example, Mosley, *Hirohito, Emperor of Japan,* pp. 331–50. The final word has yet to be typed, although MacArthur kept little written record on the topic. Thanks to recent declassifications and the personal interest of MacArthur Memorial archivist James Zobel, some worthy documentation finally emerges on the MacArthur-Hirohito tale. See William J. Sebald, U.S. Political Advisor for Japan, to H. Merrell Benninghoff, deputy director, Office of Far Eastern Affairs, State Department, Oct. 26, 28, 1948, RG 5, box 107/2, "Political Advisor to SCAP," MacArthur Archives. MacArthur quoted in Sebald to

Benninghoff. Sebald's lengthy memos to Benninghoff include summaries of conversations with General MacArthur on a Hirohito trial, abdication, or suicide. See also Willoughby interview; Elliott R. Thorpe, brigadier general, U.S. Army, ret., interviewed by J.H. Griffin, lieutenant colonel, U.S. Army, 1981, Senior Officer Oral History Program, project 81-11, RG 15, box 33/11, U.S. Army Military History Institute interviews, MacArthur Archives. Both Willoughby and Thorpe were close to MacArthur and were also advisors on the Hirohito issue.

6. Keenan's own few post-IMTFE writings on the Hirohito issue are sometimes contradictory; Keenan has, however, offered detail and substance to the MacArthur Memorial's various oral history pursuits. For "deep background" on Keenan's work and views while serving with the IMTFE, contact James Zobel, archivist and Tokyo War Crimes Trials specialist, at the MacArthur Memorial (telephone, 757–441–2965). Although modest about his knowledge of the topic, he may be the world's top expert on Joseph Baker Keenan and the IMTFE.

7. Transcript of "Testimony of Toshizo Nishio," RG 5, box 118/3, "Extracts"; Keenan to MacArthur, Sept. 3, 1946, RG 9, box 159, WC 1–110, MacArthur Archives.

8. Summaries (attached to the complete transcripts) of the Okochi, Sakai, Konoye, and Kido "Imperial Household" trials can be found in RG 5, box 118/3, "Extracts," MacArthur Archives.

9. Araneta to Truman and enclosed petition, Jan. 21, 1946, Truman papers.

10. The *Pacific Stars and Stripes* also covered the Araneta lobby effort, and those press clippings are attached to the Araneta documentation cited in note 9. Keenan's opinion of Araneta was less than flattering. Reeves interview, Apr. 1996.

11. Reeves interview, Apr. 1996.

12. "More Japanese Favoring Retention of Emperor," *Pacific Stars and Stripes,* Apr. 27, 1946, p. 2.

13. Keenan to MacArthur, Sept. 3, 1946; Henry Biffle, secretary of the U.S. Senate, to Keenan, Aug. 14, 1946; memo, "MacArthur and Japan," all in RG 9, box 159, WC 1–110, MacArthur Archives.

14. Reeves interview, Apr. 1996.

15. Ibid. "Audience Bolts Pretender's Lecture; Only 5 Remain to Hear His Claim," *Nippon Times,* Jan. 21, 1947, p. 2; "Allied Decision to Retain Emperor Was Wise Move, U.S. Editors Told," *Nippon Times,* Feb. 6, 1947, pp. 1, 2.

16. General Affairs Bureau, Japanese Foreign Office Press Release, "Katsuo Okazaki," Feb. 1947, RG 9, box 159, WC 1–110, MacArthur Archives.

17. MacArthur to Sebald quoted in Sebald to Benninghoff, Oct. 26, 29, 1948, RG 5, box 107/2, "Political Advisor to SCAP"; MacArthur to Hirohito quoted in MacArthur to Maj. Sydney Graves, July 28, 1948, RG 41, box 4/1, "Letters, Personal, 1948," MacArthur Archives. These documents were only recently made available to researchers. MacArthur usually kept his reasoning behind the "Emperor

decision" (as some of his staff called it) to himself, leading to a considerable degree of speculation from later postwar analysts. See, for example, Cohen and Passin, *Remaking Japan,* pp. 42–43, 119, 335–36, 340.

18. For Sebald's analysis of Hirohito, see Sebald to Benninghoft, Oct. 26 and 29, 1948. And especially see the "shocking" (for its time) introduction to Kurihara, *Tenno.*

19. Kyodo News, "Abdication Never an Option for Hirohito," *Japan Times,* international ed., Jan. 1–15, 1999, p. 6. May, "Keenan Sketches Crimes Trials Aims," p. 1.

20. U.S. Department of State, *Trial of Japanese War Criminals,* pp. 1–13; "Joseph Keenan Meets the Press"; Keenan, "Observations and Lessons."

21. Charter—Guidelines (IMTFE), RG 5, box 118/4, "IMTFE-Indictment," MacArthur Archives.

22. George Reeves, "Strange Journey," *Pacific Stars and Stripes,* Jan. 27, 1946, pp. 1, 2.

23. "Keenan Labels Judges' Stand 'Offensive,'" *Pacific Stars and Stripes,* Feb. 14, 1946, p. 1.

24. Tojo, *Affidavit of Hideki Tojo,* pp. 1–21; Blakeney, "International Military Tribunal." Blakeney was an American lawyer assigned to the Tojo defense; he was also the senior member of the entire defense team effort. Daily Tojo trial developments were well discussed (and made available to the Associated Press and the United Press) in the following reports published in *Pacific Stars and Stripes:* Americo Paredes, "Preparations Continue on Tojo Arraignments, Trial," Apr. 5, 1946, p. 1; Ernest Hoberecht, "Tojo Reported Admitting War Guilt in Cell," Apr. 21, 1946, p. 1; "Tanaka Told Not to Testify Against Tojo," July 9, 1946, p. 1. These same reports detail the Kiyose contribution to the trials, adding depth to the press coverage. See also "Blame for Atrocity Is Assumed by Tojo," *Nippon Times,* Jan. 9, 1947, pp. 1, 2.

25. For a decent primary record of the Tojo trial, see "Record and Review of the Verdict and Sentence of the International Military Tribunal for the Far East in the Case of Hideki Tojo" (an IMTFE verbatim case transcript and report), Nov. 1948, RG 41, box 4/5, "Occupation of Japan, Far East War Trials," Dec. 3, 1945–Nov. 18, 1948, MacArthur Archives. Brackman, *The Other Nuremberg,* pp. 263–64, 275–76; Willoughby interview; Thorpe, interviewed by James; for specific Tojo quotes on the Goering issue, see International News Service, "Tojo Offers Condolences to Goering," *Pacific Stars and Stripes,* Oct. 4, 1946, p. 1.

26. Reeves interview, Apr. 1996; George Reeves, "Japanese Developed, Tested Atom Bomb before Surrender, Paper Says," *Pacific Stars and Stripes,* Oct. 4, 1946, p. 1.

27. Nishikawa, lecture, Waltham, Mass., May 1994.

28. *The CBS Evening News with Dan Rather,* Oct. 15, 1995.

29. Reeves interview, Apr. 1996.

30. "Record and Review of the Verdict and Sentence of the International Military Tribunal for the Far East in the Case of Heitaro Kimura" (an IMTFE verbatim case transcript and report), Nov. 1948. "Tribunal Told Sadism Was General Policy of Japanese Government," *Pacific Stars and Stripes,* Dec. 17, 1946, p. 1.

31. "Tribunal Told Sadism Was General Policy of Japanese Government," p. 1.

32. Tojo case transcript and report, Nov. 1948.

33. For defense counsel complaints to MacArthur, Keenan, and Truman, including copies of specific correspondence and follow-up analyses of defense counsel actions, see Capt. B.M. Coleman to MacArthur and his lengthy report, "American Defense Activities," May 13, 1946; Lt. J.W. Guider, IMTFE, to MacArthur, May 31, 1946; Truman to MacArthur, June 2, 1946; MacArthur and Chief of Legal Section, SCAP, to Guider, June 2, 8, 1946, all in RG 5, box 1/2, "Master File, November 1945–October 1946," MacArthur Archives. Also see the following articles for details on the language barrier issue, all in *Nippon Times:* "Witness Tanaka Clears Kimura of Blame at Tribunal Session Tuesday," Jan. 8, 1947, p. 1; "Actions of Japan Which Led to War Defended at Trial," Feb. 25, 1947, p. 1; "Defense Continues to Reveal Strategy," Feb. 27, 1947, p. 1; "Tribunal Squashes Defense Attempt," Mar. 4, 1947, p. 1; "Defense Witness Grilled at Trial," Mar. 8, 1947, pp. 1, 2.

34. "Unscrambling Babel," *Nippon Times Magazine,* no. 17, 224, Feb. 27, 1947, pp. 1–8. This was a special issue dedicated to the Tokyo trials and especially interested in the problems of the defense counsel.

35. Guider to MacArthur, May 31, 1946, RG 5, box 1/2, "Master File, November 1945–October 1946," MacArthur Archives.

36. Horwitz, "The Tokyo Trial," pp. 482–98.

37. For the Togo case, especially see the following in-depth, voluminous report. It includes the full case transcript (over 900 pages alone) and lengthy addenda, such as the dissenting opinions of Justices Pal, Bernard, and Roling, a critique of the prosecution's position, and relevant correspondence, affidavits, and procedural instructions. It also represents a thorough and passionate argument by Togo's defense. Ben Bruce Blakeney, counsel for Mr. Togo, "Petition to the Supreme Commander for the Allied Powers for Review of the International Military Tribunal for the Far East in the Case of Togo Shigenori," Nov. 19, 1948, RG 41, box 4/5, "Occupation of Japan, Far East War Trials, December 3, 1945–November 18, 1948," MacArthur Archives.

38. Ibid. Counsel Blakeney assisted in the English translation of Togo's published memoirs after the former foreign minister's release from prison. See Togo, *The Cause of Japan.*

39. The trials stimulated a considerable degree of anti-Japanese sentiment across Asia, and both American and Japanese officials in Japan worried about what that might mean for the future of regional relations. See Sebald and Brines, *With MacArthur in Japan,* pp. 280–84.

40. Blakeney, conclusion to "Petition in the Case of Togo Shigenori."

41. Ibid. Bernard addendum, "The Dissenting Judgment of the Member from France of the International Military Tribunal for the Far East, November 12, 1948," to "Petition in the Case of Togo Shigenori."

42. Bernard, "Dissenting Judgment"; Webb addendum: "The Separate Opinion of the President, International Military Tribunal for the Far East, November 1, 1948," to "Petition in the Case of Togo Shigenori." Webb to MacArthur, Feb. 11, 1948, RG 5, OMS, box 60, "WE-WED," MacArthur Archives.

43. Webb to MacArthur, May 23, 1946; Webb to the Department of External Affairs, Canberra, May 25, 1946; MacArthur to Webb, May 25, 1946; Webb to MacArthur, May 29, June 1, 3, 1946; June 12, 1947; Webb to the Department of External Affairs, Canberra, June 12, 1947; Department of External Affairs, Canberra, to Webb, Oct. 3, 1947; Webb to MacArthur, Oct. 6, 1947; Col. Laurence E. Bunker, aide-de-camp, MacArthur's Headquarters, to Patrick Shaw, head of the Australian Mission—Tokyo, Oct. 7, 1947; for details and quotes on Webb's early enthusiasm and later doubts about the IMTFE's work, see Webb to MacArthur, Jan. 5, Feb. 11, 1948, and Bunker to Webb, Feb. 12, 1948, all in RG 5, OMS, box 60, "WE-WED," MacArthur Archives.

44. The Pal story is an involved and emotional one, but the researcher can find Pal's legal and political position (and in his own words) in the following archival sources: Addendum, "The Dissenting Judgment of the Member from India of the International Military Tribunal for the Far East," to "Petition in the Case of Togo Shigenori"; Webb to MacArthur, June 28, 1946, RG 5, OMS, box 60, "WE-WED"; memos, "The Agenda of Mr. Justice Pal," and "Accomodation [sic] of British Commonwealth Personnel in Tokyo," RG 9, box 159, WC 111-220, MacArthur Archives. Pal, *Military Tribunal for the Far East,* pp. 67–693.

45. MacArthur to Truman, Nov. 24, 1948; memo, "Review of Judgments of the International Military Tribunal for the Far East" (later released to the press), both in RG 6, box 118/7, MacArthur Archives.

3. "Bonehead Diplomacy"

1. Yoshida to Keenan, n.d. (most likely, July 1950), RG 5, box 3, "Off. Corres., 1950," MacArthur Archives.

2. Keenan notes to and revisions and final draft of "Address to American Bar Association Meeting: Our Relations in the Far East As They Appear in the International War Crimes Trial in Tokyo," Oct. 29, 1946, RG 41, box 4/4, MacArthur Archives.

3. Ibid.

4. Ibid.

5. Japan's postwar soul-searching over its proper Cold War relationship with the Americans has been a popular topic for scholars. Some of the best studies are still the older, straightforward narratives. See, for instance, Dunn, *Peacemaking and Settlement with Japan;* Olson, *Japan in Postwar Asia.*

6. Keenan, "Our Relations in the Far East," RG 41, box 4/4, MacArthur Archives.

7. Ibid.; Keenan to MacArthur, Oct. 30, 1946, RG 41, box 4/4, MacArthur Archives.

8. American Bar Association press release, "Prosecutor Keenan in Atlantic City," Oct. 30, 1946, RG 41, box 4/4, MacArthur Archives.

9. Yoshida's support for the trials was always well stated. His government's respect for Keenan is also a point well made in a short piece by Kentaro Awaya, trans. Barak Kushner, "Controversies Surrounding the Asian-Pacific War: The Tokyo War Crimes Trial," in West, Levine, and Hiltz, *America's Wars in Asia,* chap. 14.

10. Makabe editorials, *Tokyo Shimbun,* June 25–30, 1947, in Scholarly Resources Press, *Japanese Newspapers and Periodicals Collection,* microfilm reel L9400114, NP 803; Muneo Makabe, "Japanese National Strength and International Position," *Nippon Times,* Jan. 30, 1947, p. 4.

11. If Truman was troubled by Keenan's early public comments, he never let Keenan know about it. The two men soon saw U.S.-Japan relations in a different light, but Truman never retracted his statement that Keenan was "the right choice in Tokyo." Keenan to Truman, Aug. 1, 1946; Truman to Keenan, Aug. 8, 1946, Truman papers.

12. Wood to MacArthur (with press excerpts), Dec. 30, 1947; MacArthur to Wood, Jan. 12, 1948, both in RG 5, box 2/6, MacArthur Archives.

13. MacArthur to Wood, Jan. 12, 1948, RG 5, box 2/6, MacArthur Archives.

14. Ibid.

15. Bertrand W. Gearhart to MacArthur (with excerpts of addresses before the 78th and 79th Congresses), Aug. 6, 1947, RG 5, box 2/6, MacArthur Archives.

16. "Gearhart Warns MacArthur," *Los Angeles Times,* n.d. (most likely late Aug. 1947), pp. 1, 3, press clippings file, 1947, MacArthur Archives.

17. Makabe editorials, *Tokyo Shimbun,* Aug. 30–Sept. 3, 1947, in Scholarly Resources Press, *Japanese Newspaper and Periodicals Collection,* L900114, NP803.

18. *Reader's Digest* manuscript, "Japan's Problems Must Be Solved—Now!" RG 5, box 2/6, MacArthur Archives.

19. Dashiell to MacArthur, MacArthur to Dashiell, June 23–25, 1947, RG 5, box 2/6, MacArthur Archives.

20. Dashiell to MacArthur, June 26, 1947, RG 5, box 2/6, MacArthur Archives.

21. Wheeler to Dashiell and McEvoy, June 27, 1947, RG 5, box 2/6, MacArthur Archives.

22. "Japan's Problems Must Be Solved—Now!"

23. Ibid. The possibility that a Soviet economic package might be more successful than a capitalist American one was a novel suggestion for its time. Nevertheless, McEvoy's interest in this irony would be superseded a decade later by economist Walt Rostow. Rostow offered a much more intelligent analysis of Soviet

economic potential, in a landmark study that won him a National Security Council seat in the John Kennedy administration. See his *Stages of Economic Growth.*

24. General Headquarters, Supreme Commander for the Allied Powers, memorandum and report, "Prosecutor Keenan's Summation," Mar. 6, 1948, RG 5, box 1/4, "Master File, 1948," MacArthur Archives. This report includes various drafts of Keenan's trials record book and eventual "pamphlet," a record of his correspondence with the Japanese press on the publication procedure, and his, Washington's, and MacArthur's stated positions on the project.

25. "MacArthur Favors Early Peace Pact, Congressmen Told" (lead article); Russell Brines, "Delay in Signing Treaty Handicaps Development in Japan," both in *Nippon Times,* Feb. 27, 1947, pp. 1, 2.

26. Krug to Truman, Mar. 10, 1947, RG 5, box 1/4, "Master File, 1947," MacArthur Archives.

27. For quotes on Narahashi's "dark politics" and "criminal behavior," see Howard Handleman, "Purged Narahashi Begins Battle to Have His Name Put on Ballot"; "Big 'Purgees' Demand Early Re-Screening"; "Narahashi Asks Yoshida Take Immediate Action"; for Narahashi's position on the "plot" against him, see "The Narahashi Phenomenon" (editorial), *Nippon Times,* April 11 and 12, 1947, pp. 1, 2.

28. "The Narahashi Phenomenon" (editorial), *Nippon Times,* April 11 and 12, pp. 1, 2.

29. Furukaki interview. James's extensive interviews of Occupation Government–era figures constitute a fascinating, invaluable, and exhaustive account. Furukaki was a senator in the Diet's House of Peers from the end of the war to 1947. He then became general manager of the NHK news empire and in 1949 began a seven-year tenure as the president of NHK. He remained especially interested in Japanese political and legal opinion during the occupation period, including the Sasaki-led debate over the Japanese constitution.

30. Ibid. For the several Sasaki arguments, see Sasaki, *Fundamentals of the Japanese Constitution,* pp. v–ix; for Sasaki's specific concerns over promilitarist sentiment and the significance of the trials, see Sasaki, "Renunciation of War Clause Held Insignificant Provision," *Nippon Times,* Apr. 30, 1947, p. 1.

31. For Article 9 matters, see Sasaki, *Fundamentals of the Japanese Constitution,* pp. v–ix; for Sasaki's moral and legal concerns over renouncing war, see Sasaki, "Renunciation of War Clause Held Insignificant Provision," p. 1.

32. Furukaki interview.

33. For Sasaki's concern over the return of the "old Japan," see Sasaki, "Renunciation of War Clause Held Insignificant Provision," p. 1; for some interesting observations on Sasaki and war crimes trials symbolism, see Garcia-Mora, "Crimes against Peace."

34. General Headquarters, Supreme Commander for the Allied Powers, memorandum for MacArthur, "Sasaki and U.S. Response," May 1947, RG 5, box 1/4, "Master File, 1947," MacArthur Archives.

35. Researched in 1949 and finalized in 1950, Rusk's report was a mammoth one. Including a mountain of data, elaborate conclusions made from those data, and lengthy political summations, it was titled "Japanese Political Trends Affecting the U.S. Position in Japan," RG 5, box 3, "Off. Corres., 1950," MacArthur Archives.

36. Ibid.

37. Ibid.

38. Ibid.

39. Magruder to Rusk and memorandum, "Response to Report No. 5247," July 17, 1950, RG 5, box 3, "Off. Corres., 1950," MacArthur Archives.

40. Ibid.

41. Ibid. MacArthur also discussed the State Department–Occupation Government row with one of his closest aides, Brig. Gen. Elliott Thorpe. He also told him about Keenan's position, for Thorpe regarded the former chief prosecutor with high esteem. See Thorpe, interview by Griffin. "Joseph Keenan Meets the Press."

42. Suzukawa interview.

43. Ibid.

44. Tadakatsu Suzuki should not be confused with convicted war criminals Teiichi Suzuki and Col. Kunji Suzuki. "Oral Reminiscences of Ambassador Tadakatsu Suzuki," Tokyo, Aug. 22, 1977, interview by D. Clayton James, RG 49, box 6, "James Interviews," MacArthur Archives.

45. Ibid.

46. Ohtake interview.

47. Mansfield interview.

48. Mansfield to author, Mar. 16, 1992.

49. Keenan to MacArthur and MacArthur to Keenan, June 16–17, 1951, RG 5, box 3, "Off. Corres., 1951," MacArthur Archives.

50. MacArthur to Keenan, June 17, 1951, RG 5, box 3, "Off. Corres., 1951," MacArthur Archives.

4. Judgment on Guam

1. "Historical Overview of the War Crimes Trials," introductory file to the Murphy papers.

2. For a general background on the fall of Guam, see Rogers, *Destiny's Landfall*, pp. 163–69; Maga, *Defending Paradise*, pp. 150–73.

3. For a general account of World War II and Guam, see the works cited in note 2 and Sanchez, *Guam 1941–1945;* Hoyt, *To the Marianas*, pp. 252–78; Farrell, *Pictorial History of Guam;* Gailey, *Liberation of Guam.*

4. Murphy to the Commander in Chief, U.S. Fleet, and Chief of Naval Operations (Admiral King), Apr. 20, 1945, and "Historical Overview of the War Crimes Trials," Murphy papers; for Murphy's comments on the navy's trials legacy on Guam, see "Development of the U.S. Navy War Crimes Program," final report file, pt. 3, U.S. Navy Commission—Guam; hereafter cited as Commission Records.

5. "John D. Murphy: A Profile, Historical Overview of the War Crimes Trials," introductory file, Murphy papers.

6. For evidence-gathering issues, procedures, rules, and agenda matters, see "Organization of Navy War Crimes," pt. 1, "Early Phase of Development," and pt. 1a, "Initial Status and Scope of the Organization," final report file, Commission Records.

7. "John D. Murphy: A Profile, Historical Overview of the War Crimes Trials."

8. For the word-for-word account of the Tachibana trial, see "Transcripts of Case no. 33, the Trial of Lt. General Yoshio Tachibana et al.," Aug. 15–Oct. 4, 1946, JAG Docket no. 154578, Commission Records; for the U.S. military and Guamian reaction to the Tachbana trial, see "War Trials to Convene This Morning," *Navy News,* Guam ed., Aug. 22, 1946, p. 1; "Flesh Feasts, Bayoneting Testified to by Hidano," *Navy News,* Guam ed., Sept. 13, 1946, pp. 1, 3. The *Navy News,* Guam ed., 1945–1950, may be found at the Micronesian Area Research Center, Univ. of Guam (MARC).

9. "War Crimes Tribunal Tries 'Cannibal Case,'" *Navy News,* Guam ed., Aug. 15, 1946, p. 1; "Isogai Admits Eating 'Funny Kind of Meat' But Didn't Know It Was Human," *Navy News,* Guam ed., Sept. 14, 1946, p. 2.

10. For witness testimony, see "Transcripts of Case no. 33" (Tachibana); for witness testimony analysis, see James Young, INS staff correspondent and special to *Navy News,* "Witness Admits Ordering Men to Use Bayonet," *Navy News,* Guam ed., Aug. 23, 1946, pp. 1, 3.

11. "Middle Phase of Development, January 1946–January 1947," final report file, Commission Records.

12. For the national madness defense, see "Transcripts of Case no. 33" (Tachibana); "Chichi Jima," final report file, Commission Records; for analysis of the national madness defense, see "Spectators Startled at War Crimes Trial," *Navy News,* Guam ed., Aug. 20, 1946, p. 1.

13. For Tamamuro and the horror of this case, see James Young, INS staff correspondent and special to *Navy News,* "American-Born Japanese Witness Sensation of Day at Trial," *Navy News,* Guam ed., Aug. 24, 1946, p. 1; for Tamamuro's star witness testimony, see "Chichi Jima."

14. "John D. Murphy: A Profile, Historical Overview of the War Crimes Trials."

15. Young, "American-Born Japanese Witness Sensation of Day at Trial," p. 1.

16. "Chichi Jima."

17. "Transcripts of Case no. 31, Trial of Lt. Colonel Kikuji Ito, IJA, et al.," June 19–Sept. 1, 1946, JAG Docket no. 151334, Commission Records; James Young, INS staff correspondent and special to *Navy News,* "War Crimes Trial Upset by Ito's Testimony," *Navy News,* Guam ed., Aug. 22, 1946, pp. 1, 3.

18. Young, "War Crimes Trial Upset by Ito's Testimony," pp. 1, 3.

19. "Defense Objections Hold War Crimes Trials," *Navy News,* Guam ed., Aug. 17, 1946, p. 1.

20. "6 Japs Hanged: Pay First Death Penalties on Guam," *Navy News,* Guam ed., June 20, 1947, pp. 1, 2.

21. "Transcripts of Case no. 26, Trial of Rear Admiral Shigematsu Sakaibara, Dec. 21–24, 1945, JAG Docket no. 148331, Commission Records; G.A. Van Horn, "War Crimes Commission Imposes Death for Five Jap Officers," *Navy News,* Guam ed., July 3, 1946, p. 1; George Wilbur, "History of War Crimes Trials," *Navy News,* Guam ed., Dec. 14, 1947, p. 3. This article examined the Sakaibara case. During 1947 *Navy News,* which maintained strong daily coverage of the Guam commission's work, began a series of "historical" articles about some of the more spectacular and involved trials held on the island. The series pulled together information from that daily coverage as well as from commission testimony.

22. For the best and most comprehensive source on Wake Island during World War II, see Robert J. Cressman, *'A Magnificent Fight': The Battle for Wake Island* (Annapolis, Md.: U.S. Naval Institute Press, 1995). The Hollywood version (1942) of the battle began filming while the fighting was still going on. The scripts and action scenes were adjusted depending upon the headlines. Despite its struggles and inaccuracies, *Wake Island,* starring Brian Donlevy, was an instant box-office hit. It also created an exaggerated image of the defenders of the island, as well as a "Remember Wake Island" slogan, which stuck more in the public mind than the facts of the battle itself.

23. "Transcripts of Case 26" (Sakaibara), Commission Records; Wilbur, "History of War Crimes Trials," Dec. 14, 1947, p. 3.

24. "Historical Overview of the War Crimes Trials."

25. The author witnessed this behavior while teaching in Misawa for three years.

26. See Tweed and Clark, *Robinson Crusoe, USN.* The film version of this book, *No Man Is an Island,* starring Jeffrey Hunter, was released by Twentieth Century Fox productions in 1962.

27. "Realization of a Vow: Ghost of Guam Presents New Chevrolet to Guamanian," *Navy News,* Guam ed., Sept. 17, 1946, p. 1.

28. Adm. Charles Pownall, governor of Guam, to the Department of the Navy, Mar. 19, 1949, and enclosed newspaper clipping, "Guam Rebels at New Navy Rule," *Washington Post,* Apr. 3, 1949; memorandum of meeting between John T. Koehler, acting secretary of the navy, and the secretary of the interior, July 7, 1949, "Official Correspondence," U.S. Navy Government Records (NR); President Truman to the Interior and War Departments, May 14, 1949, box 5009, "Guam," RG 59, National Archives, Washington, D.C.

29. Louisa B. Garrido, "War Life during Japanese Rule Revealed by Student," *Navy News,* Guam ed., Dec. 14, 1947, p. 3. This was one of a series of seven long articles written by young Guamanians about the horrors of the occupation.

30. "Transcripts of Case no. 11, Trial of Samuel T. Shinohara," July 28–Aug. 27, 1945, JAG Docket no. 144704, Commission Records.

31. Ibid.

32. Ibid.

33. "Transcripts of Case no. 21, Trial of Jose P. Villagomez," Oct. 22, 1945, JAG Docket no. 142103; "Transcripts of Case no. 22, Trial of Francisco Sablan," Oct. 29–30, 1945, JAG Docket no. 142104; "Transcripts of Case no. 23, Trial of Juan Villagomez," Oct. 31–Nov. 1, 1945, JAG Docket no. 142374, Commission Records.

34. George Wilbur, "History of War Crimes Trials," *Navy News,* Guam ed., June 20, 1947, p. 2. This article was a history of the Hosokawa case; "Transcripts of Case no. 14, Trial of Akiyoshi Hosokawa," Sept. 1–13, 1945, JAG Docket no. 144574, Commission Records.

35. "Transcripts of Case no. 39, Trial of Surgeon Captain Hiroshi Iwanami," June 10–Sept. 5, 1947, JAG Docket no. 160413; "Truk and Central Carolines," final report file, both in Commission Records.

36. "Transcripts of Case 39" (Iwanami); "Truk and Central Carolines." Kenneth Maga, USMC, ret., who was Iwanami's prison guard during the trials, interview by author.

37. "Transcripts of Case no. 40, Trial of Rear Admiral Shimpei Asano et al.," Sept. 22–Oct. 24, 1947, JAG Docket no. 161779; "Transcripts of Case no. 46, Trial of Vice Admiral Seisaku Wakarayashi," July 29–Sept. 7, 1948, JAG Docket no. 166096; "Transcripts of Case no. 45, Trial of Vice Admiral Masashi Kobayashi," May 13–July 16, 1948, JAG Docket no. 165564, Commission Records.

38. Details of Abe's role on Makin were known as early as 1946. See G.A. Van Horn, "War Crimes Commission Imposes Death for Five Jap Officers," *Navy News,* Guam ed., July 3, 1946, p. 1. Pt. 3, "Final Phase of War Crimes Trials (January 1947 to May 1949)," final report file, Commission Records.

39. Pt. 3, "Final Phase of War Crimes Trials (January 1947 to May 1949)"; an interesting discussion of the developing legal arguments on "spying" as well as on the fate of missionaries in the islands during the war appears in James R. Young, "'Spies Not Allowed,'" *Navy News,* Guam ed., Aug. 21, 1946, p. 1.

40. Pt. 3, "Final Phase of War Crimes Trials (January 1947 to May 1949)"; "Transcripts of Case no. 49, Trial of Captain Akira Tokunaga et al.," Jan. 26–Feb. 16, 1949, JAG Docket no. 167716, Commission Records.

41. "Murderers Hang for Guam Crimes," *Navy News,* Guam ed., June 20, 1947, p. 2. For a fascinating account of the "straggler issue," see Ito, *Emperor's Last Soldiers;* Smith, *Diary of Sergeant Ito.*

42. "Murderers Hang for Guam Crimes," p. 2.

43. The Government of Guam even maintains a website dedicated to Yokoi, including a long and detailed history of his activities. His former hideout is now a popular tourist spot, especially for Japanese visitors to the island. He died on Sept. 22, 1997. See <http://www.ns.gov.gu/scrollapplet/sergeant.html>.

44. Pt. 3: "Final Phase of War Crimes Trials (January 1947 to May 1949),"
Commission Records. The closing statements for the defense at the end of the trials
were nearly identical to the closing statements at the end of the earlier "high profile" cases (Tachibana, Ito, Sakaibara, etc., of 1945–1946). See "Lawyers Close
Defense in War Trials," *Navy News,* Guam ed., Sept. 26, 1946, p. 1.

45. "Final Phase of War Crimes Trials (January 1947 to May 1949)"; "Lawyers Close Defense in War Trials."

46. "Final Phase of War Crimes Trials (January 1947 to May 1949)"; "Lawyers Close Defense in War Trials."

47. "Final Phase of War Crimes Trials (January 1947 to May 1949)"; "Lawyers Close Defense in War Trials."

48. "Final Phase of War Crimes Trials (January 1947 to May 1949)"; "Lawyers Close Defense in War Trials."

49. "Final Phase of War Crimes Trials (January 1947 to May 1949)"; "Lawyers Close Defense in War Trials."

50. Statement by Adm. John D. Murphy, Dec. 1, 1949, addendum to pt. 3,
"Final Phase of War Crimes Trials (January 1947 to May 1949)."

5. Rush to Judgment?

1. "Miscellaneous Correspondence—Diplomatic (Vatican), 1948," RG 5,
box 15/15, MacArthur Archives.

2. Walzer, *Just and Unjust Wars,* p. 326.

3. Portions of the Graef testimony had already been submitted (for the record)
to the IMTFE from the U.S. Eighth Army military tribunal in April 1947. For both
1947 and 1948 Graef testimony detail, see the IMTFE "'Hell Ships' Testimony
Summary," RG 49, box 2, MacArthur Archives; Graef interview.

4. IMTFE "'Hell Ships' Testimony Summary"; Graef interview. Graef's
"marbles" allusion can be found both in the testimony record and in James's interview transcripts.

5. IMTFE "'Hell Ships' Testimony Summary"; Graef interview.

6. IMTFE "'Hell Ships' Testimony Summary"; Graef interview.

7. Blakeney to MacArthur, and memo, "The Position of the Defense Division," Nov. 13, 1948, RG 5, box 15/15, MacArthur Archives.

8. Ibid.

9. SCAP to Dept. of the Army (untitled memo on war crimes budget issues), Jan. 4, 1948, RG 9, box 159, WC, MacArthur Archives.

10. MacArthur to Col. R.M. Levy, adjutant general, Jan. 13, 1948; defense
counsel and chief prosecutor responsibilities are quoted in Levy to Truman and
Gen. George Marshall, Feb. 1, 1948, both in RG 9, box 159, WC, MacArthur
Archives.

11. Blakeney to MacArthur, and memo, "The Position of the Defense Division," Nov. 13, 1948, MacArthur Archives.

12. MacArthur to Levy, Jan. 13, 1948, MacArthur Archives.

13. Mansfield interview.

14. Blakeney to Webb and MacArthur, and memo, "Dismissal of Defense Counsel," May 23, 1948, RG 9, box 159, WC, MacArthur Archives. This lengthy, detailed report offers excellent insight into the daily workings of the IMTFE in 1948.

15. Adjutant General's Office, General Headquarters, Far East Command, Radio and Cable Center, memo, "Disposition of Remains Issue," Aug. 4, 1948, RG 9, box 159, WC, MacArthur Archives.

16. Ibid.; Levy to Marshall, and memo, "Disposition of Remains of Executed War Criminals within Far East Command," July 27, 1948, RG 9, box 159, WC, MacArthur Archives.

17. Truman to MacArthur, Aug. 4, 1958 [*sic:* 1948], RG 9, box 159, WC, MacArthur Archives.

18. Adjutant General's Office memo, "31 August 1948," Aug. 4, 1948, RG 9, box 159, WC, MacArthur Archives.

19. Ibid.; Levy to the Department of the Army, Aug. 13, Sept. 3, 1948, RG 9, box 159, WC, MacArthur Archives.

20. "Dismissal of Defense Counsel," May 23, 1948; Levy to Department of the Army, Sept. 3, 1948, both in RG 9, box 159, WC, MacArthur Archives.

21. For more on the statements issue, see Webb's comments in International Military Tribunal for the Far East, *Judgment,* pp. 8–9, 14–17.

22. Ibid. The New Zealand position was well taken. Webb's original summation (available in the MacArthur Archives) was more than 650 pages long, but then it was shortened, amazingly, to 21 pages. The New Zealand position can be found in Webb's addendum to the original summation, pp. 633–34, RG9, box 159, WC, MacArthur Archives.

23. For Roxas's position, see Levy to CG PHILRYCOM, May 30, 1948; for an analysis of the Roxas position and the reasons for its rejection, see Levy to Department of the Army, including a long, involved report, "Stern Justice for War Criminals," Nov. 9, 1948, both in RG 9, box 159, WC, MacArthur Archives.

24. "Stern Justice for War Criminals."

25. Levy to Department of the Army, Feb. 4, July 2, 1949 (including attachment, Levy to the assistant secretary of the army with memo, "Confinement of Convicted War Criminals," Mar. 7, 1949), RG 9, box 160, "War Crimes, Dup. Copies," MacArthur Archives.

26. Levy and C.R. Liggit, deputy chief, Legal Section, General Headquarters, Far East Command, to Department of the Army, including a report and transcript, "Western Army Case" (Otosu), Mar. 28, 1949, RG 9, box 160, "War Crimes, Dup. Copies," MacArthur Archives.

27. Ibid.

28. Coughlin, *Conquered Press,* p. 120.

Epilogue

1. Brasher, "Tokyo Publisher Target of Attack." The role of Japanese journalism over the years in denying the reality of horrible World War II massacres, such as that at Nanjing, is a major matter of concern in the following work, which is coedited by Katsuichi Honda, a reporter for *Asahi Shimbun:* Honda and Gibney, *The Nanjing Massacre.*

2. See the "Proper Legacy" preamble to Keenan's lengthy original draft of his trials "history" publication. RG 9, box 160, "W.C. 221-320, 19 Nov. 48–29 May 50," MacArthur Archives.

3. Ibid.; see also the fascinating and idealistic introduction to Fearey, *Occupation of Japan—Second Phase.* Fearey was the former secretary to the prewar U.S. ambassador to Japan, Joseph Grew, and a member of MacArthur's political advisors staff during the postwar Occupation Government. "Judgment" (original draft and notes) by Sir William Webb, Nov. 1948, RG 9, box 160, "WC 221–320, 19 Nov. 48–29 May 50," MacArthur Archives.

4. "U.N. Khmer Rouge Trial Team" (a file of Reuters and Associated Press reports, plus Cambodian "news and information" releases from the Dith Pran Holocaust Awareness Project, Inc.), sent to the author from Dith Pran, Nov. 17, 1998.

5. Ibid. For a decent analysis of mid- to late-1990s Cambodian politics and international intrigue, see Becker, *When the War Was Over,* pp. 508–17.

6. Trueheart, "U.S. Cool to War Crimes Panel."

7. Webber, "Annan Calls War Crimes Court 'Gift of Hope.'"

8. Lippman, "War Crimes High Court Is Approved."

9. Richardson is quoted in Truehart, "U.S. Cool to War Crimes Panel."

10. Truehart, "U.S. Cool to War Crimes Panel."

11. Dith Pran to author, Dec. 9, 1998.

12. Rubin is quoted in Lippman, "War Crimes High Court Is Approved."

13. Scheffer and Dicker quoted in Lippman, "War Crimes High Court Is Approved."

14. Lippman, "War Crimes High Court Is Approved."

15. Webber, "War Crimes Court 'Gift of Hope.'"

16. "U.N. Khmer Rouge Trial Team" file.

17. Ibid. Cloud, "U.S. Crafts Plan," pp. 1, 14; Schmetzer, "Mysterious Death of Pol Pot," sec. 1, pp. 1, 4; for the Chinese statement, see Cloud, "Prosecuting War Criminals"; "Khmer Rouge Leaders 'Very Sorry.'"

18. "U.N. Khmer Rouge Trial Team" file.

19. Muller, "Stand Up to Oppression."

20. Dith Pran, "War Crimes, Cambodia, and the World," Armstrong Lecture Series, Bradley University, Peoria, Ill., Apr. 6, 1999.

21. Kyodo News Service, "Poll Shows 80% of Cambodians Want Khmer Rouge Trial," *Japan Times Weekly,* international ed., Jan. 27, 1999; "Cambodia's Surreal Beach Party," editorial, *New York Times,* Jan. 5, 1999; the U.S. position is

quoted in "Sorry about That Khmer Genocide," editorial and opinion Page, *Nation* (Thailand), Jan. 13, 1999, Dith Pran Holocaust Awareness Project, Inc., News and Archives Section, website, <http://www.DithPran.org> or <http://www. Cambodian.com>. Although precise page numbers for various news reports are not given at this on-line archive, the war crimes–related articles are gathered from around the world and published uncut.

22. Roth, "Growth and Stability in East Asia."

Bibliography

Appleman, John Alan. *Military Tribunals and International Crimes.* Westport, Conn.: Greenwood Press, 1954.

Baerwald, Hans. *The Purge of Japanese Leaders under the Occupation.* Berkeley: Univ. of California Press, 1959.

Becker, Elizabeth. *When the War Was Over: Cambodia and the Khmer Rouge Revolution.* New York: Public Affairs, 1998.

Bergamini, David. *Japan's Imperial Conspiracy.* New York: William Morrow, 1971.

Blakeney, Ben Bruce. "International Military Tribunal." *American Bar Association Journal* 32 (Aug. 1946): 10–11.

Brackman, Arnold C. *The Other Nuremberg: The Untold Story of the Tokyo War Crimes Trials.* New York: William Morrow, 1987.

Brasher, Philip. "Tokyo Publisher Target of Attack." *Milwaukee Journal Sentinel,* Jan. 9, 1999, p. 2A.

Cloud, David S. "Prosecuting War Criminals Is Much Easier Said than Done." *Chicago Tribune,* Apr. 17, 1998, sec. 1, p. 1, 4.

———. "U.S. Crafts Plan in Event Pol Pot Is Tried." *Chicago Tribune,* Apr. 10, 1998, sec. 1, p. 1, 14.

Cohen, Theodore, and Herbert Passin. *Remaking Japan: The American Occupation as New Deal.* New York: Free Press, 1987.

Command and General Staff School. *Principles of Staff Organization.* Rizal, Philippines: Fort William McKinley, 1957.

Coughlin, William J. *Conquered Press.* Palo Alto, Calif.: Pacific Books, 1952.

Dickinson, John. Papers. Archives of the Douglas MacArthur Memorial, Norfolk, Va.

Dole, Bob. "U.S. Will Suffer." *USA Today,* July 21, 1997, p. 13A.

Dower, John W. *Japan in War and Peace.* New York: New Press, 1993.

———. *War without Mercy.* New York: Pantheon, 1986.

Dunn, Frederick. *Peacemaking and the Settlement with Japan.* Princeton, N.J.: Princeton Univ. Press, 1963.

Fairman, Charles. "The Supreme Court on Military Jurisdiction: Martial Rule in Hawaii and the Yamashita Case." *Harvard Law Review* 59 (July 1946): 833–82.

Falk, Richard, Gabriel Kolko, and Robert J. Lifton, eds. *Crimes of War.* New York: Random House, 1971.

Farrell, Don. *The Pictorial History of Guam: Liberation—1944.* Tamuning, Guam: Micronesian Productions, 1984.

Fearey, Robert. *The Occupation of Japan—Second Phase, 1948–50.* New York: Macmillan, 1950.

Feis, Herbert. *Japan Subdued.* Princeton, N.J.: Princeton Univ. Press, 1961.

Feldhaus, J. Gordon. "The Trial of Yamashita." *Current Legal Thought* 13 (1947): 243.

Fuqua, Ellis E. "Judicial Review of War Crime Trials." *Journal of Criminal Law and Criminology* (May–June 1946): 58–64.

Furukaki, Tetsuro. "Oral Reminiscences of Tetsuro Furukaki, Tokyo, Japan." Interview by D. Clayton James, Aug. 17, 1977. RG 49, box 5, "James Interviews," Archives of the Douglas MacArthur Memorial, Norfolk, Va.

Gailey, Harry. *The Liberation of Guam, 21 July–10 August 1944.* Novato, Calif.: Presidio Press, 1997.

Garcia-Mora, Manuel R. "Crimes against Peace in International Law: From Nuremberg to the Present." *Kentucky Law Journal* 53 (1964): 1–33, Archives of the Douglas MacArthur Memorial, Norfolk, Va.

Geffen, Louis. Papers. Archives of the Douglas MacArthur Memorial, Norfolk, Va.

Ginn, John L. *Sugamo Prison: An Account of the Trial and Sentencing of Japanese War Criminals in 1948 by a U.S. Participant.* London: McFarland, 1992.

Glueck, Sheldon. *War Criminals.* New York: Kraus, 1966.

Graef, Calvin R. "Oral Reminiscences of Master Sergeant Calvin R. Graef, Carlsbad, New Mexico (in response to William M. Taylor, Jr.'s letter for information on 'Hell Ships')." Interview by D. Clayton James, Oct. 1, 1971. RG 5, box 15/15, "James Interviews," Archives of the Douglas MacArthur Memorial, Norfolk, Va.

"Guam." RG 59. National Archives, Washington, D.C.

Hadley, Eleanor. *Anti-Trust in Japan.* Princeton, N.J.: Princeton Univ. Press, 1970.

Hanayama, Shinso. *The Way of Deliverance: Three Years with the Condemned Japanese War Criminals.* New York: Scribner's, 1950.

Honda, Katsuichi, and Frank Gibney, eds. *The Nanjing Massacre: A Japanese Journalist Confronts Japan's National Shame.* New York: M.E. Sharpe, 1999.

Horwitz, Solis. "The Tokyo Trial." *International Conciliation* 465 (1950): 477–98.

Hoyt, Edwin F. *To the Marianas: War in the Central Pacific, 1944.* New York: Avon, 1983.

Illinois at War Collection. Bradley Univ. Library, Peoria, Ill.

International Military Tribunal for the Far East. *Judgment.* Tokyo: IMTFE, Nov. 1948.

Ito, Masashi. *The Emperor's Last Soldiers.* New York: Coward-McCann, 1967.

"Joseph Keenan Meets the Press." *American Mercury,* no. 70 (April 1950): 1.

Keenan, Joseph B. "Observations and Lessons from International Criminal Trials." *University of Kansas City Law Review* 17 (1949): 1–4.

Keenan, Joseph B., and Brendon Brown. *Crimes against International Law.* Washington, D.C.: Public Affairs Press, 1950.

Kenworthy, Aubrey. *The Tiger of Malaya: The Story of General Tomoyuki Yamashita and "Death March" General Masaharu Homma.* New York: Exposition Press, 1953.

"Khmer Rouge Leaders 'Very Sorry,'" *Chicago Tribune,* Dec. 30, 1998, sec. 1, pp. 1, 14.

Kimura, Tokutaro. *Justice and Peace*. Honolulu: Privately published/Arms Press, 1946.

Kodama, Yoshio. *Sugamo Diary*. Tokyo: Radio Press, 1960.

Kurihara, Ken. *Tenno: Showa-Shi Oboegaki* [The emperor and Showa history]. Tokyo: Yushindo, 1955.

The Law of Land Warfare. U.S. Army Field Manual. Washington, D.C.: GPO, 1956.

Lawyers Co-operative. *United States Supreme Court Reports*. Book 90. Rochester, N.Y.: Lawyers Co-Operative Publishing, 1946.

Lippman, Thomas. "Worldwide War Crimes High Court Is Approved: Delegates Overrule U.S. Objectives." *Washington Post,* July 18, 1998, p. A01.

Maga, Kenneth. Interview by author. Wauwatosa, Wisconsin. August 19, 1998.

Maga, Timothy P. *Defending Paradise: The United States and Guam, 1898–1950*. New York: Garland, 1988.

————. *Hands across the Sea? U.S.-Japan Relations, 1961–1981*. Athens: Ohio Univ. Press, 1997.

Mansfield, Michael J. (Mike). "Oral Reminiscences of Ambassador Michael J. (Mike) Mansfield, Tokyo, Japan." Interview by D. Clayton James, Aug. 16, 1977. RG 49, box 5, "James Interviews," Archives of the Douglas MacArthur Memorial, Norfolk, Va.

Minear, Richard H. *Victors' Justice: The Tokyo War Crimes Trial*. Princeton, N.J.: Princeton Univ. Press, 1971.

Mosley, Leonard. *Hirohito, Emperor of Japan*. Englewood Cliffs, N.J.: Prentice-Hall, 1966.

Muller, Lyle. "Stand Up to Oppression, Urges Pran: Killing Fields Survivor Tells Iowa City Audiences That World Pressure Works." *Cedar Rapids (Iowa) Gazette*. FYIowa: Iowa's News and Information Network, website, <http://www.gazetteonline.com/news/9810/oct110.htm>, Jan. 1999.

Murphy, John D. Papers. Hoover Institution on War, Revolution, and Peace, Stanford Univ.

Navy News, Guam ed. (1945–1950). Micronesian Area Research Center, Univ. of Guam (MARC).

Nippon Times (1945–1950). Archives of the Douglas MacArthur Memorial, Norfolk, Va.

Nishikawa, Nasao. "Japanese History in the Dock: Victory for a Viewpoint." *Perspectives: The American Historical Association Newsletter* 35, no. 8 (Nov. 1997): 5, 8.

Olson, Lawrence. *Japan in Postwar Asia*. New York: Praeger, 1970.

Ohtake, Sado. "Oral Reminiscences of Sado Ohtake, Tokyo, Japan." Interview by D. Clayton James, Aug. 17, 1977. RG 49, box 6, "James Interviews," Archives of the Douglas MacArthur Memorial, Norfolk, Va.

Pacific Stars and Stripes (1945–1950). Archives of the Douglas MacArthur Memorial, Norfolk, Va.

Pal, Radhabinod. *International Military Tribunal for the Far East: Dissentient Judgment*. Calcutta: Sanyal, 1953.

Pell, Herbert. Papers. Box 1, "War Crimes Commission File," Franklin D. Roosevelt Library, Hyde Park, N.Y.

Piccigallo, Philip. *The Japanese on Trial.* Austin: Univ. of Texas Press, 1979.

Pran, Dith. Interview by author. Bradley University, Peoria, Illinois. April 16, 1999.

Press Clippings File. "War Crimes, 1945–1948." Archives of the Douglas MacArthur Memorial, Norfolk, Va.

"The Prime Minister's Speech." *Today's Japan.* NHK Television—Tokyo. News for Overseas Viewers, WGBH, Boston, Aug. 15, 1995.

Redford, L.H. "The Trial of General Tomoyuki Yamashita: A Case in Command Responsibility." Master's thesis, Old Dominion Univ., 1975.

Reel, A. Frank. *The Case of General Yamashita.* New York: Octagon Books, 1949.

Reeves, George. Interview by author. Boston, Apr. 1996.

Rogers, Robert F. *Destiny's Landfall: A History of Guam.* Honolulu: Univ. of Hawaii Press, 1995.

Roling, B.V.A. *The Tokyo Judgment: The International Military Tribunal for the Far East (IMTFE), 29 April 1946–12 November 1948.* Amsterdam: Univ. Press of Amsterdam, 1977.

Rostow, Walt. *The Stages of Economic Growth: A Non-Communist Manifesto.* 3d ed. Cambridge: Cambridge Univ. Press, 1991.

Roth, Stanley. "Scenarios for Ensuring Growth and Stability in East Asia." Speech before the plenary session of the World Economic Forum, Hong Kong, Oct. 15, 1997. USIS Washington File (the archives section of the USIA website, <http://www.usia.gov/abtusia/posts/JA1/wwwh1543.html>), Jan. 1999.

Rovere, Richard H., and Arthur Schlesinger Jr. *The MacArthur Controversy and American Foreign Policy.* New York: Noonday Press, 1951.

Russell, Edward F.L. *The Knights of Bushido: A Short History of Japanese War Crimes.* London: Cassell, 1958.

Sanchez, Pedro. *Guam 1941–1945: Wartime Occupation and Liberation.* Tamuning, Guam: Sanchez Publishing, 1983.

Sasaki, Soichi. *Fundamentals of the Japanese Constitution.* Tokyo: Shiragikukai, 1954.

Schmetzer, Uli. "The Mysterious Death of Pol Pot." *Chicago Tribune,* Apr. 17, 1998, sec. 1, p. 4.

Scholarly Resources Press. *Japanese Newspapers and Periodicals Collection.* Wilmington, Del.: Scholarly Resources Press, 1998.

Sebald, William, and Russell Brines. *With MacArthur in Japan: A Personal History of the Occupation.* New York: Norton, 1965.

Shiroyama, Saburo. *War Criminal: The Life and Death of Hirota Koki.* New York: Kodansha International, 1977.

Smith, Craig B. *The Diary of Sergeant Ito.* Los Angeles: Whirlwind Press, 1986.

Smith, Robert Barr. "Justice under the Sun: Japanese War Crimes Trials." *World War II Magazine,* Sept. 1996, pp. 1–16.

Suzukawa, Isamu. "Oral Reminiscences of Isamu Suzukawa, Tokyo, Japan." Interview by D. Clayton James, Aug. 12, 1977. RG 49, box 6, "James Interviews," Archives of the Douglas MacArthur Memorial, Norfolk, Va.

Tanaka, Yuki. *Hidden Horrors: Japanese War Crimes in World War II.* Boulder, Colo.: Westview Press, 1996.

Taylor, Lawrence. *A Trial of Generals: Homma, Yamashita, MacArthur.* New York: Icarus Press, 1981.

Thorpe, Elliott R. "Oral Reminiscences of Brigadier General Elliott R. Thorpe, Sarasota, Florida." Interview by D. Clayton James, May 29, 1977. RG 49, box 6, "James Interviews," Archives of the Douglas MacArthur Memorial, Norfolk, Va.

Togo, Shigenori. *The Cause of Japan.* Trans. Fumihiko Togo and Ben Bruce Blakeney. New York: Simon and Schuster, 1956.

Tojo, Hideki. *Affidavit of Hideki Tojo, Individual Defense.* Tokyo: IMTFE, Dec. 19, 1948.

"Trials Set for Tokyo." *Washington Post,* Dec. 29, 1945, p. 1.

Trueheart, Charles. "U.S. Cool to War Crimes Panel: Washington May Not Back Proposal for Permanent Tribunal." *Washington Post,* July 10, 1998, p. A32.

Truman, Harry S. Papers. Box X8, "Student Research File: The War Crimes Trials at Nuremberg and Tokyo." Official File, Harry S. Truman Library, Independence, Mo.

Tweed, George R., and Blake Clark. *Robinson Crusoe, USN: The Adventures of George Tweed, RM 1/C, U.S.N. on Jap-Held Guam.* New York: McGraw Hill, 1945.

U.S. Department of State. *Trial of Japanese War Criminals.* Publication no. 2613. Washington, D.C.: GPO, 1946.

U.S. Navy Commission—Guam. Records, 1945–1949. Micronesian Area Research Center, Univ. of Guam (Commission Records).

U.S. Navy Government Records (NR), 1949. Micronesian Area Research Center (MARC), Univ. of Guam.

Walzer, Michael. *Just and Unjust Wars: A Moral Argument with Historical Illustrations.* New York: Basic Books, 1977.

Webber, Jude. "Annan Calls War Crimes Court 'Gift of Hope.'" *Excite News,* July 18, 1998. Website with Reuters Ltd. press reports, <http://nt.excite.com/news/r/980718/15/news-un>, Jan. 1999.

West, Philip, Steven I. Levine, and Jackie Hiltz, eds. *America's Wars in Asia: A Cultural Approach to History and Memory.* New York: M.E. Sharpe, 1998.

Willoughby, Charles A. "Oral Reminiscences of Major General Charles A. Willoughby, Naples, Florida." Interview by D. Clayton James, July 30, 1971. RG 49, box 6, "James Interviews," Archives of the Douglas MacArthur Memorial, Norfolk, Va.

———. *Shanghai Conspiracy.* New York: Dutton, 1952.

Index